Visions of Liturgy and Music for a New Century

Visions of Liturgy and Music for a New Century

Lucien Deiss, C.S.Sp.

French text translated by Jane M.-A. Burton
English text edited by Donald Molloy

A Liturgical Press Book

THE LITURGICAL PRESS
Collegeville, Minnesota

Cover design by Greg Becker.

1   2   3   4   5   6   7   8

Library of Congress Cataloging-in-Publication Data

Deiss, Lucien.
     [Vision de la musique et de la liturgique.   English]
     Visions of liturgy and music for a new century / Lucien Deiss ;
French text translated by Jane M.-A. Burton ; English text edited by
Don Molloy.
          p.   cm.
     Translation of an unpublished ms., La vision de la musique et de
la liturgique.
     Includes bibliographical references and index.
     ISBN 0-8146-2298-4
     1. Church music—Catholic Church.   2. Catholic Church—Liturgy.
3. Chants (Plain, Gregorian, etc.)—History and criticism.
I. Burton, Jane M.-A. trl.   II. Molloy, Donald.   III. Title.
ML3080.D45   1996
264'.0202—dc02   96-17693
                                                           CIP
                                                           MN

Contents

Introduction

In this present work we shall consider music and song in the Christian liturgy, and especially in the Eucharistic celebration.

In the first part of the book we shall look at the ministerial function of music and song, the principle which in our opinion is the key to all other questions (chapter 1).

In the second part of the book we shall look at those participants in the liturgy who are involved in the music: first, the celebrating assembly itself; then the musical roles of priest, choir, music director, and organist (chapter 2).

In the third and longest part of the book we shall examine the different chants of the Eucharistic celebration, classifying them according to their genre:

Acclamations and dialogues (chapter 3)

The Responsorial psalm (chapter 4)

The processional chants during the Entrance, Gospel, Presentation of the Gifts, Communion, and Recessional (chapter 5–8)

The litanies of the Lord Have Mercy, the Prayer of the Faithful, and the Lamb of God (chapters 9–11)

The hymns: the Gloria, the Gospel refrain, and the Thanksgiving hymn after Communion (chapter 12)

The Creed (chapter 13)

The cantillation of the readings (chapter 14).

We published a similar work five years after the Second Vatican Council as *Spirit and Song of the New Liturgy* (Cincinnati: World Library Publications, 1970, 1973, 1976. Original French edition, *Concile et chant nouveau* (Paris: Ed. du Levain, 1969). A revision that takes into account the evolution of the liturgy since that time is now necessary.

One of the principal tasks of Vatican II was to fill the gap that separated the sanctuary, where the clergy reigned, from the nave, where the people stood. The first "celebrated," the second "assisted." In order to create a single celebrating community, Vatican II used "full, conscious, and active participation"[1] as a bridge between clergy and people. Such participation represented the ideal of the liturgical movement at the time of the council. It seemed capable of resolving all problems.

Since that time, the center of gravity in the Church—and its problems—has moved. It has moved from Europe, where the Roman liturgy was born, and has come to rest in the Third World and the southern hemisphere. A new gap has thus been created between the Roman liturgy on the one hand and, on the other, the peoples of the Third World and southern hemisphere. A new bridge has therefore been built—that of inculturation. Vatican II began the journey that would open the path of inculturation: "Even in the liturgy the Church does not wish to impose a rigid uniformity; rather does [it] respect and foster the qualities and talents of the various races and nations." The council sanctioned "variations and adaptations to different groups, regions and peoples, especially in mission countries." Yet it also directed all creativity by asking "that the substantial unity of the Roman Rite [be] preserved."[2] It was thought that inculturation represented the most burning urgency of our time.

We must also note that because of the immediacy of the means of communication, the world seems to become smaller and smaller, and humanity recognizes itself as a single human family. We see more clearly today than in the past that immense human populations have not yet welcomed the gospel message; for example, no solid bridge has yet been built to effectively reach the Islamic world of almost a multimillion believers!—or the Chinese, of more than a multimillion people!

[1] Constitution on the Sacred Liturgy, *Sacrosanctum Concilium* 14.

[2] *Sacrosanctum Concilium* 37–38. A. Chupungco, *Cultural Adaptation of the Liturgy* (New York: Paulist Press, 1982), presents nos. 37–40 of the Constitution on the Liturgy as "the Magna Carta of liturgical adaptation" (42–57).

To say the same thing in terms of statistics: in 1988, the Catholic Church represented only 17.64 percent of the world population.[3]

A final remark should be made. Within the Western world, where the Christian community has not yet decided resolutely to cross the bridges that the ecumenical movement has built between Catholics, Orthodox, and Protestants, "a dramatic split has opened up between the Church and the contemporary culture."[4] The Church seems exiled from the modern world. The constant diminution of the practice of religion, especially among the young, is only the exterior sign of this exile.[5]

Vatican II strongly affirmed: "The Church has been sent to all ages and nations and therefore is not tied exclusively and indissolubly to any race or nation, to any one particular way of life, or to any customary practices, ancient or modern."[6] Yet in actual fact, our liturgy remains what it is by reason of its origin, that of Western Christianity, while the demand that adaptations should "preserve the substantial unity of the Roman Rite," seems to some "total uselessness in regard to the southern hemisphere,"[7] for there is little chance that the Roman Rite will be loved and desired, whether by the Third World, the Islamic community, the Chinese, or even by our own contemporary culture.

These reflections underline the modesty of this work. It is neither by song nor by music that the 17.64 percent of Catholics in the world will be able to deal with the problems of world evangelization. Yet music and song can be bridges that lead toward Christ. We have the right to expect that such bridges should be well built. Such is the modest aim of this book.

Changes have sometimes been imposed within the Church in an insensitive and even brutal manner. Our intention, however, is not to list the reforms that have already been carried out. Such an inventory would soon risk becoming obsolete, given the fluidity of change at the present time. It would have only a relative interest. In fact, what

---

[3] "L'Eglise dans le monde," *Documentation Catholique,* 86 (1989) 29.

[4] John Paul II, Discourse to members of the Pontifical Council for Culture, January 18, 1983.

[5] Cf. H. Küng, "La crise du service divin, crise de l'Eglise," in *Garder espoir* (Paris: Cerf, 1991) 189–91.

[6] Constitution on the Church in the Modern World, *Gaudium et spes,* 58.2.

[7] A. Hastings, "Le Christianisme occidental et la confrontation des autres cultures," in *La Maison–Dieu* 179 (1989) 34.

interests the contemporary Christian community is not so much the
re-form undertaken by the council as a response to the problems of
1962–1965, but the actual *form* of the liturgy today. Does it give a response to the problems of our own time?

Neither do we intend to project a hypothesis of what we consider
the desirable evolution of the liturgy for the future. No one can pre-
dict with any certainty what the celebrations of the Church of tomorrow will be like or toward what sort of liturgy the Spirit of Jesus
will lead the Church.

This book intends simply to reflect on what is desirable today,
while drawing on the riches of the past to inform our search.

Sometimes it is thought that the period of reform inaugurated by
Vatican II has been completed and that it is now simply necessary to
correctly apply the conciliar decisions in order to gather all the fruit
and to resolve all future problems. Perhaps such thinking hopes to
put an end to all contestable initiatives or the pursuit of endless ex-
periments. Yet such a static vision of the liturgy, as was generally in
vogue before the council, does not respond authentically to the mystery of the Church. Vatican II speaks of a "permanent reform," *perennis reformatio*[8] of the Church. This permanent reform of the Church
necessitates a permanent reform of the liturgy.

Perpetually youthful, betrothed to Christ Jesus (2 Cor 11:3), the
Church will never finish growing in the beauty of its youth. Thus its
prayer, which expresses its dialogue with the Lord, will never cease
to invent new forms with which to express its ever new love. A young
woman who refuses to update her style of dress or appearance will
soon seem like an outdated old lady. If she refuses to grow up, she is,
for all intents and purposes, as much as dead. Likewise, a Church
that refuses to change into its spring wardrobe again will soon be exiled from its time, and the face that is meant to reflect the beauty of
the Lord Jesus in the world will be made ugly by the wrinkles of old
age. For it must always be spring for the Church, that is to say, always the time of renewal; the face of the Church must always bear
the grace of a young fiancée, "without wrinkle or mark" (Eph 5:27).

This permanent renewal can be profitably lived only in permanent contact with the tradition of the Church. Not that we cast a nos-
talgic eye toward the past. But the tradition helps us to understand

[8] Decree on Ecumenism, *Unitatis redintegratio,* 6.

the future; the path already traveled reveals to us the path yet to be traveled. The more we reach out toward a renewed liturgy, the more we must know the past and learn how to discern its fundamental, essential elements.

Even the errors of the past are precious, for they show us what we should not reproduce for the present and the future.

For those who look to the future to build a new liturgy, this gaze at the past must be a peaceful and sympathetic one. When a young woman of twenty puts on her wedding dress, she does not criticize the little skirt she wore at the age of ten. Likewise, when the Church puts on its dress for the twenty-first century, and appears with a new beauty, it does not criticize the dress it wore in the past. For the Church is beautiful in every age with the splendor of Jesus Christ. Humility is necessary in liturgical reform. We are not pioneers in the process of discovering mysteries hidden from past generations. We are simply those who celebrate the liturgy according to the exigencies of our own time.

Neither the postconciliar reform, nor inculturation, nor any other reform, not even "the preservation of the substantial unity of the Roman Rite" is to be regarded as an end in itself. All these are means. The aim of a movement is not to journey perpetually but to reach the goal toward which it travels. The aim of liturgical reform is to celebrate, in an ever greater authenticity, the reality of the Father, through the Son, in the unity of the Holy Spirit.

All liturgical reform must judge itself by reference to this transcendent goal. From this perspective it is certainly always urgent to embellish the path that leads to the Father by renewing harmonies and rhythms. But it is still more urgent not to linger on the path of beauty but to reach out to God, who is infinite beauty and the source of all music.

Lucien Deiss, C.S.Sp.
Feast of the Immaculate Conception
December 8, 1993

Part One

1

The Ministerial Function of Music

THE ESSENTIAL QUESTION

From the beginning of chapter VI of the Constitution on the Liturgy, *Sacrosanctum Concilium,* a chapter concerned with "sacred" music, the council deals with the "ministerial function" of music:

> Sacred Scripture, indeed, has bestowed praise upon sacred song. So have the Fathers of the Church and the Roman pontiffs who in more recent times, led by St. Pius X, have explained more precisely the ministerial function exercised by sacred music in the service of the Lord (SC, art. 112).[1]

The instruction *Musicam Sacram* (MS) of March 5, 1967, affirms in the very first paragraph of the prologue that the council was concerned precisely with this question:

> Sacred music, in those aspects which concern the liturgical renewal, was carefully considered by the Second Vatican Ecumenical Council. It explained its role in divine services, issued a number of principles and laws on this subject in the Constitution on the Liturgy, and devoted to it an entire chapter of the same Constitution (MS, art. 1).[2]

---

[1] This text and all subsequent citations from the Constitution on the Sacred Liturgy are from Austin Flannery, O.P., *Vatican Council II: The Conciliar and Post Conciliar Documents,* new revised edition, vol. 1 (Collegeville, Minn.: The Liturgical Press, 1992) 31.

[2] Flannery, op. cit., 80.

In the second paragraph, the instruction presents itself as a response to the questions about the ministerial function of music:

> The new norms concerning the arrangements of the sacred rites and the active participation of the faithful have given rise to several problems regarding sacred music and its ministerial role. These problems appear to be solved by expounding more fully certain relevant principles of the Constitution on the Liturgy (MS, art. 2).[3]

In other words, the question of the ministerial function of music occupies a place of first importance in the Church's thought. This question is at the heart of all liturgical reform, especially the problems posed by music and song.

The expression "ministerial function" is a very poor translation of the Latin *munus ministeriale*. The word *munus* signifies function, charge, office. Tertullian speaks of *sacerdotalia munera,* priestly functions.[4] The adjective *ministerialis* signifies "who is at the service of." The expression *munus ministerialis* is redundant, almost a tautology, as if one could speak of a "functional function" or a "ministerial ministry." Yet it is useful, incisive in its precision. In the liturgy, the ministerial function of a person or thing is the service that the person or the thing renders to the community. The ministerial function of a reader is to proclaim the reading; that of the chalice, to contain the Eucharistic wine. What then is the ministerial function of song, or of a particular song, in the liturgical celebration?

This question of the ministerial function may be likened to the question, at once simple and yet of primary importance, that a child might pose when confronted with an object whose function the child does not know: "What is that for?" In the liturgy, what is an entrance chant for? a responsorial psalm? a Lamb of God? We can extend these questions and address them to all the essential actions of the liturgy: What is the ministerial function of the readings or the homily, even of the celebration of the Eucharist itself? It is clearly evident that we have not been baptized in order to sing songs or to listen to readings or homilies, or even in order to celebrate the Eucharist.

We can divine, in spite of the language used (which falsely suggests something somewhat ancient and dusty) that the question of the

---

[3] Ibid.

[4] St. Irenaeus, *Adversus omnes Haereses,* 41.8. Sources chrétiennes 46 (1957). For Tertullian *munus* and *officium* are synonyms. See *De spectaculis,* 12.1. S.C. 332.

ministerial function of each song, object, and word used in the liturgy is indeed the essential question: What is your function in the liturgy? What service do you render? It is a question of the right to exist. The question cuts to the core of every rite and action. If a symbol no longer speaks to the community, if it serves no purpose, it is better to abandon it and find another. If a homily wanders among the weeds of pious insignificance, it is better to omit it. If a song or a piece of music does not fulfill its ministerial function, it is better to be silent.

The liturgy has always taken account of the ministerial function of everything, even if, during the course of the ages, it judged this criterion by different standards. It is a law of history: No rite or song can see the light of day and remain in existence unless it fulfills a clear and precise function. Rites and songs root themselves deeply in the liturgy to the extent that they fulfill a ministerial function. If not, they dry up and harden into empty gestures and are soon carried away by the relentless tides of history. Such is the hard and healthy law of life. Yet in the preconciliar liturgy, the question of the ministerial function was scarcely posed. It certainly did not present itself with any acuity.

This was because the post-Tridentine liturgy had fixed itself into a certain immobility that was happily designated hierarchical and too easily referred to as the tradition. The liturgy was sterile. It did not attempt to reply to the new questions that new situations posed but only repeated old answers, usually adding warnings about the need to be on one's guard about "innovations." For four centuries, there had been almost no change in the Mass rite since its promulgation by Pius V on July 14, 1570.[5] In addition, the Church has not always escaped the temptation to pride itself on its rubrics. Sometimes it has continued to linger complacently while the world has continued to evolve—often toward progress, always toward change. If one reads some particular preconciliar Church documents, the impression is given that the only existing problems were those of the adaptation of the world to the Church's institutions and the obedience of the faithful to the Church's directives. Sometimes the Church even congratulated itself for a rigidity that created a certain kind of uniformity and barred the path to the free spontaneity of those who celebrated.

---

[5] P. Journel, *Les Rites de la Messe en 1965* (Paris: Desclée, 1965) writes: ". . . the *Ritus servandus* has not undergone any substantial change in the successive editions of the Roman Missal from 1750 to 1962," 13.

When the wind of reform blew over the council, everyone realized that it was the same violent wind of the first Pentecost, acting to promote adoration "in spirit and in truth" (John 4:23). What could have resisted the power of the Spirit and the joy of renewal?

Definition of Ministerial Function

What are the criteria for defining the ministerial function of liturgical chant in general and of a certain chant in particular? Who can tell us, for example, what are the ministerial functions of a *Kyrie,* a *Gloria,* a *Sanctus,* or an *Agnus Dei?* Who can tell us whether this function is effectively fulfilled?

Ministerial function may be defined:

> on the one hand, in reference to the liturgy itself, as understood and interpreted by the Church, according to its tradition and laws; on the other hand, in reference to the assembly that celebrates the mysteries of Christ.

It is certainly possible, as history illustrates, that a tension can arise between the Church authority that legislates and the faithful who obey. But normally, in times of liturgical peace and rubrical tranquillity, the head that governs and the members who obey, because they are complementary, dialogue among themselves: both constitute the one Church of Jesus Christ. "Throughout the Constitution on the Sacred Liturgy, it is the whole Church which speaks, the Mystical Body of Christ, Head and members, in such a way that it is Christ himself who speaks, He in whom all the members are unanimous."[6] To define the ministerial function of the liturgy in regard to the liturgy itself, as understood and interpreted by authority, and in regard to the celebrating assembly, is to define it according to a single reality: a single People of God celebrating Jesus Christ.

In Regard to the Liturgy Itself

First, ministerial function can be defined in regard to the liturgy itself, as understood and interpreted by Church authority, according to the Church's tradition and laws.

---

[6] H. Schmidt, *Constitution sur la sainte Liturgie* (Bruxelles: Lumen Vitae, Coll. tradition et renouveau, 1966) 200.

The tradition of the Church, the laws promulgated by competent authority, and the orientations given assign a particular function to each chant. When, for example, the Missal affirms that the Creed is the profession of faith of the whole assembly, or that the *Sanctus* is an acclamation to be chanted or recited by all the faithful, it defines the ministerial function of these two chants exactly.[7]

The instruction *Musicam Sacram* formulates a general principle that can be considered the golden rule of ministerial function:

> The proper arrangement of the liturgical celebration requires . . . that the meaning and proper nature of each part and of each song be carefully observed (MS, art. 6).[8]

To follow this golden rule is to realize the ministerial function of each chant. Each song in the liturgy must fulfill, like a good servant, the role assigned to it by the liturgy in conformity with the Church's tradition and laws.

While it may be an act of loyalty toward the tradition of the Church to deem that certain pieces of the Church's traditional musical repertoire perfectly fulfill their ministerial function, it is not a lack of loyalty to suppose that others, even when executed in the best possible conditions, do not. One must realize that they were composed according to the aesthetic tastes of their day and according to a liturgical perspective that may be different from that of Vatican II. This is equally true of both the Gregorian and classical polyphonic repertoire.

The examples are numerous. There is, for example, the admirable Gregorian melody of *Kyrie II* of the Mass *Kyrie, fons bonitatis*. This ardent supplication, which rises to God and prostrates itself before God, was in former times part of the Mass celebration for solemn feasts in almost all seminaries. The tradition had thus enriched it with great religious intensity, both affective and aesthetic. The *Ite, missa est* of this Mass takes up the same melody. The question we ask today is whether one should sing "Go in peace to love and serve the Lord" in the same way that one sings "Lord, have mercy." Can one really send the liturgical assembly away with a melody that has served to invoke the mercy of God? If the ministerial function of these chants is different, the melody must be different.

---

[7] General Instruction of the Roman Missal (hereafter GIRM) 43–44, 55. The first edition dates from 1969. All GIRM citations are from *The Sacramentary* (Collegeville, Minn.: The Liturgical Press, 1985).

[8] Flannery, op. cit., 81–82.

There is in the classical polyphonic repertory the Mass *Jesu, nostra redemptio* of Palestrina (d. 1594). The litany of the *Kyrie*, the hymn *Gloria*, the acclamation *Sanctus*, and the *Agnus Dei* are all based on the same melodic theme, that of the hymn *Jesu redemptio nostra*. It is clear that Palestrina, whose music rings out like a festive carillon, did not ask about the ministerial function of the music, as Vatican II envisions. Or rather, the ministerial function that he attributes to each piece in his Masses is different from that envisioned by Vatican II. This takes away none of the glory of the one whom Pius XI called "the Master";[9] it simply invites us to use his compositions discerningly today.

It is not enough that a chant is borrowed from sacred music's ancient "store of treasures."[10] Such treasures do not automatically fulfill their ministerial function. A treasure is only precious if it can be used in the authentic service of the liturgical rites.

In Regard to the Celebrating Assembly

A liturgical celebration does not exist in itself. It is lived and participated in by an assembly; it is incarnated in an assembly. Ministerial function must thus be judged in the context of the celebrating assembly.

The Constitution on the Liturgy marked a decisive stage in the history of the active participation of the people. The Constitution forcibly demands:

> To promote active participation, the people should be encouraged to take part by means of acclamations, responses, psalms, antiphons, hymns, as well as by actions . . . (SC, art. 30).[11]

The instruction *Musicam Sacram* tried to implement this decision of the council without reservation. No document has ever been so concerned with the people, and none has demanded with such insistence that their thoughts, desires, and capacities be taken into account:

> In selecting the kind of sacred music to be used, whether it be for the choir *or for the people, the capacities of those who are to sing the music must be taken into account* (MS, art. 9).

---

[9] Pius XI, *Divini cultus*, December 20, 1928, *Acta Apostolicae Sedis* [hereafter AAS] 21 (1928) 38.

[10] Flannery, op. cit., art. 121, p. 33.

[11] Flannery, op. cit., 11; see also arts. 28, 114.

In order that the faithful may actively participate more willingly and with greater benefit, it is fitting that the format of the celebration and the degree of participation in it should be varied as much as possible, according to the solemnity of the day and the *nature of the congregation present* (MS, art. 10).

The faithful fulfill their liturgical role by that full, conscious, and active participation (MS, art. 15).

One cannot find anything more festive and more joyful in sacred celebrations than a *whole assembly expressing its faith and devotion in song* (MS, art. 16).

The formation of the whole people in singing should be seriously and patiently undertaken together with liturgical instruction, according to the age, status and way of life of the faithful and degree of their religious culture (MS, art. 18).[12]

Liturgical chant is thus to be judged within the context of the community that sings it.

In the past the rubrics scarcely concerned themselves with the community itself; all the attention went into seeing that the chant conformed not to the spirit of a people but to the letter of rubrical laws. All the Christian communities throughout the world were made to sing the same Gregorian melodies, for example, the triple Alleluia of the Vigil Mass of Easter, whether they liked it or not. Indian Christians might have protested: "We don't like this melody. We prefer to sing music written in the five notes of our own musical scale. How beautiful are our five notes! But the seven notes of your Western scale and that Alleluia appear vulgar to us, as ridiculous as if a young Indian woman should dress in European style, in shorts or in slacks!" The rubrics would reply: "No matter! You must sing it nevertheless, as it is written!" Christians in the African bush might implore: "Let's have a bit more rhythm please for this Alleluia! For rhythm is our joy, through which we love to sing praise to the risen Christ. But your Alleluia resembles a burial chant!" The rubrics would reply: "No matter! You must sing it as it is written!" Christians in the suburbs might say: "We are not able to sing this Alleluia together as an expression of the union of our hearts. Rather, it reduces us to silence, as our voices slide and slip on the notes as if on ice." Again, the rubrics would reply: "No matter! You must sing it as it is written!"

---

[12] Flannery, op. cit., 83, 84. Italics mine—L. D.

In the past, the rubrics used to say: "Look at the Gregorian hymn-book that we have given you!" Today they say: "Look at the assembly!" The most appropriate music is not that which is best in a certain book but that which is best for a particular assembly.

Who can pretend that this problem no longer exists even though we now sing in the vernacular? Who can pretend that priest, choir, director, or guitarist no longer impose their personal musical preferences on the assembly? Who would not hope that those who are responsible for the music and song might feel themselves first of all responsible for the assembly? Who can be convinced that certain songbooks have been put together solely with the needs of the assembly in mind, and not with other priorities?

Neither music, song, organ, choir, nor guitar holds center place in the liturgical celebration: the central place belongs to the People of God.

We shall often have to refer to the question of rubrics. It is easy to criticize the exaggerated role they exercised over the celebration in former times. It is naive to think that Vatican II suppressed them all. It is equally naive to think that the liturgy of the future will suppress them. In theory, like all laws, they exist to aid the community and its celebration. The constraint they impose is often lighter than the decisions taken by individuals and imposed on the whole assembly. It is indispensable to know both what the universal Church desires and authorizes and what the needs of the local celebrating community are. The good of the celebrating community is the supreme law, beyond all rubrics.

MINISTERIAL FUNCTIONS

The instruction *Musicam Sacram* of 1967 enumerates the ministerial functions that song serves in the celebrating community:

> Liturgical worship is given a more noble form when it is celebrated in song. . . . Through this form, prayer is expressed in a more attractive way, the mystery of the liturgy, with its hierarchical and community nature, is more openly shown, the unity of hearts is more profoundly achieved by the union of voices, minds are more easily raised to heavenly things by the beauty of the sacred rites, and the whole celebration more clearly prefigures that heavenly liturgy which is enacted in the holy city of Jerusalem (MS, art. 5).[13]

---

[13] Ibid., 81.

The instruction is very optimistic about the power of music and song. Let us accept such optimism. It is evident, however, that this power varies according to the assembly and, even more, according to persons present. What can be said of those who are allergic or insensitive to music? The instruction must be moderately interpreted.

The different "ministries" of song can be classed under the following headings:

Song adds solemnity to the celebration

It gives a greater efficacy to texts

It imbues the liturgical celebration with beauty

It helps create unity in the assembly.

Song Adds Solemnity to the Celebration

In the motu proprio *Tra le sollecitudini* (November 22, 1903) Pius X affirms:

Sacred music, as an integral part of the solemn liturgy . . . tends to increase the decorum and the splendor of the ecclesiastical ceremonies.[14]

Some fifty years later, Pius XII, in the encyclical *Musicae Sacrae Disciplina,* December 1955, teaches that sacred music:

by its very beautiful modulations and its magnificence, must embellish and enhance both the voice of the priest who offers the sacrifice and that of the Christian people who praise the Almighty.[15]

The Constitution on the Liturgy of Vatican II affirms that sacred music "[confers] greater solemnity upon the sacred rites" (art. 112).[16]

These words are full of good sense. They do not, however, enrich our liturgical knowledge. For this we must turn to the instruction *Musicam Sacram:*

Liturgical worship is given a more noble form when it is celebrated in song, with the ministers of each degree fulfilling their ministry and the people participating in it (MS, art. 5).

---

[14] Cited in R. K. Seasoltz, *The New Liturgy* (New York: Herder and Herder, 1965) 4.
[15] AAS 48 (1956) 12.
[16] Flannery, op. cit., 32.

It should be borne in mind that the true solemnity of liturgical worship depends less on a more ornate form of singing and a more magnificent ceremonial than on its worthy and religious celebration, which takes into account the integrity of the liturgical celebration itself, and the performance of each of its parts according to their own particular nature (MS, art. 11).[17]

Thus the "true solemnity of liturgical worship" does not depend on "a more magnificent ceremonial" but on the authenticity of the rites; a celebration is "more noble" when each celebrant, whether presider, reader, psalmist, or assembly, participates according to his or her position. In such a celebration the communal and hierarchical character of the liturgical assembly is manifested.

The advance in such an affirmation in comparison with the preconciliar documents is evident. In the past, a celebration was considered solemn if it was carried out according to the rubrical norms of the solemn High Mass, even if the people were not present or did not participate. The instruction *De Musica Sacra et Sacra Liturgia* of September 3, 1958, defines the solemnity of the Mass in excessively clerical terms, that is, in regard to the singing of the priest, without any reference whatsoever to the people: "The Mass is called *sung* if the celebrating priest truly sings the parts which the rubrics say he must sing; otherwise, it is called *said*" (3). In such a scenario, a Requiem Mass could be called a sung Mass even if there were only a single priest and an organist to give the responses. Likewise, a Mass could be called "said" even if a thousand of the faithful sang at it. Vatican II inaugurated the end of such rubrical nonsense. Rubrics, too, must reflect life.

To affirm that song brings an element of solemnity to the liturgy is also to ask the community the question: "Does every song that is sung enrich the celebration?" Sometimes we sing out of habit, without real need or profit. We must submit our liturgical celebrations to the following rule: each time the quality of the music is not equal to the quality of the silence it breaks, it is preferable not to sing. To put it in a more positive way: singing must always be done with such a perfection that the community is really "edified," that is to say, really built up by the celebration. Vatican II spells the end of all badly executed music.

But we have not yet arrived at this point. All liturgies, whether Eastern or Western, Catholic, Orthodox, or Protestant, can question

[17] Flannery, op. cit., 81, 83.

themselves on the effective edification and enrichment of their particular liturgies through music and song.

Song Gives the Texts a Greater Efficacy

In *Tra le sollecitudini,* Pius X writes that

> since [the] principal office [of sacred music] is to clothe with befitting melody the liturgical text proposed for the understanding of the faithful, its proper end is to add greater efficacy to the text, in order that by means of it the faithful may be more easily moved to devotion and better disposed to receive the fruits of grace associated with the celebration of the most holy mysteries (art. 1).[18]

According to the Constitution on the Liturgy, sacred music gives a more suave expression to prayer: *"orationem suavius exprimens"* (art. 112). The instruction *Musicam Sacram* expresses the same idea in identical terms.[19]

That song is almost automatically able to give a "suavity," that is, a mellifluous and pleasing quality, to the expression of prayer may be called into question. Prayer may also express itself violently; music then adds not suavity but rather brings out prayer's tragic beauty. If one thinks, for example, of the anguish and then the triumph expressed in the Gregorian antiphon of Holy Week *Christus factus est,* the flamboyant colors of Palestrina's *Stabat Mater,* the poignant palpitations of the chorale *Denn alles Fleisch* of Brahms' *German Requiem,* there is no suavity but rather a violence that grips the heart.

This said, it is clear that song does give—sometimes—"a greater efficacy" to the text. In clothing it with splendor, it makes it more persuasive. A luminous harmony between song and prayer can be found in the Gregorian repertoire, such as in the *Gloria* of certain Masses, the unforgettable introits, such as the *Ad te levavi* (first Sunday of Advent) or *Spiritus Domini* (Pentecost), and in certain Bach cantatas in which the music seems to lift the prayer to heaven. Song is thus to the word what poetry is to prose or a painting is to a photograph. And the Church has decided that song has a certain importance. The Church also remembers that God, in God's self-revelation through the Word, made use of poetry, and that the most decisive revelations

---

[18] Seasoltz, op. cit., 4–5.
[19] See arts. 5, 11.

come to us clothed in the mantle of poetry dressed in the splendor of rhythmic beauty.

The harmony between prayer and song can be broken, however, when the music dominates and takes attention away from the text. A certain melodic rhetoric obscures the prayer. Sometimes Gregorian chant gets drunk on its own beauty and drowns the Word of God in the meandering of its neumes. In the offertory chant *Jubilate Deo,* which sings of the wonders of God in the words of Psalm 66, the Gregorian melody leaps about in successive waves from lower *do* to upper *fa.* There are no longer any words to be heard. There is only the immense jubilation of forty-eight notes sung on the vowel "a." What festive joy in this outpouring of notes! Yet who listens to the psalm? Such a distortion between music and prayer is even more common in classical religious music. Mozart's *Exsultate Jubilate* finishes with an ecstatic round of thirty-three Alleluias. One of them is stretched out through a hundred and two notes. The melody rejoices to such an extent that words are no longer necessary: who could be bothered with them?

In conclusion: When it is affirmed that song gives a greater efficacy to a text, what is really meant is that it *should* do so.

Song Imbues the Liturgy with Beauty

In *Tra le sollecitudini,* Pius X reacted strongly against the worldly babble that was rampant in the liturgical music of his time. When he speaks of a *Tantum ergo* in which the first verse was a slow cavatina and the second an allegro, he reveals to us the depths to which Church music had fallen. He desired that Church music should be "a true art" and possess "goodness of form" (arts. I, 2).[20]

Pius XI desired an artistic clergy. In *Divini cultus* he stated that seminarians should be formed

> in that highest art which can justly be called "aesthetic," that of Gregorian chant and the knowledge of music, and that of polyphony and of the organ. . . .[21]

Such a vision of a clergy who "must absolutely" possess a knowledge of music is a rich inheritance from the past. For centuries the Church was the context in which polyphony and the art of the organ

---

[20] Seasoltz, op. cit., 5–8.
[21] AAS 21 (1928) 37.

were developed, from the early organ of the twelfth century to the splendors of the classical period. Priests must have possessed a certain knowledge of music. Nowadays, the ordained ministry is not considered intrinsically linked to musical knowledge. It is, however, linked to the creation of a beautiful environment in which music plays an important part.

Pius XII wrote with a touch of Roman lyricism:

> The dignity that is the exalted goal of sacred music consists in this: by its most beautiful modulations and its magnificence, it should embellish and enhance both the voice of the priest offering the sacrifice and that of the Christian people who praise the Most High; it raises the hearts of the faithful toward God by its impetus and by a kind of intrinsic virtue; it makes the liturgical prayers of the Christian community more alive and more fervent, so that God, One and Triune, may be praised and invoked by all with greater force, fervor, and efficacy. By its art, it makes the unfolding of the sacred rite more splendid.[22]

The best formulation of the ministerial function in music is without a doubt to be found in the instruction *Musicam Sacram:*

> Minds are more easily raised to heavenly things by the beauty of the sacred rites, and the whole celebration more clearly prefigures that heavenly liturgy which is enacted in the holy city of Jerusalem (MS, art. 5).[23]

Vatican II should have marked the proscription of all music that is not beautiful, the end of all that is poorly executed. May this be granted to us!

What a grace it would be if every liturgical celebration opened the door to heaven, if each song uplifted the soul toward the harmony of invisible realities! Even if our songs do not fully radiate such a grace, we must, nevertheless, continue to pursue the path of beauty toward the One whose beauty is inexpressible. Human beings have need of earthly splendors to contemplate God, who is the source of all splendor. Our piety is not only nourished by theological concepts and perfectly performed rubrics. Something deep within us knows that it is God who has created all beauty: the tenderness expressed in a melody, the pleasure of a harmony, the feel of a stirring rhythm, as well as the smile of a child and the elegance of a woman. The name

---

[22] AAS 48 (1956) 12–13.
[23] Flannery, op. cit., 81.

of God is proclaimed and praised when the poet writes a hymn, when the musician clothes it with a melody, and when the sculptor carves the smile of a saint out of stone. The liturgy must use all these gifts. It gives each of them its highest value by consecrating them to God. To grasp such beauty as though it were God would be sinful; to receive it as pointing to and revealing something of God is a grace:

> If through delight in the beauty of these things
>   people assumed them to be gods,
> let them know how much better than these is their Lord
>   for the author of beauty created them. . . .
> For from the greatness and beauty of created things
>   comes a corresponding perception of their creator (Wis 13:3, 5).

The Christian people have always had this appreciation of beauty as a path to God. Innumerable cathedrals testify to it by their architecture; Gregorian chant and polyphony testify to it by their music.

It remains true that the criteria used to judge music generally, and a particular song, have varied from one epoch to another, and from one cultural tradition to another. They may even vary within the same community from person to person. Thus the members of the council of the evangelical community of Arnstadt reproached J. S. Bach for "having lately introduced (in 1706) into the choir accompaniment a number of surprising *variations,* of having broken up the melodies with strange sounds, and of having thus disturbed the community of the faithful."[24] The members of the council were not able to distinguish between the "surprise" that genius evoked and the platitudes with which their musical sensibilities were content. Such an incident displays the Christian wisdom of respecting the musical abilities and tastes of the community and of not judging those in charge of the music even if sometimes one experiences the temptation to judge after the model of the bourgeoisie of Arnstadt.

"Beauty will save the world."[25] Beauty will also save the liturgy with its music and song. In the future, there will be no place for ugliness and vulgarity.[26]

---

[24] A. Schweitzer, *Joh. Sebastian Bach* (Wiesbaden: Breitkopf and Hartel, 1952) 88.

[25] N. Berdyaev, *Destin de l'homme dans le monde actuel* (Paris: 1936) 318. Cited in M. M. Davy, "La musique du monde nouveau," in *Encyclopédie de Mystiques* (Paris: Laffont, 1972) 426.

[26] In its message of December 8, 1965, the council wrote: "The world in which we live has need of beauty if it is not to sink into despair. Beauty, like truth, is what puts joy

One has remarked that, in some parishes, the liturgical reform was so hasty and so violent that one forgot sometimes the presence of some gratuitous beauty which came from the past and still could embellish celebrations today. The thorough cleaning from the house of liturgy of all that was not absolutely necessary, even if it was beautiful, created much emptiness. The new celebrations were correct, but all beauty of the past was gone. The Latin language, for instance, was still proclaimed to be the official language of the Roman Rite (CSC 36), but there was no more singing in Latin. No one wants to pass judgment on communities or on their celebrations, but each community should ask itself if, on the way toward some newness, it did not lose some treasures of past beauty.

Song Helps to Create Unity

Finally, the last "service" that song renders to the liturgical community—not a small service—is to promote the unity of the assembly.[27] The instruction *Musicam Sacram* is strongly worded in this regard:

> The mystery of the liturgy, with its hierarchical and communitarian characteristics, is more openly manifested; the unity of hearts is more profoundly attained by the unity of voices (MS, art. 5).[28]

This is a fact of experience. A gathering of the faithful, in any given place, remains an indeterminate group, a body without a soul, if it does not express its unity in a communal activity.

In the context of a liturgical celebration, these communal activities are quite limited: praying with a single voice, sharing in a procession, giving the kiss of peace. . . . It is chiefly through song that the deepest unity, that of "one heart and soul" (Acts 4:32) is experienced, as each person joins his or her voice to that of their sisters and brothers. What began as a crowd has become an assembly.

---

into human hearts. It is a precious fruit which resists the wear of time, and which unites generations in a common admiration."

[27] *Sacrosanctum Concilium*, art. 112. [Translator's note: the Flannery book's translation does not quite express the force of the text as rendered by the author, so it is translated accordingly. J. B.] The tradition liked to underline this unifying role of song. See J. Basurco, *El Canto cristiano en la tradicion primitiva* (Madrid: Marova Coll. Christus Pastor, 1966) especially ch. 4, "El Canto communitario como expression ecclesial," 93–115.

[28] Flannery, op. cit., 81.

This unity brought about by song is akin to both the unity between different local churches and the unity of the faithful of a particular community.

In the past, the preconciliar texts insisted on the *unity of particular
local churches* with the Church of Rome, thanks principally to the adop-
tion of the same Latin language and the same Gregorian chant:

> If, in the Catholic churches of the whole world, Gregorian chant re-
> sounds in its purity and its integrity, it will have also, like the Roman
> liturgy itself, a universal character; thus, in the whole world this har-
> mony will become familiar to the faithful; they will have the impres-
> sion of being at home, and thus they will have the satisfaction of
> feeling in their hearts the admirable unity of the Church. This is one
> of the principal reasons why the Church so ardently desires that
> Gregorian chant be intimately linked with the Latin words of the sa-
> cred liturgy.[29]

This sign of unity that the use of the same language and the same
chant affords remains fully relevant today. It is particularly needed in
small missionary communities in which members find themselves im-
mersed in an often indifferent, sometimes hostile, environment.
Singing in Latin gives them a sense of being united with the immense, universal Catholic community.

Yet the evolution of the liturgy has emphasized more the *unity of
the faithful* in a single local community. Vatican II decreed that Latin
was to remain the language of the Roman Rite. It even said that the
faithful should be able "to say or sing together in Latin those parts of
the Ordinary of the Mass which pertain to them."[30] But the desire for
the vernacular was so strong that only a few fragments of Latin remain. Communities preferred to express their unity by singing in
their own language rather than expressing their attachment to the
Roman Church by singing in Latin or by having the choir sing in
Latin. Besides, they remembered that it is the Spirit of Jesus who seals
the unity of the Church, not Latin or any other language.

Like other ministerial functions, that of song is not carried out
through some kind of enchantment. Song can bring a community together, but it can also disperse it. Such is the case when cantors, instead of putting themselves at the service of the community, put

---

[29] Encyclical *Musicae Sacrae Disciplina,* December 25, 1955, art. 21. AAS 48 (1956) 16.
[30] Flannery, op. cit., 13, 18.

themselves in place of the community and muzzle it, demanding that it be only an admiring audience. Whether the song is that of a guitar soloist, a Gregorian schola, or a choir singing Palestrina, the problem is the same; and it makes no difference that the quality of performance may be quite professional.

Lovers of God's beauty have always sought to pray and praise the Lord in all splendor. The Church, in the course of centuries, has made an alliance with God's lovers. Today, it asks them not to stop singing but to sing even better.

A Sacred Music?

What should music used in the liturgy be called? Religious music? Sacred music? Is there such a thing as sacred music?[31]

The expression *religious music* seems a convenient term but in fact remains too vague. How should we define "religious?" Paul recommends that "whatever you do, in word or deed, do everything in the name of the Lord Jesus, giving thanks to God the Father through him" (Col 3:17). Every word and every action–and thus all musical activity–is invited to praise the Father and to give thanks to him in Jesus Christ. Yet, in the immense religious celebration of life, not all is liturgical. The most vital aspects of life–being born, giving birth, fathering a child, dying–all happen under the watchful eye of God but we experience them without benefit of liturgy. All music used in the liturgy is therefore religious, but all religious music is not appropriate to the liturgy.

At first the term *sacred music* seems most appropriate. It is the term favored in the official documents. It is used in the motu proprio of Pius X, *Tra le sollecitudini* (1903), in the encyclical of Pius XII, *Musicae Sacrae Disciplina* (1955), in the instruction *De Musica Sacra et Sacra Liturgia* (1958), and in the instruction *Musicam Sacram* (1967). The council used it without considering the inherent problems in its use. Chapter 5 of the Constitution on the Liturgy is entitled "Sacred Music." Yet history reveals that this expression is as ambiguous and problematic as that of "religious music." The idea that some music is "sacred" while other

---

[31] To help define various notions about sacred music, the Instruction *De Musica Sacra et Sacra Liturgia,* September 3, 1958, art. 4 says: "By sacred music is to be understood: Gregorian chant, sacred polyphony, modern sacred music, sacred music for the organ, popular religious song, religious music." AAS 50 (1958) 633.

music is "profane" is problematic. The masters of classical polyphony, such as Josquin des Près (ca. 1440–1521) or Orlande de Lassus (1532–1594), used to write both very pious Masses and quite impious madrigals—all with the same ink! For his famous air "Bereite dich, Zion," J. S. Bach, Christian though he was, did not hesitate to recycle an air he had composed for a profane cantata the preceding year. At that time people "did not perceive anything diametrically opposed between liturgical music and nonliturgical music, and they ignored any connection between the sacred and profane."[32] Luther, who was knowledgeable about music, set a number of religious texts to secular music. The Christmas chorale *Vom Himmel hoch da komm'ich her* was written using the melody of a popular dance tune: Luther insisted that it was not good to let the devil have all the best tunes. The melody of the famous chorale of the Passion, *O Haupt voll Blut und Wunden,* comes from a lively song that Hans Leo Hassler (1564–1612) had published in an album entitled "The Garden of Pleasure of New German Dances," and whose worldly words proclaimed "My feelings are troubled by a tender virgin" *(Mein G'müt ist mir verwirret von einer Jungfrau zart)*. J. S. Bach took the melody from "The Garden of Pleasure," transplanted it into the setting of the Church, changed its three-quarter time to a majestic four-four time, and clothed it with a sumptuous harmony that still tears at our hearts today.[33] A profane melody can become sacred. Inversely, a sacred melody can become unsacred and bear the words of a profane song. The most famous French ditty, "Le roi de Renaud de guerre revint," took its inspiration from the Gregorian hymn *Ave maris stella* from the Office of the Blessed Virgin Mary.[34]

This hymn also inspired the Lutheran chorale *Erschienen ist der herrliche Tag.* There is not, therefore, properly speaking, "sacred music," even less a "Christian melodic form, harmony, or rhythm." To state this more positively: All music, if it is able to "be converted," that is to say, to put itself at the service of the liturgy, can be welcomed into the liturgical celebration.

It is therefore neither technical perfection nor a "sacred" character that opens the gate of the liturgy, even if in past centuries a work

---

[32] A. Basso, *Jean-Sebastian Bach* (Paris: Fayard, 1985) vol. 11, 486.

[33] According to Schweitzer, op. cit., 16, Bach created the melody of the chorale based on numbers 21 *(Erkenne mich, mein Hüter)*, 63 *(O Haupt voll Blut und Wunden)*, and 73 *(Wenn ich einmal soll scheiden)*, using a different harmonization each time.

[34] According to H. Davenson, *Le Livre des chansons* (Neuchâtel: de la Bacconière, 1946) 162.

has been welcomed fervently and is recommended by the tradition. The *Sanctus* of J. S. Bach's Mass in B minor, in spite of its majestic resonance, the Masses of Lassus, in spite of the surprising brilliance of their harmonies, the Gregorian *Sanctus* of the Mass *Kyrie, rex splendens,* in spite of its gentle, melodic arabesques, are not suited to the liturgy of Vatican II. Why? Simply because the *Sanctus* is a chant to be sung by the entire celebrating community,[35] and not the chant of the choir alone or of the Gregorian schola.

Today, rather than speak of religious music or of sacred music, it is preferable to speak of *music of the Christian liturgy* or the *ritual music of Christians,*[36] music that accomplishes the ministerial function the liturgy calls for as part of the celebration. Thus, it can be called *ministerial music.* There is no intended slight toward music in such a phrase. On the contrary, it is an affirmation of the dialogue between music and rite, beauty and prayer. When this dialogue is authentic, music and rite become prayer.

When this dialogue becomes a monologue, whether in the rite or in the music, the ministerial function is degraded and the rhythm of the celebration is broken. Thus the *Ite, missa est* of the Gregorian Mass *Kyrie, fons bonitatis,* in spite of the melodic splendor of its thirty-four notes, which unfurl like a festive garland, is really quite unsuitable for the ministerial function of the *Ite, missa est,* which is to say that such festivity is excessive for signaling the community that the celebration is finished. The simple notes of the *Go in peace,* in spite of the modesty of its melody, are well adapted to their ministerial function. They express clearly what needs to be said. *Music for the Christian liturgy, Christian ritual music, ministerial music:* in the end, it does not matter what term is used. The essential thing is *what is,* what is the reality. The reality is a situation in which music and rite are harmoniously joined, welcomed into the liturgy, and become prayer together.

The adage "The one who sings prays twice" is well known. It is believed to have sprung from the Augustinian tradition. Luther's followers adopted it in the form *Doppelt betet wer singt.*[37] The formula is an attractive one. Yet it is meaningless if its premise is tested. One

---

[35] GIRM 55a.

[36] The document produced by *Universa Laus,* the international study group on song and music in the liturgy, preferred "music of the Christian liturgies" or "Christian ritual music."

[37] Basso, op. cit., 109.

wonders how the Missal, usually so judicious in its judgment, could cite it and attribute it to a vague, unnamed tradition: "According to an ancient proverb: he prays twice who sings well."[38] What naivety! And what of those who sing badly? And those who do not sing at all? Who among us could truly say that they have never been seduced so much by the music that they did not pray at all? Are the most excellently performed chorales necessarily the most prayerful? What about silence as a form of prayer? It can be a crying out to God. When Moses remained silent before God—and before the Red Sea that he wanted to cross with the people—God questioned him: "Why do you cry out to me?" (Exod 14:15). In brief, sometimes song can be an aid to prayer; and sometimes it can be an obstacle to prayer. In the context of the liturgy, the demand is that music be an aid to prayer.

The Essential Question

Is the question of the ministerial function of music an important one? Indeed, it is *the* essential question, the fundamental question that has always been answered by the most authentic reforms, by a deeper understanding of the liturgy, and by which we are able to proceed today.

Very simply, this question may be expressed:

> What is the function of song in the liturgy? What is the function of this particular song?

> What needs to be done so that the music can fulfill this "service"?

These are questions that may challenge the most traditional positions as well as the most radical revisions. For from such a stance, it is no longer a question of adapting ancient liturgies but of discerning the needs of the present situation. It is not sufficient for the future to be able to capitalize on the past and to restore an ancient liturgy, as if the fabrication of some great fossil, perfectly executed, were sufficient to resolve contemporary questions.

Liturgical song after Vatican II is faced with new questions and confronted by the demand of an authentic ministerial function. It has been liberated from certain useless constraints and is thus able to re-

[38] GIRM 19.

cover the spontaneity of Christian freedom. It should remember the prodigious affirmation of the Constitution on the Church in the Modern World, *Gaudium et spes:*

> The Church has been sent to all ages and nations and, therefore, *is not tied* exclusively and indissolubly to any race or nation, to any one particular way of life, or *to any customary practices,* ancient or modern (art. 58–italics mine).[39]

Liturgical song, which is therefore not tied to any custom, ancient or modern, must not, however, let itself err, becoming intoxicated with such liberty. For its liberty, like that of the children of God, is a liberty in the service of the Lord Jesus. In the liturgical celebration, it is a *ministerial* liberty, carried out as a service to the celebrating community.

Christians will use such liberty to place every possible beauty and richness at the service of the liturgical community; they will seek to express in their sometimes unconventional melodies a trace of God's own smile.

---

[39] Flannery, op. cit., 952.

Part Two

2

The Participants in Liturgical Song

INTRODUCTION

The Church, the People of God

In the past when one asked "Who celebrates?" the answer was "the priest." Since Vatican II, however, the answer is "the community."

In the past when one asked "Who sings?" the answer was "the choir." Today, after Vatican II, the answer must be "the community."

How should we understand such assertions? How can we justify them?

These assertions are based on the theology of the Church as presented by Vatican II in the Constitution on the Church, *Lumen Gentium* (LG). The evolution of this conciliar document was a masterpiece of significance. On June 5, 1960, John XXIII appointed a theological commission and charged it with the task of preparing a preparatory schema on the Church. From 1960 to 1964 the commission produced texts based on the following schema:

Christ, the head of the Church

The hierarchy in the Church

The laity

This pyramidal schema, seemingly classical and inoffensive, reflected well the sort of theology that was considered traditional in certain environments. It was at one with the emphasis of Vatican I, which had exalted papal authority and the charism of infallibility. The distance between the hierarchy and the laity, between the clergy and the faithful, was quite marked. Following such a theological line and prolonging the thought of Vatican I, Leo XIII taught that "in the Church of God two parts can be distinguished in the most absolute fashion: the taught and the teachers, the flock and the pastors."[1] In 1906 Pius X taught that "the Church is par excellence an unequal society; that is, there are two categories of persons: the pastors and the flock. . . . In the pastoral body alone resides the power and necessary authority. . . . As for the multitude, it has no other duty than to let itself be led, as a docile flock which follows its shepherds."[2] Stupefying teaching to our modern sensitivities!

It is precisely this kind of theology that Vatican II called into question. The council developed the following schema, which was approved on November 18, 1965:

Christ, the head of the Church (LG 7–8)

The people of God (LG 9–17)

Its articulation in the hierarchy and the faithful (LG 18–38)

In the vision of Vatican II, the Church is thus first the people of God (the expression "people of God" is found thirty-nine times in *Lumen Gentium*). The existence of this people is primary, its hierarchical organization—as important as it is—is secondary. A communion (a *koinonia,* as the tradition says) exists among the members of the faithful. Paul VI speaks of the "fraternity which unites all the members of Christ in a single communion."[3] This fraternity is suggested by Jesus' own words: "For you have one teacher, and you are all students" (Matt 23:8). It is sealed in love by the Holy Spirit.

If the Church defines itself as the people of God, then the whole people of God celebrate the liturgy. "The integral subject of the liturgical action is the Church, even when, at the level of necessary 'pow-

[1] *Epistola tua* of Cardinal Guibert, in H. Legrand, "Le développement d'Eglise-sujets," in *Les Eglises après Vatican II,* Coll. Théologie historique 61 (Paris: Beauchesne, 1981) 152.
[2] Encyclical Vehementer nos, AAS 39 (1906) 89. See H. Legrand, op. cit., 152.
[3] Discourse of November 11, 1969, to the Synod, *Doc. Cath.* 62 (1969) 957. On the theme of the Church as communion, see J.M.R. Tillard, *Eglise des Eglises, l'ecclésiologie de communion,* Coll. Cogitatio fidei 143 (Paris: Cerf, 1987).

ers,' the ordained priest acts alone."[4] It is, therefore, the whole people of God who participate in liturgical song and music. We may even affirm that it is the only participant, since all who have a part in the music or song of the liturgy belong to the people of God.

Such a statement does not imply that everyone must sing everything. The whole people celebrate the Word, but this does not mean that everyone must proclaim together the readings or give the homily. The whole people celebrate the Eucharist—even in the Middle Ages we read that "the priest does not sacrifice alone, or consecrate alone, but all the assembly of the faithful who assist consecrate with him, sacrifice with him"[5]—but this does not mean that everyone must recite the Eucharistic Prayer. Likewise, the whole people sing, but each participates according to his or her charism and in a way that enhances the beauty and balance of the celebration.

A New Vision of the Liturgy

The theology of the Church as communion changes our vision of the liturgical celebration and especially of liturgical song.

On December 4, 1963, the council called the faithful to a "full, conscious, and active participation" in the actions of the liturgical celebration.[6] This phrase, "full, conscious, and active participation," has become the antiphon for the chant of liturgical renewal.[7] Is it a good antiphon?

To answer this question, it is necessary to see the invitation to participation in its historical context. In 1963 it represented a magnificent victory over the type of ecclesiology and liturgical celebration that had reigned for a number of centuries. The liturgy of the Church was the liturgy of the clergy who celebrated it. The people, the "docile flock," were invited to look on and admire with their eyes what the priests in the sanctuary were celebrating and to participate according to what was asked of them.

[4] Y. Congar, "L'Ecclesia, ou communauté chrétienne, sujet intégrale de l'action liturgique," in *Vatican II, La liturgie après Vatican II,* Coll. Unam Sanctam 66 (Paris: Cerf, 1967) 282.

[5] Attributed to Guerric d'Igny, Sermon 5, 15, PL 185.87 AB. Cited in Y. Congar, "L'Ecclesia," 252. On the authenticity of this statement see T. Morson and H. Costello, *Dictionnaire de Spiritualité,* vol. 6, col. 1115.

[6] *Sacrosantum Concilium* 14.

[7] In *Sacrosanctum Concilium,* the concept of participation is mentioned twelve times: in nos. 11, 14, 19, 21, 27, 30, 41, 48, 50, 79, 113, and 124.

Is this sufficient? It was in 1963. It was no longer sufficient in 1965, when the council, in the Constitution *Lumen Gentium,* presented the Church as the people of God. If the Church is the people of God, a communion of sisters and brothers, the celebration of the liturgy must also be a communion of this people of sisters and brothers around Jesus Christ.

Does the word *participation* adequately express the role of the community in the celebration?

In fact, the word *participation* was not new. It had already appeared sixty years before Vatican II in the *motu proprio* of November 22, 1903, *Tra le sollecitudini.* Yet at that time, the meaning of participation was restricted to what the hierarchy decided to allow the laity to do. Pius X asked that "efforts must especially be made to restore the use of Gregorian chant by the people, so that the faithful may again take *a more active part* in the ecclesiastical offices, as they were wont to do in ancient times."[8] Sixty years of effort have revealed that the vision of Christian communities singing Gregorian chant was a utopian dream.[9] Such participation was also selective: women were excluded from choirs, since cantors "fulfilled an authentic liturgical office in the churches; women, regarded as incapable of such an office, may not be admitted to be part of the choir or the choir school."[10]

To participate means to have a part. But what part? The word is a snare.[11] The community *per se* does not have a part, whether large or small, to play in the celebration: it celebrates the totality of the liturgical action. Rather, all members of the faithful, by reason of their baptism, are wholly engaged in every part of the celebration.

This vision of the Church as communion that celebrates as one, in and through each of its members, was responsible for the introduction of the most significant and most important changes in the new liturgy. It also renews our understanding of music and song in the liturgy.

---

[8] Art. 3, in Seasoltz, op. cit., 5–6. Italics mine–L.D.

[9] In some countries, a few parish communities knew some parts of the Commons of certain Gregorian Masses, which they chanted in their own manner!

[10] *Les Enseignements pontificaux: La Liturgie* (Tournai: Desclée and Cie, 1961) 176.

[11] It is good to note that the GIRM, which in its first edition spoke of the priest as the "celebrant," speaks in the second edition of the "priest celebrant," for all the community are celebrants. See *Enchiridion Documentorum Instaurationis Liturgicae* (Torino: Marietti, 1976) 483, n. *u.*

What Importance?

How important are these questions? In them, the Church's institutional credibility is at stake. According to the Constitution on the Liturgy, "the principal manifestation of the Church consists in the full, active participation of all God's holy people in the same liturgical celebrations, especially in the same Eucharist . . . (SC art. 41).[12] What does this epiphany of the Church reveal, and, because song is a particularly important form of participation, what type of community do our songs reveal?

Our celebrations reveal a community in which the clergy—exclusively male—govern, teach, and celebrate for the benefit of the laity, and men and women who are governed, taught, and "ritualized" by the clergy. We cannot avoid asking whether such a separation between clergy and laity, between men and women, is really willed by Christ? Does it authentically represent the message of the gospel? Or, inversely, is a people that is governed, taught, and ritualized only and solely by clerics, and only and solely by men, the true people of God, the people God has formed for God's praise and glory?[13]

Our assemblies become increasingly more sparse. Young people are often noticeably absent. No one protests against our celebrations; they just ignore them. What should we think of a society that is no longer capable of handing down its custom of celebrating its faith and of praising God in an enthusiastic, convincing manner? These are important questions. And anguish surrounds them.

Our joy must lie in seeking to answer these questions in a manner worthy of Jesus Christ. The songs of our communities reveal who we are.

THE PRIEST

The priest presides in the celebrating community, a community called together in the name of Christ. His position and his ministry may be envisaged from a double point of view.[14]

---

[12] Flannery, op. cit., 14–15.
[13] See Isa 43:7 and 1 Pet 2:9.
[14] See J. Lécuyer, "Le Célébrant," in *La Maison-Dieu* 61, 5–29.

In the Name of Christ

He presides in the assembly as representing Christ, *in persona Christi*.[15] He is the sacrament, the sacred sign of Christ.

From this point of view, the most worthy song of the priest—and of the whole Eucharistic celebration—is the sung recitation of the words of institution (Eucharistic Prayer).

The Eastern liturgies have understood the dignity of this chant that is at the heart of the Eucharistic celebration. The priest sings the words of institution in a solemn recitative. The people make the presider's prayer their own by ratifying it with acclamations. In the Liturgy of St. James, for example (and in the Mozarabic Rite), they acclaim each consecration by a triumphant Amen. In the Ethiopian liturgy, they sing a triple Alleluia followed by a profession of faith:

> Amen, amen, amen!
> We believe, we confess,
> we praise you, our Lord and God.
> This is true, we believe![16]

In the Coptic liturgy the people intervene in the institution narrative itself, creating a joyous and solemn dialogue with the priest:

> Jesus Christ, the night when he gave himself up to undergo the Passion . . . took bread in his holy, immaculate, pure, blessed, and lifegiving hands, and lifting his eyes to heaven, toward You, his Father, God, and Master of the universe, gave thanks,
> –Amen!
> said the benediction,
> –Amen!
> sanctified it,
> –Amen!
> broke it . . . and said: Take and eat of it all of you. For this is my body broken for you and for the multitude, for the remission of sins. Do this in memory of me.
> *–Amen, amen, amen!*
> *We believe, we confess,*
> *and we give you glory.*[17]

---

15 *Sacrosanctum Concilium* 33.

16 See F. L. Brightman, *Liturgies Eastern and Western* (Oxford: Clarendon Press, 1965) 232.

17 See Brightman, op. cit., 176–77.

Lastly, we find in almost all the rites an acclamation of praise:

> We praise you,
> we bless you,
> we give you thanks, O Lord . . . .[18]

In this acclamation, the liturgy admirably manifests that the Eucharist is first a thanksgiving of a celebrating, grateful people. From the beginning, the liturgy has been pleased to express itself with tremendous joy and praise. Toward the middle of the second century, Justin Martyr testifies to this festive ambiance when he writes:

> When we have finished praying, bread, wine, and water are brought up. The president then prays and gives thanks according to his abilities, and the people give their assent with an "Amen!"[19]

The rubrics of the Roman Rite had accustomed us to keep a profound silence during the Canon, which was called "sacred"[20] but which in reality was burdensome. It did, however, express the veneration with which the Christian community surrounded the mystery that it was celebrating. Yet the priest accomplished the essential rites alone, without ever inviting the people to exteriorize their participation in the great Eucharist Prayer. Condemned to silence, they took refuge in individual prayer and united their hearts to the Eucharistic Prayer said by the priest. This served to separate the priest and the community at the very moment when the celebration reached its height. If the whole community celebrates, and if the high point of the celebration is the Eucharistic Prayer, it is precisely here, at the heart of the Eucharistic Prayer, that the participation of the community ought to be the most intense.

The aloneness of the priest and his isolation from the people was further accentuated by the architectural arrangement of certain churches. Choirs and altars were elevated, true "Tabors" that one climbed by a long series of steps, and from which the clergy dominated over the people, and imposing communion rails that would have been more aptly called "separation" rails. In addition, the entry into certain choirs was prohibited by solid, imposing grills, the fossilized witnesses of the richness of a past age, witnesses of the separation of

---

[18] Ibid., 178.

[19] *First Apology*, 67, in L. Deiss, *Springtime of the Liturgy* (Collegeville, Minn.: The Liturgical Press, 1979) 93.

[20] Instruction *De Musica Sacra* of September 3, 1955, art. 27: "After the consecration, unless the *Benedictus* is still to be sung, a sacred silence is recommended until the *Pater noster.*" AAS 50 (1958) 641.

clergy and people. The priest presided, moreover, by turning his back to the people and speaking in Latin.

All these dispositions were in perfect response to the theology of the Council of Trent, which had strongly insisted on defining the priesthood of the ordained priest as different from the priesthood of the faithful. But they did not fully reflect the theology of Vatican II, which saw the Church as the people of God, of which 1 Peter 2:9 affirms: "But you are a chosen race, a royal priesthood, a holy nation, God's own people . . . ."[21]

Some Considerations and Suggestions

The proclamation of the Canon should be solemnized as much as possible, especially the words of institution.

This solemnization is usually brought about by singing (in the form of a cantillation or recitative). This presupposes a priest who can master the technique of solo singing and has the voice to do so.

The cantillation of the Canon is especially necessary in the case of a concelebration in which a fair number of priests are present. Everyone knows how difficult it is to get a group of priests—each of whom has a well-developed personality, not to say singularity—to recite together in a way that preserves a certain exterior dignity. Often the priestly prayer degenerates into disorder, an anarchic muttering, without rhythm or life. Only song is able to accomplish the miracle of unifying these priestly voices so that all keep the same tone and the same verbal pace. If sung, one can realize one of its ministerial functions: to help bring unity to a celebration.

When cantillation does not seem appropriate or possible, the priest must take care to proclaim the words of institution with dignity and solemnity. This text is not merely a history that one presents to the community, or a prayer that one murmurs to oneself. From the beginning—the most ancient text, that of the First Letter of Paul to the Corinthians (11: 23-25), which dates from about 54 C.E.—the account presents itself as an official account, sculpted by the tradition and em-

---

[21] The council cites this text in the Constitution on the Church, 9, in the Constitution on the Liturgy, 14, in the decree on the Apostleship of the Laity, 3, and in the Decree on the Missionary Activity of the Church, 15; see also the Decree on the Ministry of Priests, 2. For the separation since the Middle Ages of the choir in which the clergy celebrated and the nave where the laity prayed, see B. Chédozeau, "Le Missel des fidèles et la participation à la messe," in *La Maison-Dieu* 191, 69–82.

bellished by the liturgy. It is in such a form that Paul, after having noted that he is transmitting what he himself received, presents the account in a solemn manner: "The Lord Jesus on the night when he was betrayed took bread . . . ."

In order for the people to fully participate in the Canon, we might envision that eventually there should be an acclamation of praise and thanksgiving after each consecration, in addition to the *Sanctus* and the Great Amen that concludes the Canon. The ancient liturgies provide excellent texts:

> We praise you,
> we bless you,
> we give you thanks.

It is possible to use the following acclamation:

We wor-ship you, we give you thanks, we sing your praise and

glo - ry, Lord, our God.

Other formulas are also desirable. One might suggest:

- For Advent, "Blessed is the one who comes in the name of the Lord."

- For Christmastime, "Glory to God in the highest heavens."

- For the Easter Season, the triple Alleluia.

The best formulas are those acclamations that integrate themselves easily into the movement of the Eucharistic Prayer itself: "We praise you" *(eulogoumen),* "We give you thanks" *(eucharistoumen* = we make "Eucharist").

In the Name of the Church

The priest presides in the assembly in the name of the Church, *in persona ecclesiae.* The prayers he makes to God are made in the name of all the people, principally in the name of those who participate and celebrate with him.

From this point of view, the most worthy songs are those in which the priest presents the prayers of the whole ecclesial community to the Father, through the mediation of his Son, in the unity of the Holy Spirit, that is to say, the prayers and the preface.

Further Reflections

The prayers are the presidential prayers. They are proclaimed in the name of the community by the one who presides over its prayer. The solemnization of the texts goes hand in hand with a simple and clear diction. This solemnization is inherent in the texts themselves, and does not depend on the emphases given by the voice of the celebrant.

The Singing of the Prayers

The singing of the prayers poses a particular problem. Before the reform of Vatican II, when Masses were considered "sung" by the rubrics, priests had to sing the prayers and the prefaces.[22] When the liturgy came into the vernacular, priests continued to sing in their native tongue what they had been used to singing in Latin, victimized by force of habit. Such cantillation on three or four notes raises questions.

As stated above in regard to the singing of the institution narrative: In order to sing solo, one must have a solo voice. Such a statement is simple common sense. The charism of ordained ministry does not confer it automatically. In the past, priests who could not put two notes together in tune felt, nevertheless, that it was their duty to sing. Some of them—God forgive them!—had the habit of singing at a pitch below the notes, and they floundered about singing only an approximation of the written melody. The era of such hideous experience must truly come to an end.

Does cantillation really help prayer? Does it help the community to understand the text? Does it clothe the text in a splendid garment? Or, to use the words of the official texts, does "the whole celebration more clearly [prefigure] that heavenly liturgy which is enacted in the holy city of Jerusalem" (MS, art. 5)?[23]

---

[22] As previously mentioned in the first chapter, the instruction *De Musica sacra et sacra Liturgia,* 3, of September 3, 1958, defined a sung Mass in a very clerical manner by considering only what the priest sang.

[23] Flannery, op. cit., 81.

A last, decisive question: Is the text singable? Does it possess certain literary qualities that invite song? In the past the Latin prayers were written in rhythmic prose, which gave them a literary feel of great nobility.[24] When human beings come before the majesty of God and, as beggars, hold out their hands toward God's tenderness, they clothe their words in a solemn gravity. But the passage from Latin to one's native language has sometimes been a passage from nobility to banality. The translation strips the text of its literary cloak. Only a skeleton remains; sometimes not even a skeleton. Do the remains deserve to be highlighted by song?

The Singing of the Preface

We can make analogous remarks about the prefaces. Coming before the great Eucharistic Prayer, they should be like a cry of joy and gratitude for the salvation that the Father gives us in his Son Jesus. Instead, they usually sound like a teacher's lecture. Certainly it is often excellent theology, but how can one experience true joy and sing that today "You [God] have revealed in Christ your eternal plan of salvation . . . and have renewed humanity in his immortal image" (preface for Epiphany), or that we venerate "three Persons equal in majesty, undivided in splendor, yet one Lord, one God" (preface for Trinity Sunday)?

The preface is introduced by a solemn dialogue. Many priests sing it in dialogue with the assembly. On the whole, it is pleasant. The dialogue is short: twenty to twenty-five seconds. It promises hope of God's marvels. "Let us give thanks to the Lord our God," the priest sings. "It is right to give him thanks and praise," the assembly replies. But then the preface sinks into platitudes when the priest begins a simple recitation: "We come to you, Father, with praise and thanksgiving . . ." (Eucharistic Prayer I). A good musical beginning that only leads to prose without music. Would it not be better to sing everything if the text lends itself and if the presider has the gift of a good voice or, if not, to recite everything?

---

[24] The 1,030 prayers—with about two exceptions—that the Leonine Sacramentary (6th c.) contains finish in a rhythmic clause. The three usual clauses are: the *cursus planus*, which carries the accent on the fifth and second syllables before the end *(nostris infunde);* the *cursus tardus*, which carries the accent on the sixth syllable and on the antepenultimate syllable *(incarnationem cognovimus);* and the *cursus velox*, which carries the accent on the seventh and second syllables before the end *(gloriam perducamur).*

What would be desirable for the "priestly song" in the future? It is the heritage of the Latin liturgy that allows the priest to sing, no matter how and no matter what, even to jump over an accent, or even a word in the text of the Missal, without provoking any reaction from the assembly. The demands of the vernacular are severe: song must be exceptional when the voice of the presider is exceptionally good and when the text is exceptionally lyrical. Otherwise, a dignified proclamation, with the judicious use of a microphone, will replace to advantage a mediocre cantillation of a text that does not demand it. Perhaps there is still hope for an imminent and peaceful end of the priest's song, with a discreet departure from our celebrations.[25]

THE SINGING ASSEMBLY

The Assembly's Songs

Two questions: the first, "Which songs should the assembly sing?" and the second, "Which songs should the choir sing?" If we can give a clear answer to these questions, we shall make smooth a path that is often rough.

We must reply: "All the songs belong to the assembly," and "All the songs belong likewise to the choir."

There is only one celebrant in the liturgical celebration: the assembly. There is, therefore, only a single celebrating and singing assembly. All those who exercise ministries in the service of the assembly—priest, choir, soloist—do so as members of the assembly.

In the songs sung by the assembly, the choir intervenes because it is part of the assembly. It may do so by sustaining the assembly or by being in dialogue with it.

In the songs sung by the choir alone, the choir must sing them in such a way that the listening assembly can say: "We are happy with what you are doing in our place. We form a single choir with you."

The Problem of Quality Singing

Vatican II brought about an intense participation in the singing role of the people throughout the Christian communities of the world.

---

[25] Cantillation characterizes at such a point the "ecclesiastical" style that the media automatically uses in public announcements to evoke "the religious."

Communities that had been mute for centuries, or muzzled by choirs who, burning with the desire "for the greater glory of God," had monopolized all the musical space, suddenly set about singing in their mother tongue. This singing did not always attain the desired perfection. Some asked whether our worshiping assemblies, sometimes made up of musical "philistines," were capable of singing worthily. The problem, moreover, did not begin with the council, as though before the council the quality of the singing had always been good. Let us look at this issue closely.

The aim of the liturgy is not to promote the musical formation of the people, with the goal of thus obtaining the best possible musical performance. The Church is a mystery of salvation, not a musical academy. The people's singing must always be prized insofar as it expresses the participation of the baptized in the liturgical celebration. It is absolutely unthinkable that the people be forbidden to express this participation simply on aesthetic grounds. The Church knows well that among holy people not everyone has the voice of a nightingale! Yet the Church also knows that participation in the mystery that is celebrated is essential and of primary importance.

This having been said, it must also be said that the participation of the people will be expressed more perfectly if the singing is of a better quality. We must therefore do all in our power to improve the quality of the singing, both that of the people and that of the choir. Every effort made in the service of beauty is a service offered to God.

In addition, the people's singing possesses a particular beauty that even the most perfectly trained choir cannot attain. Of course, the people sometimes drag out the final note, fail to observe the eighth-notes, upset the melody, bellow the high notes: all defects that can be corrected in time. But we must not judge the people's singing solely by the criteria that may be used for the choir. The assembly is not a choir placed in the nave; the assembly is the people of God. When the choir sings, all the people listen, and if the choir's execution is mediocre, the people notice, the assembly's prayer is disturbed, and the people have the right to criticize. But when the whole assembly sings, no one listens—except God—for everyone joins in as an expression of his or her participation in the liturgy. It is in this union of all the voices present that the particular beauty of the assembly's singing resides: the innocent voices of the children, croaking voices of the elderly, voices that are well placed, voices that are nasal; all these numerous, diverse voices express what no single voice can express alone: the mystery of the Church that unites everyone in common praise of Christ so that, as Paul wrote to the Christians of Rome, "together you may with one voice glorify the God and Father of our Lord Jesus Christ" (Rom 15:6). Those ignorant of the musical art of solmization and those well trained in it, the "philistines" as well as the seasoned musicians, all proclaim together the joy of their faith and together build a community of praise.

This miracle can be understood only by those who have lived it in the liturgical celebration, whether as part of the assembly or as a musician who has experienced the honor of accompanying the singing of the baptized community.

The Assembly's True Potential

It is important never to underestimate the musical potential of the assembly or its artistic sense. The people have a feel for beauty; they are capable of creating it. They can also progress, sometimes prodigiously, in the ability to sing together. Think of how impossible it seemed ten years ago for the people to sing the varied and rhythmic melodies that were being written. Now even doctors, lawyers, and bricklayers whistle them while they work! It would therefore be a gross error to limit the assembly's singing only to the outlines of the music, simple antiphonal lines without melodic weight. We must not reduce our liturgies to the kindergarten level. On the contrary, we must allow the people to fully express their joy, their sadness, and all their prayer, in antiphons animated by a mighty, melodic dynamic that offers the possibility of exulting in the movement of the rhythm: in other words, we must treat them as adults. It is a fact of experience that those antiphons which can be learned in a minute are those the assembly forgets . . . the minute afterwards . . . those which make little impact on the memory or the heart. The antiphons possessing a certain fullness, which demand a certain effort at the beginning, a going beyond what comes easily, are those which the assembly can use more lastingly, which do not wear out so quickly.

THE CHOIR

The liturgical reform has profoundly changed the liturgical landscape in which the choir moves. In certain Third World countries, especially in Africa, new choirs have sprung up out of communities like spring jonquils in a field. They dress themselves in dazzling colors, they rejoice and dance to the rhythm of their drums, they are given to inventing new songs in their tribal languages: a real celebration of joy! Sometimes the same community has at its disposal several choirs, each of which animates a particular Mass. In some missionary settings there is no problem about finding choirs and songs: the only problem is in directing the superabundance of all these resources. In some countries where Christianity has long been established, the reform has, contrary to the experience of the Third World, evoked a certain suspicion, often even sadness and regret and a desire for the past: How are we going to continue with the new liturgy when even the existence of the choir is threatened by solo guitarists? How are we going to preserve the "treasure" of the old liturgy when the new songs constantly bombard the sound system?

After this time of exultation for some and anguish for others, we may hope to return to a certain liturgical tranquillity. More than ever the liturgy has need of choirs. Immense work needs to be done: the integration of songs old and new in a Vatican II liturgy.

The Members of the Choir

In the motu proprio *Tra le sollecitudini,* Pius X presented the choir as the "choir of levites" and concluded that:

> singers in the church have a real liturgical office . . . and that therefore women, as being incapable of exercising such an office, cannot be admitted to form part of the choir or of the music chapel (art 13).[26]

Women may not sing in the choir. Such was the law in force until recently. We should note that it was not enforced everywhere, but it clearly reflected a certain clerical mentality. Besides, in order to show that the choir represented the "choir of levites," the men were dressed in cassocks, even when they were elderly fathers of families, and the boys (who sang the soprano or alto parts) were disguised as miniature priests, dressed in albs and wearing crosses on their chests. This clericalization corresponded perfectly to the teaching of Pius X, who affirmed: "It [is] fitting that singers while singing in church wear the

---

[26] Seasoltz, op. cit., 8.

ecclesiastical habit and surplice, and that they be hidden behind grating when the choir is excessively open to the public gaze" (art. 14).[27]

Then came Vatican II. The Church suddenly discovered that it was not made up solely of men, but also of women—about 50 percent women! The instruction *Musicam Sacram* of 1967 drew the conclusions from this discovery and affirmed:

> The choir can consist, according to the customs of each country and other circumstances, of either men and boys, or men and boys only, or men and women, or even, where there is a genuine case for it, of women only (MS, art. 22).[28]

We are part of a certain declericalization of the choir. This evolution must logically bring, then, a certain declericalization of the musical repertoire. Here we touch on an enormous problem. The contemporary repertoire must express not only the style of past centuries but also the words, rhythms, and melodies of people today. Just as it is no longer necessary to dress in a cassock and surplice to carry out a liturgical function, so it must not be necessary to borrow the so-called "ecclesiastical" style for liturgical song.

To sum up: Vatican II's understanding of the mystery of the Church as the people of God opens us to an understanding of the choir's role as not simply that of the "choir of levites," according to the dictum of Pius X, but as the choir of the people of God. The ancient chants lose none of their nobility, and the new songs are not placed in an inferior position, for all songs are the songs of the people of God.

The Ministerial Function of the Choir

The ministerial function of the choir varies, depending on whether it is a cathedral choir, a parish choir, or one or two cantors who alone act as the choir. Yet this ministerial function always has the service of the assembly as its aim.

---

[27] Idem.

[28] Flannery, op. cit., 86. The encyclical *Musicae sacrae disciplina* 36, of December 25, 1955, had already said that where it was not possible to constitute a *schola cantorum* of men or of boys, it was possible to admit women to the group, "as long as the men are completely separated from the women and girls and everything unbecoming is avoided." (!) Those who direct mixed choirs know that such a separation is impossible and does not represent how things work in real life! Art. 74, cited in Robert F. Hayburn, *Papal Legislation on Sacred Music 95 A.D. to 1977 A.D.* (Collegeville, Minn.: The Liturgical Press, 1979) 355.

To the question "Which songs belong to the choir?," we may reply "All of them!" Now to explain!

As in the past, and according to what the new rubrics anticipate, the choir may sing alone in order to nourish the prayer of the assembly and to increase its joy by the beauty of the choir's singing. The "treasury of sacred music" of which the Constitution on the Liturgy (art. 114) speaks—whether of Gregorian chant or of classical polyphony—offers to all choirs a repertoire of exemplary beauty. This beauty has survived the changes in artistic tastes of past centuries. The new liturgy eagerly welcomes such beauty.

The choir intervenes not only in the dialogues and acclamations that concern the entire assembly, but also in the other songs the choir sings in unison with the assembly or in dialogue with it. The instruction *Musicam Sacram* notes that the choir "support[s] and promote[s] the participation of the people . . ." (MS, art. 18).[29] An immense task never completed. Practically, the choir is irreplaceable, whether for sustaining, correcting, or encouraging the singing of the assembly or for promoting a new song that demands a certain application. It is a fact of experience: Where the choir is good, whether on the musical level or on the liturgical level, there the people will sing well also; there, too, the community is usually alive and vibrant. On the contrary, where the choir is mediocre, whether on the musical level or on the liturgical level, there also the parish community is often weak and asleep. It is really true that song integrates itself into a whole pastoral approach and reveals the vitality or the weakness of a community.

The choir may also intervene by casting the song that the community is singing in unison into four-part harmony. It may do this by following the melody note by note. The traditional choirs of the Protestant tradition furnish good examples of this type of harmonization. Most of the recent liturgical creations have chosen this kind of harmonization. The choir may also harmonize in a complementary fashion. Bach's *St. Matthew Passion* provides a supreme example of this type of harmonization in the passion chorale *O Lamm Gottes unschuldig*. The very simple melody of the chorale is sung by an independent group while the choir weaves around it, as though with vines of compassion. The execution of such music requires not only a good choir but also an assembly that is confident of its own part. Such music has been rarely used in recent liturgical compositions.

---

[29] Flannery, op. cit., 85.

It is apt that the instruction points out that the choir, "because of the liturgical ministry it performs . . . deserves particular mention. Its role has become something of yet greater importance and weight by reason of the norms of the council concerning liturgical renewal" (MS, art. 19).[30]

Thus, in the Church's judgment, not only does the new liturgy not put the choir in the shade but emphasizes its importance. It is a joy for musicians and liturgists to see that the council brought about the resurgence of numerous parish choirs and communities that sing, whereas in the past, silence and sometimes boredom reigned.

THE NEED FOR LITURGICAL FORMATION

The Constitution on the Liturgy *(Sacrosanctum Concilium)* states that "great importance is to be attached to the teaching and practice of music. . . . Composers and singers, especially boys, must also be given a genuine liturgical training" (SC, art. 115).[31] The instruction further stated that:

> Besides musical formation, suitable liturgical and spiritual formation must also be given to the members of the choir, in such a way that the proper performance of their liturgical role will not only enhance the beauty of the celebration and be an excellent example for the faithful, but will bring spiritual benefit to the choir members themselves (MS, art. 24).[32]

The Constitution emphasized the musical training of children. Yet it may happen that certain musicians, although adult in musical knowledge and virtuosic in playing the keyboard, are children when it comes to liturgy. It may also happen that certain priests, even good priests, are illiterate in music. It is possible to meet good Christians who have a solid piety and an excellent musical formation who are underdeveloped in liturgical and biblical knowledge and understanding.

It would be utopian to expect that perfectly formed choirs might spontaneously arise in the Church. The Lord of glory can certainly create from nothing, but he asks for our effort and collaboration.

---

[30] Idem.
[31] Ibid., 32.
[32] Ibid., 86.

Surely, the Holy Spirit can help us to improvise successfully in difficult moments, yet it is preferable that we trust the Holy Spirit to help us to work toward acquiring the sort of liturgical formation of which Vatican II spoke.

The Repertoire

The repertoire is the bread that nourishes the choir. Here we shall not speak of the repertoire appropriate to cathedrals or basilicas. They have a particular repertoire as well as particular festive celebrations. We shall speak rather of parish type choirs.

In the past, these choirs were assured of their nourishment each Sunday. They also sang to an easily satisfied audience, whether that audience was enthralled by the beauty of their singing or merely endured a mediocre performance. What has happened in recent times is that this passive audience has begun to be awakened liturgically, and has become the primary agent in the singing. It seems that the bread has been taken out of the mouths of the choir and been replaced not by some noble Palestrinian cake but by the everyday fare of plain, unadorned basics. Some choirs naturally ask: "What shall we eat tomorrow? What shall we sing tomorrow?"

The traditional Gregorian or polyphonic repertoire is usually very beautiful, but it does not necessarily adapt itself well to the new liturgy. We need time and the experience of different styles in order to learn how to create new masterpieces that will allow the people to sing with the choir. We also need to remember that the patristic era and the Middle Ages produced innumerable hymns, of which 30,000 are already catalogued and published. Of these 30,000, only 75 are represented in the ancient Roman breviary.[33] The people know only two or three, and then only part of them.[34] It has taken centuries to build up the classical Gregorian and polyphonic repertoire; only the masterpieces of that repertoire have survived, and only a few pieces are actually known by the people. We still have a long way to go! Perhaps we shall always be in a stage of transition, and that is the price we pay for remaining alive. It is unrealistic to hope for a return

[33] See P. Salmon, "La prière des heures," in A. G. Martimort, *L'Eglise en prière: Introduction à la Liturgie,* 3rd ed. (Paris: Desclée and Cie, 1965) 848.

[34] Such knowledge is probably restricted for most of the Christian community to the last two stanzas of *Pange Lingua* (i.e., *Tantum ergo* and *Genitori*), the first and last stanzas of *Veni Creator,* and perhaps also *Ave Maris Stella.*

to the liturgical tranquillity of the generations that preceded us. Many of the traditional pieces, even if they do not fit perfectly into the new liturgy, will continue to be used in our celebrations. Many new pieces, even if they are no better adapted to the new liturgy than the old ones, will continue to be introduced into liturgical celebrations.

Each piece of the ancient repertoire must be analyzed according to the new needs of the liturgy. If a piece is no longer suitable for the function it was originally created for, it must no longer be used for that particular function. This does not necessarily mean that it cannot be used at all. It may be possible to use it authentically elsewhere, primarily perhaps in the celebrations of the Word of God. The instruction *Musicam Sacram* affirms that:

> in . . . popular devotions *(pia et sacra exercitia)*, and especially in celebrations of the word of God, it is excellent to include as well some of those musical works which, although they no longer have a place in the liturgy, can nevertheless foster a religious spirit and encourage meditation on the sacred mystery (MS, art. 46).[35]

History has shown that the vision of *Musicam Sacram* about *pia et sacra exercitia* was too optimistic. Some pieces die and disappear from our celebration; others come and go: such is the law of life. Wisdom sees to it that the best pieces are preserved, but it is also necessary to create others.

Modesty is required when seeking to create new pieces to enrich the repertoire. We have to keep in mind that new additions to the repertoire are provisional. Each generation must invent the songs and musical forms that it needs: it must bake *today* in the oven of *present* inspiration the bread it needs *today* to nourish its faith. Tomorrow, those who come after us will bake their own bread. If they find that our bread is still good, we shall be delighted that they take advantage of it. But we shall leave to them the joyful responsibility of expressing their own faith.

The Place of the Choir

The Missal gives the following directions concerning the place of the choir and the organ:

---

[35] Flannery, op. cit., 91–92; see also art. 53. By *pia* or *sacra exercitia* are meant such celebrations as the Way of the Cross or the Rosary, which do not fulfill the meaning of liturgical action in the sense used in ecclesiastical legislation. See the instruction *De Musica Sacra,* September 3, 1958, art. 1, AAS 50 (1958) 632.

In relation to the design of each church, the *schola cantorum* should be so placed that its character as a part of the assembly of the faithful that has a special function stands out clearly. The location should also assist the choir's liturgical ministry and readily allow each member complete, that is, sacramental participation in the Mass.

The organ and other lawfully approved musical instruments are to be placed suitably in such a way that they can sustain the singing of the choir and congregation and be heard with ease when they are played alone.[36]

These are words of wisdom. But their practical application is often difficult.

The best place for the choir is, theoretically, and if the building lends itself, at the junction of the sanctuary and the nave. Such placement testifies that the choir is part of the assembly. It testifies to the choir's perfect integration into the celebration. Yet it is inconvenient because the choir is exposed to all eyes and draws the attention of the assembly to itself. Moreover, choir directors lose some of their comfortable directing freedom before and during a piece, when it proves necessary, perhaps, to correct a tempo or bring out one of the parts through some technical nuancing.

From a liturgical point of view, the least acceptable place for the choir is the balcony. It is true that the choir is near the organ and organist there and, not able to be seen by the assembly, has a certain freedom to function and be directed in singing. The voices also carry better from the balcony. Yet the choir is separated from the assembly and less integrated into the whole celebration. And anyone who has ever sat in the balcony knows how difficult it is to keep attuned to a boring celebration or homily from that location.

Ancient churches were not built for the liturgy of Vatican II. There is no ideal place for the choir. There are simply different churches and diverse communities. Each poses its own particular problems.

---

[36] GIRM 274–75.

THE MUSICAL DIRECTOR

The Role

The leader's role is to "direct and sustain" the assembly's singing so as to facilitate its prayer. The director is the "insurance policy" of the singing assembly.

In exercising this ministry, the human factor is of utmost importance. The director must be so well accepted by the assembly that they are unaware of his or her presence and direction. The role of the singing director, whether one likes it or not, is always that of a critic: here the critique is carried out from the position of being involved in the unfolding of a song. The execution of one piece does not necessarily resemble the execution of another piece. Each has its own strengths and weaknesses and needs to be sung in a particular way. Directors must strive to observe the special needs of any piece and to set the correct tempo for it. It is their duty to quicken the pace if it is too slow, and slow it down if it is too fast. They must always be critically aware, for it is their job to assure the melodic and rhythmic security of the community. Critics accomplish their task more effectively and are more easily accepted when they criticize amiably. Directors of the assembly's singing must therefore always remain calm, cheerful, and modest.

Let them not equate a sad look with a "pious" appearance: the children of light have no need of sadness or false masks of piety. A glum face makes the assembly ill at ease and saps its vitality. Rather, let them radiate a calm and confident joy and a contagious enthusiasm. They ought to be so attractively persuasive that, in the words of Scripture, if the assembly does not sing, "the very stones will cry out . . ." (Hab 2:11).

The role of singing director is somewhat akin to the cantor's role prescribed by *Musicam Sacram:*

> Provision should be made for at least one or two properly trained singers, especially where there is no possibility of setting up even a small choir. The singer will present some simpler musical settings, with the people taking part, and can lead and support the faithful as far as is needed (MS, art. 21).[37]

---

[37] Flannery, op. cit., 86.

Outward Appearance

The director must have a convivial appearance because he or she is part of a celebration that is always festive. The director must also have an impeccable appearance. The most popular liturgy must never become a "T-shirt" liturgy but must always remain dignified, even if this dignity does not express itself as in the past.

Directors may, according to the custom of certain countries, dress in a liturgical vestment. Pius X, in *Tra le sollecitudini,* recommended that cantors wear ecclesiastical dress because they represent the "choir of levites." This custom has been continued in certain countries as well as in some children's choirs. We may ask if it is not better to declericalize the ministries that are not truly clerical. A layperson may certainly direct the assembly's singing without hiding his or her lay clothes under an alb. However, an alb may sometimes be useful for hiding the stigma of bad taste.

Gestures and movement must be convivial; they must also be appropriate. If directors must move about, let them do so calmly and devoutly. Discretion and artistic economy are essential qualities.

Their Placement

The location of the assembly's songleader depends partly on their function and partly on the church's layout. Each church poses a particular problem. The following points are in order:

> Directors must be visible to the entire assembly. This is a "must" if they are to be effective.

> Directors are not the central focal point; they must not hide the altar or overshadow the presider.

> Their place is not at the ambo (pulpit). This is reserved for the proclamation of the Word (epistle, responsorial psalm, gospel, homily) and the prayers that are attached to it.[38]

It is possible to have within the area of the sanctuary a fixed ambo of a certain size and importance on one side of the sanctuary, which harmonizes with the architecture of the altar and the presider's chair, and

---

[38] It is better for the commentator, cantor, or choir director not to use the lectern. GIRM 272.

a simple, unadorned lectern on the other side, from which it is possible to direct the assembly's singing. The ambo and the lectern have separate and different functions.

The ambo is the venerable place where the mystery spoken of by Vatican II is accomplished, for "it is [Christ] who speaks when the holy Scriptures are read in the Church."[39] The dignity of the ambo may be compared only to the dignity of the altar.

The lectern is the place where all the necessary cues are given to the assembly, whether about the singing, the rites of the celebration, or about anything concerned with the life of the parish community.

The Director's Goal

The goal of the music director is not primarily to ensure better singing but rather better prayer through a better execution of the singing.

No one may direct the assembly's prayer if they do not pray themselves.

The Golden Rule

The golden rule for leading the singing is: minimum intervention, maximum effect.

D. Julien has cleverly expressed this principle in the following wisdom, which every music director should learn by heart:

When a phrase suffices, don't give a speech.

When a word suffices, don't utter a phrase.

When a gesture suffices, don't utter a word.

When a look suffices, don't make a gesture.[40]

This discretion of the music director can become absolute. When the community sings a song in unison that it knows well, direction is irrelevant. And if irrelevant, it becomes harmful if it distracts.

It is wise not to direct at all whenever direction might hinder the quality of the community's prayer. This prayer that sometimes uses

[39] *Sacrosanctum Concilium* 7. The ambo and the altar are the two "tables" where "the two parts which in a sense go to make up the Mass, viz., the liturgy of the word and the eucharistic liturgy . . ." (ibid., 56) are celebrated.

[40] D. Julien, "Direction du chant d'assemblée, in *Eglise qui chante* 81 (1967) 15.

song must never be changed into a song about prayer, and thus merely a simple musical performance.

The Direction of the Singing

The direction of a professional choir has its own precise rules.[41] The direction of a parish choir has similar rules as well as its own customs, chiefly those of its director. The direction of an assembly is different. Outside the liturgical assembly, the assembly often sings well without direction. In the liturgical celebration, a good organist, playing on a good instrument, can give direction to the assembly. All direction of an assembly's singing is geared to facilitate the community's prayer. Particular directors have their charisms, and each assembly has its unique personality. The following are simply a few remarks of general interest.

Rhythmic Direction

The direction of the rhythm is the most useful one. It consists of establishing the basic rhythmic pattern.

It is easy to establish rapport with the first row; however, one should make conducting motions as if directed to the last row in the church. By doing this, the whole assembly, right to the back row, will find it easy to follow the director.

The dimension of the motions should correspond to the size of the assembly:

When directing a small assembly, gestures can be modest.

When directing a large assembly, gestures should be grander; the larger the assembly, the larger the gestures.

The larger the gestures, the fewer they should be. Placed in front of the assembly, and visible—in principle—to all, the director of singing must avoid all theatrical gestures.[42]

To give greater force to a gesture, the hand must be used as an extension of the forearm. It must not be just a dead weight on the end of the arm but rather an extension of the forearm.

---

[41] See the excellent work by W. J. Finn, *The Art of the Choral Conductor* (Evanston, Ill.: Summy-Birchard, 1960) vol. 2.

[42] See Finn, op. cit., 1.

The body should remain still. The director should not bob up and down or adopt a peculiar stance.

Melodic Direction

This sort of direction spells out the melodic line to the assembly, with its progression through different notes of the scale.

This method was particularly common in ancient times. It is useful above all when the assembly does not know the melody well; it also is effective with children.

In Conclusion

It is not surprising to know that some parishes do not always have good music directors. Good musicians are the result of training, study, and practice.

Neither should we believe that the grace of ordination or religious profession automatically confers a charism for directing an assembly well. Here, as elsewhere, grace does not replace hard work.

One final remark. The principles we give here are not given as gospel. They are to be taken with a certain good humor and freedom; they are to be applied flexibly, knowing that there are many ways of doing things well, but also many ways of doing things not so well.

Music directors might lovingly remember their Model, I mean Jesus himself, whom tradition has been pleased to call "chorègos," the conductor of a communal dance, for he directs the prayer of redeemed humanity, as Clement of Alexandria (d. ca. 215) so magnificently says:

> The Word of God, leaving the lyre and the harp, instruments without a soul, adapted himself to our world, and especially to human beings, microcosms [of the whole], and to their soul and body. He made use of this instrument of a million voices to praise God, he himself sang in harmony with this human instrument. . . . A human being is an instrument of God, tuned and holy.[43]

[43] *Protrepticus* 1.5, 3–4.

THE ORGANIST

A good instrument and a good organist are indeed a blessing for a celebrating community. If community and organist are as one, they can save a celebration from mediocrity. If celebrations succeed, organists no doubt have contributed to that success.

Accompanying the Singing

In speaking of the ministerial function of instruments, and therefore of the organ, *Musicam Sacram* gives them the role of accompanying the singing as their principal task:

> The use of musical instruments to accompany the singing can act as a support to the voices, render participation easier, and achieve a deeper union in the assembly. . . . In sung or said Masses, the organ, or other instrument legitimately admitted, can be used to accompany the singing of the choir and the people (MS, arts. 64–65).[44]

These statements seem banal. Yet, in terms of history, they codify a recent practice in the Church. Until the nineteenth century, plainsong was sung without accompaniment,[45] and the Great Organ, when it was used, was always played alone. It was only when orchestras were suppressed—often for economic reasons—that the organ began to be used to play the instrumental parts. Its role became increasingly important. So-called "accompanying" organs were installed in the choirs of churches and were used to accompany the singing, a role for which the Great Organ had not been designed.

The ministerial function of the organ in this area can be a major one. In practice, in the majority of parishes that have a good organ, the organ takes over the function of leading the assembly's singing. It sustains the melody and renders rhythm and pitch.

A good organist will always choose the range[46] that is best suited to the community. The composer has written the music in the key that is best for the music. But the organist must accompany the song in the key that is most suited to the community. Organists must

---

[44] Flannery, op. cit., 96.

[45] See J. Bonfils, "Note historique sur le rôle de l'orgue dans la liturgie catholique," in *L'Eglise qui chante* 16 (1959) 7–8.

[46] The span of notes within which most tones of a voice part or melody lie.

therefore be masters of transposition, so that they may adequately accompany the voices of women, of men, or of children.

There is a fundamental difference between the execution of a classical musical piece and the accompanying of the community's singing. The first must be played strictly, according to the composer's intentions. The aim is a sort of re-creation. The assembly's singing, sustained by the organ accompaniment, is like a new creation.

It should be noted that the singing range of an assembly that is used to singing is greater than that of an inexperienced assembly. For the experienced congregation, an upper E on the staff is easily sung; for the inexperienced, a C or C# is about as high as the assembly can sing without disagreeable notes making themselves heard. For both, it is not the extreme passing notes that are the most important, but the middle range where the melody is situated. The middle range in which the voices are most at ease are the notes E, F, G, A on the lower part of the staff, or F, G, A, B-flat; or even, for a well-trained assembly, G, A, B, C.[47]

A well-accompanied assembly is the supreme art of the liturgical organist. What a joy it is to have in his hands some hundreds of singing voices, and to sustain them in the praise of the Lord! In this art, knowledge and technique must be perfect. Mediocrity is unforgivable.

Solo Playing

The organ frames the songs by introducing them with preludes or prolonging them with postludes. The choral preludes of Bach's *Orgelbuchlein* are masterpieces that show to what heights song embellishment can attain.

Usually the organ intones the song by playing a brief introduction. It is the organ that creates a lyrical environment in which the assembly can sing.

The beginning strains must create a melodic pattern that blends easily into the melody of the song. It should seduce and invite the community to sing. The musical introduction must not detract from the melody that comes after it. A melody has a pattern and a dynamic, just as human beings have faces and life-force. One must not mutilate the "face" of a melody or shoot it down as hunters shoot down birds in full flight!

[47] See the excellent remarks on this subject by G. Nassoy, in *Le guide liturgique de l'organiste,* Coll. Kinnor (Paris: Fleurus, 1965) 125–34.

Organists should write out their introductions in musical notation, especially for songs most often used. Four or five well thought-out measures are worth much more than an improvisation that busies itself in some melodic chatter.

When one does not have time to prepare, often the best solution is to play the first phrase of the song in its entirety as the introduction.

The Rhythm

It is the rhythm given in the opening measures that the community will take up. It must therefore be played with clarity and precision.

The rhythm of the song must be maintained throughout the introduction, right into the opening measures of the song. To have a pause after the organ has intoned the opening is a sure way to disturb the assembly, which knows almost intuitively the precise moment at which it must begin to sing. If the assembly is to sing at ease, it must be given the greatest possible sense of security.

The tempo indicated by the composer is usually the ideal tempo for the song. Yet the ideal tempo for the assembly is the one most comfortable. Ideally, the assembly should follow the composer's tempo marking. Yet it is easily understood that a little group celebrating a Eucharist in someone's home may find themselves singing more in an allegro vein rather than in a Sunday assembly's moderato.

A tempo is usually set somewhat slower when there is a large architectural volume in the church or prolonged reverberation. One must always take reverberation into account or the song will be ruined by the sound lingering at the end of a phrase and into the beginning of the next.

The organ must also "breathe" with the assembly. If phrases are linked without a breath, the singing will be drowned out by the organ.

Harmony

Harmony is sometimes useful, sometimes necessary, to bring out the "feel" of a melody.

To announce the melody clearly, it is wise at times to begin the piece in unison, adding the harmony once the community has recognized the melody. A brilliant harmonization that obscures the melody is a disservice to the hesitant ears of the faithful. It is, rather, the organist who should be brilliant in introducing the piece and skillfully and richly voicing the harmonic organ accompaniment.

Other Considerations

Musicam Sacram (art. 65) speaks of solo organ playing before the celebration, at the presentation of the gifts, at communion, and at the end of the liturgy. We might add to that the brief moments of silence after the penitential rite and after the homily.

Let organists not be timid! Let them welcome the community as though having long awaited its arrival; and at the end of the celebration, let them prolong their playing as though they regret having to leave the congregation.

If organists master the art of improvisation, they will be able to hint at the entrance song at the beginning of the Mass, and lengthen the recessional at its conclusion.

Solo organ playing must be appropriate to the celebration. It is not the time to present one's free-concert repertoire before a captive audience: this is to betray the liturgical service demanded. The temptation is certainly present: what artist can count on having such a patient audience each and every Sunday? Yet to play the great works on every occasion is the surest way to devalue them. Certain toccata, if they could speak, would cry out in anguish at having been dragged into every procession. Christian organists must serve the community and its prayer-life, not their own reputations.

The instruction does not allow solo organ playing during Advent, Lent, and Holy Week (art. 66),[48] which is regretful. Such an attitude derives from an era when organ playing was considered festive and joyous. But the organ may also serve the community in times of penitence or mourning. Some of Silbermann's organ pieces weep, and some of Bach's chorales are very maudlin. Besides, an organist who cannot help the community to pray in times of penitence will scarcely know how to make it rejoice in festive times.

The special ministry of the organist is to lead the community to God through the path of beauty. On this path toward God, the organist walks at the head of the assembly. The organist's task is prayer.

Bach used to decorate his scores with the letters J. J., which signified *Jesu juva*, that is, "Jesus help." He signed them with the letters S.D.G., *Soli Deo Gloria* = "to God alone be glory." Not every organist can imitate the greatness of Bach. Yet all must imitate his prayer.

48 Flannery, op. cit., 96.

Part Three
The Songs of the Mass

Songs that the liturgy uses in its Eucharistic celebrations do not all have the same form or structure. There is a world of difference between the ornate chant of a jubilus on an Alleluia and the simple and unadorned cantillation of the responsorial psalm. There are also different structures, motivated by the liturgical action itself: a litany has a different structure from that of a hymn. Each song has its own personality and pattern. It is at its most authentic when it fulfills the particular ministerial function the liturgy assigns to it.

In the past, communities would sometimes choose four canticles to "animate" the liturgy: one as an entrance chant, one at the offertory, one for communion, and one for the recessional. Perhaps this formula still exists. This provision of a "Mass of four canticles," while much better than total improvisation, nevertheless seriously depersonalized the songs and made them all canticles. The Mass was unbalanced by drowning it in uniformity. The structure of the Mass is shown to best advantage when each song fulfills its ministerial function in the liturgy. It is obvious that the entrance, presentation of the gifts, communion and closing rites, and the songs that accompany them all, have different ministerial functions.

We may distinguish:

The dialogues and acclamations

The responsorial psalm

The litanies of the Lord have mercy, prayer of the faithful, and Lamb of God

The entrance, gospel, presentation of the gifts and communion processional songs

The *Gloria* and the hymn at the gospel

The thanksgiving hymn and the final song

The Creed.

3

The Dialogues and Acclamations

The dialogues and acclamations that punctuate the celebration are:

The greeting at the opening of the celebration

The Amen that concludes the prayers

The acclamation that follows the first and second readings

The dialogue that proceeds the proclamation of the gospel and concludes it

The dialogue that opens the preface

The acclamation of the *Sanctus* (Holy, holy, holy)

The anamnesis (Memorial Acclamation)

The doxology that concludes the Eucharistic Prayer

The doxology of the Lord's Prayer

The greeting of peace before communion

The final benediction and the sending forth at the end of the celebration.

All these acclamations and dialogues are to be submitted to the principle of human authenticity, a principal that may be enunciated as follows: Whatever its form, whether sung or said, a dialogue should be engaged in as a true dialogue, and an acclamation should be executed as an authentic acclamation.

The dialogue must truly be just that. It is addressed to someone and asks for a response. If the priest says "The Lord be with you" while bowing his head or gazing vaguely into space, he is not dialoguing with the assembly. If the assembly replies in a mournful voice, bowing its own head, one has the right to believe that it has not taken the priest's greeting seriously!

The presider must constantly watch the quality of his presence before the assembly. There is a way of addressing the assembly that is so lifeless that it evokes no response. There is also another way, which, while it keeps all the modesty fitting for a liturgical celebration, evokes the assembly's united and joyous response. We must take our bodies seriously, especially our voices that reveal our souls, so that dialogues remain authentically human. This problem, which is situated beyond the problem of music, is first a problem of human authenticity.

The acclamation must also be authentically human. It is a tautology to say that an acclamation is only an acclamation if it acclaims effectively. We do not say "Praise to you, Lord Jesus Christ" in the same way as "Lord have mercy." It is not a question of asking the faithful to sing louder but simply of asking them to be more authentic!

Several acclamations and dialogues present no particular problem. It suffices to accomplish them with dignity, according to what the liturgical rules demand. Others are worth particular consideration.

THE LORD BE WITH YOU . . . AND
WITH YOUR SPIRIT

At the beginning of the Eucharistic celebration the priest greets the assembly. The Missal gives three formulas as models. The simplest is the traditional *The Lord be with you.* This phrase appears in many other celebrations. It would be a mistake to consider it and use it as a simple stock phrase intended to rouse the attention of the assembly. It is a biblical formula, full of meaning. It contains one of the most essential revelations of the Word of God.

Biblical Meaning

The affirmation of God's presence among his people is part of the covenant formula that God makes with Abraham:

"I am the God of your father Abraham; do not be afraid, for *I am with you* and will bless you and make your offspring numerous for my servant Abraham's sake."[1]

In Deuteronomy, the formula *I am with you* evokes the saving protection with which God surrounds his people.[2] In the literature of the Exile, it is found in the themes of return and restoration:

> But as for you, have no fear, my servant Jacob, says the LORD,
> and do not be dismayed, O Israel;
> for I am going to save you from far away,
> and your offspring from the land of their captivity
> Jacob shall return and have quiet and ease,
> and no one shall make him afraid.
> For *I am with you,* says the LORD, to save you . . .[3]

God's saving presence that accompanies his people all along the path toward the New Covenant is fully realized in the Incarnation of Christ Jesus. He is Emmanuel, *God-with-us.*[4] The messianic age begins when the angel says to Mary, the daughter of Zion:

> Greetings, favored one! *The Lord is with you.*[5]

Thus the definitive dwelling of God with his own is inaugurated. To the affirmation of the Gospel,

> And the Word became flesh and lived among us, and we have seen his glory, the glory as of a father's only son, full of grace and truth (John 1:14).

the prophecy of Revelation responds:

> See, the home of God is among mortals.
> He will dwell with them as their God;
> they will be his peoples,
> and God himself will be with them (Rev 21:3).

When the priest says to the people "The Lord be with you," the mystery of the descent of the Eternal One into time, of Jesus' compassion

---

[1] Gen 26:24 [italics mine–L. D.]. Cf. Gen 26:3 and 46:3. For a detailed analysis of the formula *The Lord is with Thee,* see L. Deiss, *Mary, Daughter of Sion* (Collegeville, Minn.: The Liturgical Press, 1972) 67–75.

[2] Cf. Deut 20:1-4; Pss 46:8 and 12. Italics mine–L. D.

[3] Jer 30:11 [italics mine–L. D.]; cf. Isa 41:8-14; 43:1-5.

[4] See Isa 7:14; 8:14; Matt 1:23.

[5] Luke 1:28 [italics mine–L. D.]; see Deiss, *Mary, Daughter of Sion,* 67–111.

for human misery, and of the God whom one cannot see without dying, present in Word and Bread, is signified: it is the whole mystery of God's saving design. The promise of the Lord is realized in the liturgy:

> "And remember, *I am with you* always, to the end of the age" (Matt 28:20; italics mine–L. D.).

In the reformed Missal of 1969, the greeting "The Lord be with you" appears four times (seven times in the old Missal). Each greeting underlines an aspect of the liturgical mystery.

In the first greeting, "the priest reminds the assembled people that the Lord is present. This greeting and the congregation's response express the mystery of the gathered Church."[6] In coming together, Christians form the body of Christ.

The second greeting, before the proclamation of the gospel, reminds the assembly of Christ's presence in the Word, "[for it is Christ] who speaks when the holy Scriptures are read in the church" (SC, art. 7).[7]

The third greeting is part of the dialogue with which the preface begins: it is together with Christ himself that the assembly gives thanks to the Father.

The last greeting is placed before the final blessing and dismissal: Christ accompanies those who go to carry the good news to their sisters and brothers in the world.

In saying "The Lord be with you," the priest remembers the name of Jesus, Emmanuel, *God-with-us*. The Christian community also bears this name itself before the world.

AND ALSO WITH YOU

The original Hebrew phrase, followed by the Latin of the *editio typica,* is literally "And with your spirit." It can simply be translated "And with you," as in the contemporary English translation of the *Ordo Missae.* Paul greets the Galatians in a quasiliturgical way: "May the grace of our Lord Jesus Christ be with your spirit, brothers and sisters. Amen."[8] The Christian assembly thus accepts the desire the

---

[6] GIRM 28.
[7] Flannery, op. cit., 5.
[8] Gal 6:18. See also Phil 4:23; 2 Tim 4:22.

priest expresses; the assembly replies that Christ is likewise with the one who presides.

The liturgical tradition, attested to since the time of Hippolytus of Rome (ca. 215 C.E.), retained this Hebrew formula and never substituted an equivalent. It was enriched with a new dimension. The "spirit" of the presiding priest is a spirit in which the Spirit lives and works, a spirit gifted with the charism of priesthood. In replying "And with your spirit," the assembly recognizes in the priest a sort of spokesperson of its own prayer, and venerates the charism of ministerial priesthood present in him. It is as if the assembly says to him, "May God's Spirit truly dwell in your spirit, so that you may express our prayer forcibly, and present it to God."[9]

Song

The priest will only be able to say to the community "The Lord be with you," and the community "And also with you," with the infinite respect that the density and religious depth of the text require regardless of the degree of solemnity attributed to a particular celebration. The question is "Should this dialogue be sung?"

Should it be sung at every Mass? When two friends meet, they do not sing "Hello," at least not in the context of contemporary society. When the priest meets the community—in a contemporary setting—should he sing this greeting?

The "official" chant that is generally used does not evoke much enthusiasm. It is not meant to do so. It is simply meant to be suitable for most priests to sing—as it is. Intelligently used, it can carry the text perfectly.

Among the different ministerial functions performed by song, *Musicam Sacram* mentions the ability that song has to express the unity of the celebrating community.[10] If a small community crowded into a limited area can reply to the greeting of the priest, a large assembly, especially if it is dispersed in a nave where there is lingering reverberation, has difficulty in so doing. The voices are dispersed, lack cohesion, and are lost in a reverberating hum. A large assembly reveals its unity and clearly expresses it when its voices are gathered together

---

[9] See *Apostolic Tradition* 4. See also L. Deiss, *The Springtime of the Liturgy* (Collegeville, Minn.: The Liturgical Press, 1979) 121ff.

[10] See n. 27, p. 17.

in a determined rhythmic pulse and given pitch; in other words, when it sings. It seems fitting, then, that a large assembly should generally sing the dialogues and acclamations if it wants to express itself with a certain unity.

This rule is followed by instinct in the linguistic groups that use tonal languages, in equatorial Africa, for example, or in the Far East. In these languages, which are sometimes poor in concepts but very rich in expressive possibilities, all words are song and all song is rhythm. Communities express themselves communally; the faithful, in "saying" their prayers, cannot say them except by saying them together, and this "saying" is more like "singing." There, one never hears the confused buzz of our Western assemblies. The voices instinctively unite and harmonize in rhythm and pitch. A great musical sound rises up from the assembly. They "sing" like this whether it is the Our Father, the act of contrition, a catechism lesson, or a gospel passage. Once you hear this sort of cantillation, you can never forget it. It is a rhythmic balance full of majesty, like the sway of the palm trees that dance in the evening breeze; or like the waves of the Congo rapids, a flowing melody that endlessly renews itself; or like the melody that breathes and flows in the interval of a fourth or even a fifth, while remaining a word.

Most of our European languages have neglected the sense of rhythm and melody by excessive concentration on conceptualizing. Our personalities, through excessive individualism, have lost some of their ability to express things communally. To give voice to unity, we must sing!

Further Reflections

Including "The Lord be with you," the Missal suggests two other formulas as models.

The first takes up the end of the Second Letter to the Corinthians:

> The grace of Our Lord Jesus Christ, the love of God, and the communion of the Holy Spirit be with all of you. [And also with you.]

Of all the concluding Pauline formulas, this one is the most trinitarian. It is thought that it may reflect the liturgical usage of the Pauline Churches.

The other formula suggested by the Missal must have been very familiar to Paul. It is found at the beginning of the Letter to the

Romans (1:7), the Letter to the Galatians (1:3), and the First Letter to the Corinthians (1:3):

> Grace to you and peace from God our Father and the Lord Jesus Christ. [Blessed be God now and forever!]

Thus the community responds to the priest by blessing God. Such benedictions are found in the purest biblical tradition.

Note that this greeting is a pleasing combination of Hebrew and Greek. Greek-speaking people would greet each other in the time of Christ by saying *Chaire* = "Rejoice!" *Chaire* is similar to *charis*, which means grace. Hebrew-speaking people would greet each other by saying *Shalom* = "Peace." In wishing grace and peace, Paul, who had mastered both Hebrew and Greek, happily united the wishes of the Greek culture with those of the Hebrew culture.[11]

The Missal gives these formulas as examples. Priests must be creative and draw deeply from the treasury of New Testament formulas. Here are some other examples:

> Grace, mercy, and peace from God the Father and Christ Jesus our Lord (1 Tim 1:2).

> Sisters and brothers,
> may God the Father and our Lord Jesus Christ
> grant [you] peace, charity and faith.
> Grace be with all who love our Lord Jesus Christ!

The doxological repertory is particularly rich.[12] It is little known in the Christian community, no doubt because we no longer have the grateful soul that sang praise in the primitive Church. Here is a superb formula that sees the Church as the receptacle of glory in which Christ lives:

> To [God] be glory in the church and in Christ Jesus
> to all generations, forever and ever. Amen (Eph 3:21).

A last suggestion. It is possible to compose the blessing formula either by evoking the mystery about to be celebrated or by taking as a starting point the Word about to be proclaimed.[13] As an example,

[11] See M. Carrez, *Les Langues de la Bible* (Paris: Le Centurion, 1983) 86–87.
[12] See *Springtime of the Liturgy*, where we give the principal New Testament doxologies.
[13] See, for instance, the introductory blessings in L. Deiss, *Reflections of His Word* (Chicago: World Library Publications, 1980, 1981, 1982).

after the usual greeting "The Lord be with you," one might use for Christmas Day:

> Glory to God in the highest heaven,
> and peace on earth to all on this feast of Christmas,
> for God our Father in heaven loves us!
> He has given us his Son, Jesus, Emmanuel,
> to be our Savior and our brother.
> He fills our hearts with the joy of his Spirit.
> Yes, glory to God our Father
> forever and ever! Amen.

For the opening blessing—after the usual greeting—for the feast of the Epiphany, one could say:

> We bless you, God our Father.
> You have lighted the star of faith in our souls.
> Keep its light shining in us
> until the day when the Star of morning,
> Jesus Christ, your Son,
> will rise in our hearts,
> he, our Savior and our brother,
> forever and ever! Amen.

This first word of the priest to the community, the first meeting with his sisters and brothers in the presence of the Lord of glory, must radiate the joy of being gathered together with Christ in order to listen to his Word and celebrate his covenant according to the ancient ritual formula of Deuteronomy:

> And you shall rejoice before the LORD your God (Deut 12:12).

AMEN: ITS BIBLICAL MEANING

Amen is one of the smallest words sung but one of the most powerful in the liturgy, a word full of majesty and glory.

Amen comes from the Semitic root *aman* that means firm, solid. From this first meaning, Hebrew passes to the idea of *truth* and *fidelity*. This development may seem to us a spiritualization of a primitive image, but for a Semite it is only the obvious application of the first meaning: what is true is what we can feel with our hands, something that has a certain consistency and solidity; one who is faithful is someone on whom we may lean, a friend who is "solid" and "firm."

Amen can be both an affirmation (in the sense of "this is") and a prayer (in the sense of "may this be").

The Book of Revelation reveals the full importance of the solemn *affirmation* of the Amen when it juxtaposes "yes" to the affirmation, in the vision of Christ Jesus, the First-born from the dead:

> to him be glory and dominion forever and ever. Amen.
> Look! He is coming with clouds;
>   every eye will see him,
> even those who pierced him;
>   and on his account all the tribes of the earth will wail.
> So it is to be. Amen (Rev 1:6-7).

The Amen that concludes this plea for God's blessing or the invocation of God's name over the assembly is a prayer. The benediction formula that is found in the Book of Numbers (6:24-26) may be cited in this context: each invocation is acclaimed by the Amen of the community.[14]

Amen, the Name of Jesus Christ

In the Old Testament, God reveals himself as the God-Amen:

> Anyone in the land invoking a blessing on himself
> will do so by God whose name is Amen,
> and anyone in the land taking an oath
> will do so by God whose name is Amen . . . (Isa 65:16–*Revised English Bible*).

The God-Amen is the sure and firm God on whom we may lean as against an immovable rock, and the faithful God who fulfills all his promises.

In the context of the New Covenant, Christ Jesus himself is the God-Amen, according to the witness of the Book of Revelation:

> These are the words of the Amen, the faithful and true witness (Rev 3:14).

---

[14] See also Deut 27:15-26. Each curse is ratified by the Amen of the assembly at Shechem, which is given the sense of "so be it!" This self-curse represents a particularly solemn form of commitment.

Amen is Jesus' personal name, it is part of his royal and messianic title, and it introduces his other names: Witness (literally, martyr = one who gives witness), The Faithful One, The True One. In giving the Lord this superbly fitting name, John signifies not only that God remains faithful to his promises in Jesus, but also that God's faithfulness is revealed in and through the person of Jesus.

When Christians reply "Amen," do they know that they are pronouncing the Lord's name?

Jesus' Amen

Jesus himself used the Amen in a totally unique way not found elsewhere: "Amen, I say to you." This expression, so full of authority, must have struck his contemporaries.[15] By introducing his words with Amen, Jesus was proclaiming that they were absolutely sure, solid, and worthy of trust; he was speaking as *the* Amen, *the* True, *the* Faithful:

> Amen, Amen, I say to you,
> we speak of what we know,
> and we testify to what we have seen (John 3:11–New American Bible).

The Amen of the Church, Response to the "Yes" of God

Christ is the supreme gift the Father offers to humanity. He is also the living way by which humanity returns to the Father. It is in him that we receive God, and by him that we return to God. Paul illustrates well this double aspect:

> For in him every one of God's promises is a "Yes." For this reason it is through him that we say "Amen" to the glory of God (2 Cor 1:20).

God's "Yes," the realization of his promises, is Christ, and it is through Christ that the Father says his "Yes" to humanity. The Church's Amen is also Christ, and it is also through Christ that this Amen reaches the Father.

The Amen of the Doxologies

Amen normally concludes the doxology that gives glory (*doxa* in Greek) to God.

---

[15] Matthew gives it thirty-one times, Mark, thirteen times, Luke, six, and John, five times (John doubles the Amen).

The most significant doxologies of the Old Testament are those that conclude the first four books of the psalms (Pss 41:14; 72:19; 89:53; 106:48). The doxology of the second book is particularly solemn:

> Blessed be the LORD, the God of Israel,
>   who alone does wondrous things.
> Blessed be his glorious name forever;
>   may his glory fill the whole earth.
> Amen and Amen (Ps 72:18-19).

These doxologies not only concern the four concluding psalms but refer to the whole psalter. Jewish tradition saw the psalter as the "book of praises," *sepher tehillim*. This book of praises is "the book of songs and prayer of the postexilic community."[16] The prayer of the covenant people is essentially doxological. The Amen carries the community's praise.

In the New Testament, doxologies take all sorts of forms. They may be a simple acclamation, a sort of ejaculatory prayer that is inserted into the text to suddenly raise the soul to God "who is blessed eternally. Amen."[17]

> To our God and Father be glory forever and ever. Amen (Phil 4:20).

> To [Jesus Christ] belong the glory and the power forever and ever. Amen (1 Pet 4:11).

In these citations[18] Amen is found in the context of a *glory* that is proclaimed as eternal, *forever and ever;* this glory is not a glory God receives from human praise but is first and essentially that glory which God possesses in himself, the weight of the glory of God's riches, power, and light. Human praise can add nothing to this Reality; it can only recognize it by its Amen.

Other well-crafted doxologies develop in a quasiliturgical style. This is especially true of the two solemn acclamations that are found in the First Letter to Timothy. Their vocabulary, which is typically Greek, suggests that they find their origin in the Greek-speaking synagogues, and that they reflect the liturgical prayer in the Diaspora:

---

[16] H.-J. Kraus, *Psalmen* (Neukirchen: Neukirchener Verlag, 1960) XVIII.
[17] See Rom 1:25; 9:5.
[18] See also Eph 3:21; 2 Tim 4:18; Heb 13:21; 1 Pet 5:11; 2 Pet 3:18; Jude 25.

To the King of the ages, immortal, invisible, the only God, be honor and glory forever and ever. Amen (1 Tim 1:17).

To the blessed and only sovereign
to the King of kings and Lord of lords,
to him who alone possesses immortality,
who dwells in unapproachable light,
whom no one has ever seen or can see;
to him honor and power for ever! Amen (1 Tim 6:15-16).[19]

Seen in this context of glory, power, honor, and eternity, our Amen takes on a surprising relief: it is no longer the "little" word that we add to a prayer to signify that it is completed. Rather, it is an acclamation that is full of power, drawing us into the eternal world of praise.

The Amen of Myriad Angels in the Heavenly Liturgy

Finally, the Amen is found in the heavenly liturgy described in the Book of Revelation. It belongs to the four living creatures (angels) and ratifies the praise of the myriads of angels and of each and every other creature:

Then I looked, and I heard the voice of many angels surrounding the throne and the living creatures and the elders; they numbered myriads of myriads and thousands of thousands, singing with full voice,

"Worthy is the Lamb that was slaughtered
to receive power and wealth and wisdom and might
and honor and glory and blessing!"

Then I heard every creature in heaven and on earth and under the earth and in the sea, and all that is in them, singing,

"To the one seated on the throne and to the Lamb
be blessing and honor and glory and might forever and ever!"

And the four living creatures said, "Amen" (Rev 5:11-14).[20]

Bossuet comments: "In the Book of Revelation, the elect are represented as always saying Amen before God. Amen, in the holy languages, that is, 'Yes,' but an eager and affirmative yes that carries away

[19] Translation—L. D. See also the two solemn doxologies in Rom 11:33-36 and 16:25-27 and Gal 1:5.
[20] See also Rev 7:12 and 19:4.

acquiescence, or rather the heart. God is so loved in heaven: shall we not love God in this way on earth? O church that journeys in this place of exile, the blessed Jerusalem, your dear sister who triumphs in heaven, sings this Amen to God; will you not respond to this divine song, as a second choir, enlivened by the voice of Jesus Christ himself?"[21]

Liturgical and Musical Significance of the Amen

If music must faithfully serve the liturgical text, the melodies used for the Amen must communicate glory, power, and majesty. The problem is that the Amen is a very short word, and there is scarcely time to notice it before it is gone.

The author of the Book of Revelation prolonged the Amen by adding Alleluia to it: "Amen. Alleluia" (Rev 19:4). Gregorian chant extended the melodic line of the Amen in order to amplify it. The chant takes nineteen notes for the Amen that concludes the Creed in *Credo IV.* Palestrina also prolonged it: the Amen that concludes the *Credo* of the Mass of Pope Marcel lasts for twelve bars. The Amen of Bach's *Mass in B Minor* lasts for some one hundred and one bars; the sopranos alone take up the Amen fifteen times in melodies worthy of Bach's genius. All this is to say that the acclamation Amen is a meaningful and beautiful word with which to make music. Here we can no longer speak of a liturgical acclamation but only of musical splendor.

At a pastoral level, we must see clearly what is possible. The Amen is said twelve times in the Mass. All these Amens do not have the same importance. Here is a general principle: The importance of the Amen is in direct proportion to the importance of what it confirms.

The Amen of the Collects

The celebrating community ratifies the presidential prayer of the presider. This presidential prayer is said in the name of the community at the opening of the Mass, then over the gifts, and finally, after communion.

If we believe St. Jerome, the Amen resounded in the Roman basilicas like a clap of thunder coming from heaven.[22] Would that the

[21] *Oeuvres oratoires,* ed. Lebarcq, t. 4 (Paris 1930) 291–92, cited by B. Botte, *L'Ordinaire de la Messe,* Coll. Etudes liturgiques (Paris, Louvain: Cerf, Abbaye du Mont César, 1953) 103–4.

[22] *In Gal. Comm.,* 1.2–PL 26.355.

people's Amen might ring out decisively, even perhaps tumultuously. This would presuppose, however, that the presider prompt the acclamation by his own clarion call!

Certain communities like to accompany the Amen with the organ or with the choir's harmonious accompaniment. In principle, nothing that highlights the Amen is to be rejected. The organ and choir, however, should not substitute for the assembly's participation but rather should support and intensify it.

The Amen of the Eucharistic Prayer

If the importance of the Amen is proportionate to the importance of what it confirms, the Amen that concludes the doxology and the entire Eucharistic Prayer is the most important. It must flow from the community as a glorious and majestic acclamation.

We possess a testimony to this Amen in the earliest account we have of the Mass; it comes from Justin Martyr and dates from ca. 150 C.E.:

> Then bread and a cup of wine mixed with water are brought to him over the brethren. He takes them and offers prayers glorifying the Father of the universe through the name of the Son and of the Holy Spirit, and he utters a lengthy eucharist because the Father has judged us worthy of these gifts.
>
> When the prayers and eucharist are finished, all the people present give their assent with an "Amen!" "Amen" in Hebrew means "So be it."
>
> [Then] those whom we call "deacons" distribute the bread and the wine mixed with water over which the eucharist has been spoken, to each of those present. . . . This food we call "eucharist" . . . .

In the description of the liturgy on the Day of the Lord, Justin writes likewise:

> As we said earlier, when we have finished praying, bread, wine, and water are brought up. The president then prays and gives thanks according to his ability, and *the people give their assent with an "Amen!"*[23]

The liturgy Justin describes develops into an atmosphere of praise, thanksgiving, and an enthusiasm strong enough to make us

---

[23] *Apology 1,* in Deiss, *Springtime,* 92–93. Italics mine–L. D.

jealous. The president *gives thanks,* the people sing their Amen in thanksgiving, and what they receive is called thanksgiving.

Justin, a layperson, has a marked sense of his own participation as a member of the faithful, and of the role that is his in the Eucharistic celebration: to make the presider's thanksgiving his own by the acclamation "Amen." *The people give their assent by saying "Amen!"*

What is to be done today? The two syllables *A-men* are evidently too short to create an acclamation of a certain weight. The triple Amen, which is inspired by some of the Eastern liturgies, provides a solution that the community can easily manage.

Here is a formula that goes with the chant: "Through him, with him, and in him . . ." and the melody suggested by the Missal:

FORMULA I

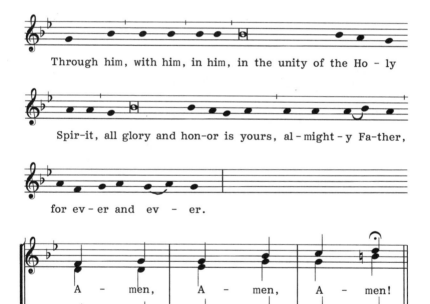

This formula goes with the "official" tone of the doxology, a tone that takes its inspiration from the Latin melody (the B-natural of the final chord is optional).

Here are two other tonal formulas. The first is best when the presider has a tenor or baritone voice:

Formula II

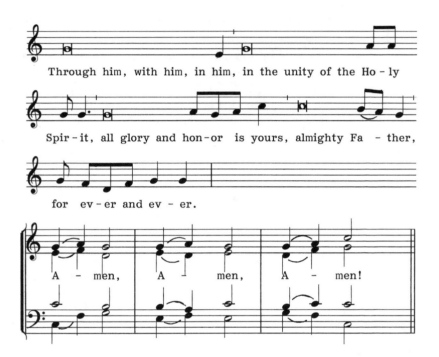

Formula III

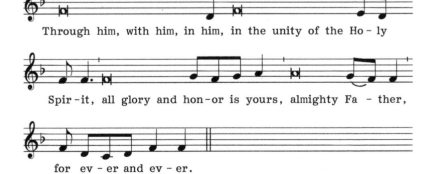

Instead of singing the doxology, the presider may also simply proclaim it if he judges it more appropriate (or at least proclaim the final *forever and ever*) on the note G (first formula and second formula), or the note F (third formula), in such a way as to "call forth" the assembly's triple Amen.

These formulas may also be sung a tone lower if the presider is more comfortable with a lower pitch.

In other formulas, the Amen is integrated into the doxology itself according to the following scheme:

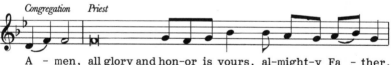

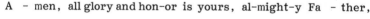

Lastly, inspired by the heavenly liturgy of Revelation 19:4, where the angels celebrate God's triumph by singing Amen-Alleluia, we can create an acclamation of a certain length that can easily be set to music:

A - men, Al - le - lu - ia, A - men, Al - le -

lu - ia. A - men, Al - le - lu - ia!

The Doxology of the Lord's Prayer

The last petition of the "Our Father," *Deliver us from evil* . . . , is expanded by a prayer called the embolism (from ἐμβόλισμα, additional piece): *Deliver us, Lord, from every evil* . . . . This prayer itself is concluded by a doxology:

> For the kingdom, the power and the glory are yours
> now and forever.

This doxology is sometimes joined to the text of the Our Father given by the Gospel of Matthew. It does not belong to the original text of the Gospel. It is, rather, a liturgical acclamation coming from the first or second century that was inserted later—maybe in the third century—in the text of Matthew.[25] It was formerly used by the Eastern churches and by the Protestant denominations. It is now a prayer that is a common treasure for all Christians.

It is always appropriate to sing God's praise and glory. Nevertheless, there are some questions about the place of this doxology in the Roman Mass.

First of all, a doxology always manifests a certain climax in the celebration. After the solemn doxology *Through him, with him, in him* . . . that concludes the Eucharistic Prayer, it does not seem right to have another climax in the ensuing doxology *For the kingdom* . . . . The doxology of the Eucharistic Prayer hides in some way the importance of the doxology of the Lord's Prayer. That is the reason why this last doxology is sometimes reduced to a prayer having no more importance than the prayer *Deliver us, Lord, from every evil* . . . .

Secondly, when the Our Father is prayed in the Mass, the congregation concludes it with the doxology, but only after the priest

---

[24] Fiche A1 197, music by J. P. Lécot, is an excellent setting for this formula.
[25] See J. Carmignac, *Recherches sur le "Notre Père"* (Paris: Letouzey & Ané, 1969) 333.

pronounces some intervening phrases, beginning with *Deliver us, Lord, from every evil . . .;* often, the congregation seems to want to add the doxology immediately, without waiting for the priest. It is an awkward situation. In any case, this phrase was an addition. It could become an omission.

Finally, the doxology of the Eucharistic Prayer, *Through him, with him, in him . . .* is prayed by the priest alone, whereas the doxology after the Our Father is said by the entire congregation.[26] There is no clear theological reason to reserve one doxology to the priest alone and the other one to the congregation. It sometimes happens that the entire congregation—even if it is not according to the rubrics—says the doxology of the Eucharistic Prayer. And many priests do not see a theological reason to prevent them from adding *all glory and honor is yours, almighty Father . . . .*

A certain erosion of the rubrics is not necessarily a sign of rubrical nonchalance or of liturgical disobedience. It can also be a sign of the true life. The sacramentary is not a dead book but a living one, given to a living community.

The Amen at Communion

Liturgical reforms have reclaimed the ancient way of receiving communion, such as this one recommended by Cyril of Jerusalem (d. ca. 387):

> When you come forward, do not draw near with your hands wide open or with your fingers spread apart; instead, with your left hand make a throne for the right hand, which will receive the King. Receive the body of Christ in the hollow of your hand and give the response: "Amen."[27]

The custom of the communicant saying Amen seems to be from an early tradition. In *Apostolic Tradition* (ca. 215), Hippolytus witnesses to the rite in use at Rome:

> After breaking the bread, he distributes each piece, saying:
> The bread of heaven
> in Christ Jesus!
> The person receiving it is to answer: "Amen!"[28]

---

[26] In the Eastern liturgies, this acclamation is reserved for the priest. See R. Cabié, "L'Eucharistie," in A. G. Martimort, *L'Eglise en prière,* vol. II (Paris: Desclée, 1983) 230.

[27] *Mystagogical Catecheses* V.21, in Deiss, *Springtime,* 289.

[28] *Apostolic Tradition* 21, in Deiss, *Springtime,* 144.

About the same time, Tertullian witnesses to a similar practice in the African church.[29]

Augustine explains that this Amen expressed the faith of the one who communicates, not only in the mystery of the Eucharist but also in the mystery of the Church, the body of Christ:

If you wish to understand what the body of Christ is, listen to what the Apostle says to the faithful:

> You are the body of Christ and his members (1 Cor 12:27). If therefore, you are the body of Christ and his members, it is your mystery that is celebrated on the table of the Lord, it is your own mystery that you receive. You respond Amen to what you are, you assent to it in responding. You hear, "The Body of Christ," and you respond, "Amen." Be therefore, a member of the body of Christ, so that your Amen may be true.[30]

ACCLAMATIONS OF THE WORD OF GOD

After the First and Second Readings

After the first and second readings it is possible to add "Word of the Lord." The assembly responds to this acclamation with "Thanks be to God."

This acclamation, which translates the ancient *Deo gratias* seems to go back to the apostolic age. It is found in Paul in the form Τῷ Θεῷ Χάρις = "Thanks be to God." Paul writes to the Corinthians: "But thanks be to God, who gives us the victory through our Lord Jesus Christ" (1 Cor 15:57).

The *Deo gratias* later became a customary acclamation signifying approbation[31] in the churches of North Africa. It could also be used as a greeting between Christians. The *Rule of St. Benedict* envisages that when someone knocks on the door of the monastery, or when a poor person approaches and calls for the monks, the doorkeeper "will reply *Deo gratias* . . . and with all the gentleness that the fear of God inspires, let him make haste to respond with the fervor of charity."[32]

---

[29] *De spectaculis*, XXV.5 (ca. 197). See M. Turcan, Sources chrétiennes 332, 43. In T. Camelot, "Un texte de Tertullien sur l'Amen de la communion," *La Maison-Dieu* 79 (1964) 108–9, an account of the most ancient patristic witnesses on the *Amen* at Communion.

[30] *Sermon* 272. PL 38.1247.

[31] See F. Cabrol, *Le Livre de la prière antique* (Paris: Oudin, 1900) 72–74.

[32] *Rule of St. Benedict*, 66.3. See *RB 1980* (Collegeville, Minn.: The Liturgical Press 1980).

In acclaiming the Word with thanksgiving, the community signifies that it is welcoming not primarily a holy text but the Lord himself who speaks to the community. "It is a living word that is received in this very act of prayer."[33]

THE ACCLAMATIONS OF THE GOSPEL

The proclamation of the gospel is solemnized by the procession of the Gospel Book, and usually accompanied in the West by the Alleluia and, in certain Eastern liturgies, by the Trisagion.

The reading of the gospel is introduced by the acclamation *Gloria tibi, Domine* = "Glory to you, Lord." This phrase can be found from the sixth century in the most ancient Gallican Ordo.[34] The end of the reading is marked by the acclamation *Laus tibi, Christe* = "Praise to you, Lord Jesus Christ." In the twelfth century, the acclamation taken from Psalm 118 (v. 26), "Blessed is he who comes in the name of the Lord," begins to be used.[35]

Song

It seems that communities have not tried very hard to improve upon the acclamations of the Word of God. Undoubtedly, the celebration of the Word is regarded—perhaps unconsciously—as a simple reading rather than as a celebration of Christ speaking to the community. Yet the community does not acclaim the Book of the Gospel but rather Jesus Christ when it says "Glory to you, Lord" or "Praise to you, Lord Jesus Christ." There is much work yet to be done in regard to these acclamations. Care must be used in harmonizing the song used for the procession of the gospel and the other songs, e.g., the sequence before the gospel or the hymn after it.[36] Moderation must be the rule. Too much singing tends to devalue the celebration.

It is the custom of a certain African tribe in Gabon to acclaim the gospel by handclapping and the refrain "Bravo, Jesus, you have spoken well!" European communities are usually more restrained. They must, however, find formulas that are just as joyful to acclaim Christ.

[33] Cabié, op. cit., 82.

[34] K. Gamber, *Ordo Antiquus Gallicanus* (Regensburg: Pustet, 1965) 18.

[35] J. A. Jungmann, *Missarum Solemnia*, vol. 2 (Paris: Aubier) 218.

[36] See pp. 212ff.

HOLY, HOLY, HOLY . . .

If the dignity of a song is determined by its relation to the Eucharist, then the *Sanctus,* which today is situated at the heart of the Eucharistic Prayer, is the most important acclamation of the Eucharistic liturgy. If the community sings only one song, it should be the *Sanctus.*

This chant is for the people what the preface is for the priest. The preface, said by the priest alone, invites the community to join in thanksgiving to the Father, through the Son, in the Holy Spirit. The *Sanctus,* sung by all, introduces the community to the ecstatic praise of God.

Biblical and Liturgical Meaning

The *Sanctus* is a chain of individual biblical acclamations linked together. In using them in the celebration, the liturgy does not strip them of their original biblical "density" but enriches them by placing them in the context of the Eucharist and its light. There are four acclamations, one of which is repeated:

> Holy, holy, holy, Lord God of power and might.
> Heaven and earth are filled with your glory.
> Hosanna in the highest.
> Blessed is he who comes in the name of the Lord;
>   Hosanna in the highest.

Holy, Holy, Holy, Lord God . . .

The first acclamation is taken from the account of the vision that began Isaiah's ministry. The prophet was in the Temple when suddenly the heavens opened and God appeared to him in majesty and glory. God was seated on a high throne. The train of God's royal cloak covered the enormous staircase that descended from the holy of holies and filled the whole sanctuary. The seraphim, beings of light and fire, served as acolytes around the divine throne. Carried away in ecstasy, Isaiah heard them singing:

> Holy, holy, holy, is the Lord of hosts;
>   the whole earth is full of his glory (Isa 6:3).

The triple repetition of the word "holy" has no symbolic significance: it is simply a superlative.[37] It is thought that the acclamation was used in the Jerusalem Temple liturgy.[38]

Exegesis is hesitant and controversial about the exact idea of holiness in the Bible.[39] The root *qds* of the Hebrew *qadosh* = holy, often rendered in Greek by *hagios* (cf. the term trishagion or trisagion, which is often used to designate the *Sanctus*), evokes the idea of separation (from the profane). God All-Holy appears as "Separated, Transcendent, The Wholly Other."[40] A more recent interpretation, based on the analysis of nonbiblical Semitic texts, links the root *qds* with the idea of consecration, belonging, purification.[41]

It is not impossible to reconcile these two concepts when speaking of God's holiness. It is probable that the concept of holiness developed as Israel developed an awareness of God's holiness. The ideas of separation and transcendence can well be linked to that of belonging by consecration.

In the account of Isaiah's vocation, Yahweh Sabaoth appears as the Lord of glory, the Transcendent One, the Wholly Other: in God's presence the seraphim veil their faces and Isaiah pleads his unworthiness as a person of unclean lips to join his voice to the angelic praise. Yet at the same time the God of glory draws near to his creature, the train of God's royal cloak reaches the sanctuary, the radiance of God's glory fills the whole earth, and God deigns to call Isaiah into his service. The theophany of God's inaccessible majesty is also the theophany of God's intimate presence among human beings.

---

[37] It was only during the period of the anti-Arian battles that a trinitarian significance was attributed to the triple invocation. According to Victor de Vita, the African bishops, when saying the *Sanctus* during the Mass, "adore and exalt the Most Holy Trinity" (*Historia persecutionis africanae provinciae,* published in 488/489, vol. II, 100), cited by R. Cabié, in A. G. Martimort, *The Church at Prayer,* II (Collegeville, Minn.: The Liturgical Press, 1985–1986) 95.

[38] According to H. Wildberger, *Jesaja,* Biblischer Kommentar, vol. X (Neukirchen: Neukirchener Verlag) 248. The triple repetition is rare in the Hebrew Scriptures; it is found in Jer 7:4 (in regard to the *Temple*), in Jer 22:29 (in regard to the *earth*), and in Ezek 22 (in regard to the *ruined* city).

[39] See C. B. Costecalde, "Sacré et Sainteté," in *Supplément au Dictionnaire de la Bible,* vol. X (Paris, 1985) col. 1342–1415.

[40] See A. Gelin, "La sainteté de l'homme selon l'Ancien Testament," in *Bible et vie chrétienne* 19 (1957) 35.

[41] See C. B. Costecalde, op. cit., n. 30. Costecalde studied in depth the texts from Mesopotamia (col. 1361–72) and Ugarit (col. 1372–82). He recognizes, nevertheless, that "the original meaning of the root *qds* is impossible to recover" (col. 1379).

It is a worthy preface to the Book of Emmanuel, God-with-us (Isa 7:14; 8; 9:10).

It is also a worthy preface to the Eucharistic Prayer in which a sinful people comes before the holiness of its Lord. The inaccessible God will make himself present among his people under the sign of bread and wine; a people with unclean lips will welcome its Lord and celebrate God's holiness.

The idea of holiness is paramount in the Book of Isaiah. The title of God, "the Holy One of Israel," is characteristically Isaian vocabulary. It is as if the seraphic singing of the inaugural vision never left Isaiah's consciousness. The supreme revelation of God's holiness is manifested in the oracle:

> The holy God shows himself holy by righteousness (Isa 5:16).

God's justice, according to Isaiah, is his mercy:

> Therefore the LORD waits to be gracious to you,
>   Therefore he will rise up to show mercy to you.
> For the LORD is a God of justice . . . (Isa 30:18).

The song of God's justice is the song of God's pity that forgives.

The Lord Sabaoth

Sabaoth is usually considered the plural of the Hebrew *saba* = *army.* Yahweh Sabaoth therefore means "God of the armies." This appellation appears 279 times as a divine title in the Hebrew Scriptures. The title has the feel of a victorious savior, and calls to mind the times when Yahweh, as chief of Israel's army (1 Sam 17:45), used to march at its head, scattering the enemy and fighting for the beloved people. The war cry that links the name Sabaoth with that of Emmanuel (God-with-us), expresses confidence of victory:

> The LORD of hosts is with us,
>   the God of Jacob is our refuge (Ps 46:7).

Besides these military armies, we should also remember the "heavenly" armies, the stars that God mobilized at critical times when the enemy seemed to be getting the upper hand:

> The stars fought from heaven,
>   from their courses they fought against Sisera (Judg 5:20).

Under the influence of the prophets, the celestial armies are spiritualized and become the angelic armies. These servants of God form God's "camp."[42] The angelic armies join with the heavenly army of stars in enthusiastic praise at the creation of the world, when the Lord places the foundation stone of the cosmos:

> when the morning stars sang together,
> and all the heavenly beings shouted for joy?[43]

Heaven and Earth Are Full of Your Glory

The biblical concept of *glory* is a technical term for referring to the radiant and luminous presence of God among God's people. This glory first appears to the people in the desert after the crossing of the Red Sea; then at Sinai at the time of the Covenant; it fills the Tent of Meeting, and later, Solomon's Temple.[44] John takes up this theme in the Prologue to the Gospel:

> And the Word became flesh and lived among us, and we have seen his glory . . . .[45]

The liturgy makes two changes to the Isaian text. The biblical text says that "the whole earth is full of *his* glory" (Isa 6:3). The liturgy boldly substitutes: "of *your* glory." The somewhat impersonal chant that the seraphim pass back and forth with covered faces, out of respect for God's transcendence, becomes a personal act of praise that we address to the Father in the liturgy. *His glory* is a recognition. *Your glory* is a cry of praise. This change of tone is further registered by the second substitution. The biblical text reads: "The *whole earth* is full of his glory." The liturgy substitutes: *"Heaven and earth* are full of your glory." The perspective has been enlarged; it is immense. Earthly praise links up with heavenly praise; the earth is linked with heaven. It is no longer in the Temple that the Trisagion rings out but

---

[42] When Jacob returns to Canaan, he meets some angels: "'This is God's camp!,'" he cries (Gen 32:2).

[43] Job 38:7. The "heavenly beings" are the angels.

[44] See Exod 24:16; Lev 9:6, 23; Num 14:10; 1 Kgs 8:10-13.

[45] John 1:14. The Latin tradition has known a certain hesitation in translating the Hebrew word (*kabod*) and its Greek translation (*doxa*). It has used *gloria,* but also *maiestas* or "honor." Sometimes both terms have been used together, as if two terms had a better chance of adequately expressing the density of the original—cf. the *Te Deum:* Pleni sunt caeli et terra *maiestatis gloriae* tuae.

now; both on earth and in heaven, angels, humans, and all of creation unite in a common act of praise and exaltation, eternally celebrating the glory of the Father. The liturgy appears as the descent of the Eternal into Time, or the ascent of earthly acclamation and its insertion into heavenly praise.

Hosanna in the Highest

Hosanna literally means *save* or *give salvation!* The expression is taken from Psalm 118:25:

> Save us, we beseech you, O LORD!
> O LORD, we beseech you, give us success!

This psalm is part of the Hallel (Pss 113–18) and, in that context, was recited by the Lord at the Last Supper.[46] The acclamation Hosanna became so popular that it lost its original significance. On the last day of the feast of Tabernacles a procession made its way around the altar seven times, and the crowd, waving palm branches, cried out "Hosanna!" The day was called the *Great Hosanna*. We know that the people took up this acclamation spontaneously in the joyous, rowdy chaos of an improvised procession, when Jesus made his solemn entry into Jerusalem:

> Hosanna to the Son of David!
> Blessed is the one who comes in the name of the Lord! (Matt 21:9)

> Blessed is the coming kingdom of our ancestor David!
> Hosanna in the highest! (Mark 11:10)[47]

"In the highest" is a Hebraicism. It means "To God who dwells in the highest heaven." Out of respect for God's transcendence, Jewish piety avoided pronouncing God's ineffable name and used circumlocutions. Jesus conformed to this custom when he spoke of the kingdom of *heaven* (that is, the kingdom of *God*).

---

[46] Matt 26:30 and Mark 14:26 explicitly mention that at the end of the meal Jesus and the Twelve sang hymns *(ὑμνήσαντες)*.

[47] On the meaning of *Hosanna* in the time of Christ, see Strack-Billerbeck, *Kommentar zum Neuen Testament aus Talmud und Midrasch,* vol. 1 (München: C. H. Beck) 845–50.

Blessed Is the One Who Comes in the Name of the Lord

Like the preceding acclamation, this acclamation comes from Psalm 118, verse 26. The priests reply to the hosannas of the pilgrims who process into the Temple with the welcoming:

> Blessed is the one who comes
> in the name of the LORD.

This is a blessing "in the name of the Lord" pronounced over the pilgrim who enters the Temple. But the temptation was too great and the primitive sense of the phrase was transformed into a blessing on the one *who comes in the name of the Lord*. The Septuagint gives the following text that would easily lend itself to a messianic interpretation:

> Blessed be
> the one who comes in the name of the Lord!

It is in this form that the Gospels cite the psalm, whether at Jesus' solemn entrance into Jerusalem (Matt 21:9; Mark 11:9; Luke 19:38) or in the eschatological logion about the city that kills the prophets (Matt 23:39; Luke 13:35).

The primitive community heard the name *the-one-who-comes* in an apocalyptic sense, as the personal name of the Messiah. When John asks Jesus, "Are you the one who is to come?", the question being asked is "Are you the Messiah?" This name admirably expressed the mission of Jesus Christ: he is the one who has come in the mystery of his incarnation.[48] Yet he does not cease to come. The Book of Revelation implores: "Come Lord Jesus!", and the Eucharistic liturgy is celebrated "until he comes."[49] He it is who will come in majesty and glory on the Day. The name *The-one-who-comes* may equally well refer to the coming of Christ in the flesh, his sacramental coming in the Eucharistic celebration, or his eschatological coming at the Parousia. In using the acclamation *Blessed is the one who comes in the name of the Lord* in the liturgy, the Church remembers once again its pilgrim condition, that it is journeying toward an eternal celebration, and that it already touches, in some sense, the shores of eternity. The heavenly liturgy evoked in the Book of Revelation, a liturgy that is the archetype of our earthly liturgy, sings both of God's holiness and of his eternity:

---

[48] There is a series of *I have come* or *I have been sent* phrases in the gospels.
[49] See Rev 22:20 and 1 Cor 11:26.

> Holy, holy, holy,
> the Lord God Almighty,
> who was and is and is to come.[50]

If we take account of the biblical significance of the *Benedictus,* we will not sing it softly, as a contrast to the beginning of the *Sanctus.* The custom of singing it softly comes from the polyphonic Masses in which the *Benedictus* was sung after the consecration, and where, from a musical point of view, it was appropriate to have an adagio after the allegro of the beginning, a piano after the forte, and a piece for a soloist or three voices (usually soprano, alto, and tenor in the Palestrinian Masses) after the initial singing by the whole choir. Yet this musical treatment cannot be justified in any way from a biblical point of view: the *Benedictus* is the cry that the crowd of disciples shouted at Jesus when he entered as Messiah into the city of Jerusalem. This *Benedictus* is neither an adagio nor a piano: we should give the *Benedictus* all the vigor and dynamism of the preceding acclamations.

To summarize: The biblical climate of the *Sanctus* is that of an enthusiastic celebration of immense joy: a royal theophany of the Lord God of hosts, myriads of angelic and celestial armies, cosmic praise of the Maker of the universe, heavenly glory enveloping the earth, the royal Messianic liturgy of palms, the return of the Lord that the New Testament describes so joyously; the *Sanctus* must evoke all this festive joy. A *Sanctus* sung at half force, breath jealously guarded, sounds gently ethereal, and has nothing to do with the song of the Isaian seraphim who make the columns of the Temple shake! We shall never have *enough* breath to do that, never enough notes to express that . . . !

The *Sanctus* in the Eucharistic Prayer

The most ancient extant anaphoras, those of the *Apostolic Tradition* of Hippolytus of Rome (ca. 215) and the Eastern anaphora of Addai and Mari (third century),[51] do not give a *Sanctus.* On the other hand, the *Sanctus* appears to be well integrated into the anaphora of Serapion, bishop of Thmuis, in Lower Egypt (d. after 362), and in that of the *Apostolic Constitutions* (ca. 380). The place of the *Sanctus* remains fluid until the sixth century, at least in the West: the Council of Vaison

---

[50] Rev 4:8. God Almighty *(Pantokrator)* translates *Yahweh Sabaot* (cf. Micah 4:4).
[51] See Deiss, *Springtime.* For Hippolytus' *Apostolic Tradition* see pp. 121ff. For the Anaphora of Addai and Mari, see pp. 156ff.

(529) prescribed its use at all Masses,[52] thus confirming that it was in fact absent from certain anaphoras until the sixth century.

We do not know exactly how the *Sanctus* was introduced.[53] We may reasonably suppose that it was by way of the Jewish custom of blessing. These blessings, so familiar to Jesus, gave birth to the Christian anaphoras. The *Kirkat Yotser*[54] blessing that accompanied the daily prayer of the *Shema Israel* used the *Sanctus* acclamation in its center:

> Be blessed, our Rock, our King, our Redeemer, you who created the holy angels. . . . Your angels dwell in the high places of the universe, they proclaim in awe, with one voice, the works of God. . . .

> > "Holy, holy, holy, is the LORD of hosts;
> > The whole earth is full of his glory" (Isa 6:3).

> It was the sound of the wings of the living creatures brushing against one another and the sound of the wheels beside them, that sounded like a loud rumbling.[55]

> > Blessed be the glory of the Lord
> > in the place of his dwelling!

The *Benedictus* is first attested as a communion acclamation in the *Apostolic Constitutions*. At the bishop's proclamation, "Holy things for the holy," the people respond with the acclamations:

> One only holy One, one only Lord,
> Jesus Christ, who is blessed for ever,
> to the glory of the Father Amen.

> "Glory to God in the highest heaven,
> on earth, peace,
> among men, good will (of God)" (Luke 2:14).

---

[52] Cabié, op. cit., 113.

[53] B. D. Spinks, *The Sanctus in the Eucharistic Prayers* (Cambridge: Cambridge University Press, 1991), speaks of "one of the unsolved mysteries of Christian liturgy" (Intro., 1). Spinks cites only the most ancient attestations of the *Sanctus* from Syria and Palestine. See also the notes of E. Lanne, "The *Sanctus* and the ancient anaphoras," in *Dictionnaire de Spiritualité*, vol. 9 (1976) col. 894ff.

[54] See Deiss, *Springtime*, 24–26.

[55] Ezek 3:12. Literally the "Ophanim" (Wheels) and the holy Hayyot (living creatures). These heavenly beings intervene in the vision of "Yahweh's chariot" (Ezek 1:14ff). Jewish tradition made them a class of angels resembling the cherubim and seraphim.

"Hosanna to the son of David!
Blessed be he who comes in the name of the Lord."
God the Lord has shown himself among us.
"Hosanna in the highest heaven"[56] (Matt 21:9).

It is in the works of St. Caesarius of Arles (d. 542)[57] that we find
the first extant attestation of the linking together of the *Benedictus* and
the *Sanctus*. This became common in the East, beginning in the eighth
century.

THE SONG OF UNITY

The *Sanctus* is the Eucharistic community's most important song
of unity:

Unity among the angels who "exult in a common joy," *socia ex-
ultatione*.

Unity among human beings who, like the angels, sing with one
voice, *una voce*.

Unity among angels and human beings who join together to
sing: "with the angels and archangels, with the cherubim and
the seraphim, and all the heavenly hosts, we sing the hymn of
your glory," *cum quibus et nostras voces*.

Christian antiquity liked to emphasize the unity of the angelic
world and the human community in a common praise of God. In his
letter to the Corinthians, which dates from the years 95–96, Clement
of Rome writes:

Let us contemplate the entire multitude of angels and consider how
they stand ready and serve his will. For the Scripture says:

Ten thousand times ten thousand stood near him,
and thousands upon thousands served him.
and they cried out,
"Holy, holy, holy is the Lord of hosts!
All of creation is filled with his glory!"

---

[56] *Apostolic Constitutions,* VIII, 13.13, in Deiss, *Springtime,* 237–38.
[57] *Sermo* 73.2, *Corpus Christianorum,* vol. 103 (Turnhout: Brepols) 307–PL 39.2277.

We too, then, should assemble in oneness of mind and cry out to him perseveringly, as with a single mouth, that we might share in his great and glorious promises.[58]

The Isaian seraphim, acolytes of Yahweh's throne, have become ten thousand myriads and thousands upon thousands, an innumerable army standing before the heavenly throne. The Isaian seraphim have recruited these myriads from the vision of the heavenly liturgy before the "Ancient of Days,"–the eternal God–in the Book of Daniel (7:10). The liturgical tradition eagerly accepted these new recruits for the Trisagion. It can be said that the Isaian seraphim will never again remain alone in their role as cantors.

The anaphora of Serapion, bishop of Thmuis, represents the tradition of certain Egyptian circles of the fourth century. The text that is given as an official prayer of the Church is undoubtedly the most ancient prayer. It reflects the angelology of the Jewish apocryphal literature that has been welcomed into the Christian tradition:

> You are attended by thousands upon thousands
> and myriads upon myriads
> of Angels and Archangels,
> of Thrones and Dominations,
> of Principalities and Powers.
>
> Beside you stand
> the two august Seraphim with six wings:
> two to cover their face,
> two to cover their feet,
> two with which to fly.
> They sing to your holiness:
> Holy, holy, holy is the Lord Sabaoth!
> Heaven and earth are filled with your glory.
> Heaven is filled, earth is filled with your wonderful glory![59]

The witness of the *Apostolic Constitutions* dates from the 380s and comes from Syria or Constantinople:

> It is you who are adored by the countless companies of Angels and Archangels, Thrones, Dominions, Principalities, Virtues, and Powers,

---

[58] Clement, *Letter to the Corinthians*, 34.5–7. See Deiss, *Springtime*, 82; *Sacrosanctum Concilium* 167 (1961) 154, 156.

[59] *Euchology of Serapion of Thmuis*, 13, in Deiss, *Springtime*, 194; A. Hanggi and I. Pahl, *Prex Eucharistica* (Freibourg: Ed. Universitaires, 1968) 128, 130.

the hosts of eternity, as well as the Cherubim and the Seraphim. . . .
With the thousand thousands of Archangels and the myriad myriads
of Angels they sing without respite an uninterrupted song. And let all
the people say with them:

> Holy, holy, holy
> is the Lord Sabaoth.
> Heaven and earth are filled with his glory!
> Blessed is he for ever. Amen.[60]

It is therefore in full conformity with the tradition that the instruction *Musicam Sacram* (1967)–two years after Vatican II–invited
the community to make the *Sanctus* the song of the whole celebrating
assembly:

> It is preferable that the *Sanctus,* as the concluding acclamation of the
> Preface, should normally be sung by the whole congregation together
> with the priest (MS, art. 34).[61]

Two years later, the *General Instruction of the Roman Missal* of 1969
transformed this invitation into a rubrical obligation. Enumerating
the principal elements that form the Eucharistic Prayer, it noted:

> Acclamation: joining with the angels, the congregation sings or recites
> the *Sanctus*. This acclamation is an intrinsic part of the Eucharistic
> Prayer and all the people join with the priest in singing or reciting it
> (GIRM 55b).

FURTHER REFLECTIONS

The Music

The *Sanctus* we know today has been part of the Christian tradition for two thousand years. Inspired initially by Gregorian chant, it
was seduced by the splendor of Gregorian *melisma;* in the twelfth and
thirteenth centuries it let the organ sumptuously embellish its
melodies while it progressively took on the exaltation of classical six-
teenth-century polyphony–whether one thinks of the melodic purity
of Josquin des Près, the festive harmonies of Palestrina, the keen

---

[60] *Apostolic Constitutions,* VIII, 12.27b, in Deiss, *Springtime,* 232; *Sacrosanctum Concilium* 336 (1987) 192.
[61] Flannery, op. cit., 88–89.

sweetness of Vittoria, or the flamboyant colors of Lassus; it let itself be clothed in the exulting music of Bach and the jubilation of Mozart; it was draped in the dreaminess of the Romantic period.

Remembering this rich past, the Constitution on the Liturgy of Vatican II affirmed: "The musical tradition of the universal Church is a treasure of inestimable value" (SC, art. 112).[62] Yet a treasure is of no use to the present unless it can be used to enrich today's liturgy. It is not unusual to find that a past masterpiece, created for a specific ministerial function, proves inappropriate for a present-day one or is no longer used in the liturgy. This is the case with the most marvelous *Sanctus* of Bach's B-minor Mass; it will always remain the most marvelous *Sanctus* of all, but this polyphonic piece from the classical period is no longer sung, neither in the Roman Catholic Mass nor in the Lutheran Communion Supper. It has become "a masterpiece suspended in a void."[63]

The reform undertaken by Vatican II assigned a precise function to the *Sanctus*. It is to be acclaimed by the entire community.

This assigned function allows us to judge the *Sanctus* of the polyphonic repertoire. They cannot be integrated into the contemporary Mass. However well executed a choir's *Sanctus* may be, it cannot take the place of the assembly's acclamation.

Even if in particularly solemn circumstances we could envisage an exception, and even if the community felt totally at one with their choir, as if it were saying "What you sing, we should like to sing with you, but you do it so well that we feel at one with you," there would still remain a structural problem. The polyphonic *Sanctus* lasts an average of five to six minutes.[64] This was not particularly irritating in the past, since the priest was saying the Eucharistic Prayer in silence, and since the Consecration separated this *Sanctus* from the *Sanctus* of the *Benedictus*. But today, can we reasonably interrupt the Eucharistic Prayer for five or six minutes of music, even if that music is sublime? Can we destroy the structure of the Prayer by making the choir's singing the focus of the Prayer?

At first, it might seem that the Gregorian repertoire would be more successful. We must keep in mind, however, the question of ministerial

---

[62] Flannery, op. cit., 31.

[63] Basso, op. cit., vol. 2, 573.

[64] So, for example, the *Sanctus* of Palestrina's *Missa brevis*. Note that the work is entitled *brevis!*

function. The *Sanctus* is an acclamation. An acclamation is not an acclamation unless it truly "acclaims." Is this the case for the twenty-one settings of the *Sanctus* in the *Liber Usualis?* We have to say that certain Gregorian melodies, while very beautiful, are not at all "acclamatory." We must not be seduced by the beauty of a melody. Beauty alone does not transform a melody into an acclamation. Among the *Sanctus* settings that seem to be adaptable to the ministerial function of the *Sanctus* as envisaged by Vatican II, we may point out:

> Ferial *Sanctus XVIII.* When sung with vigor, it has an unbelievable majesty. Otherwise it is practically unusable, as the melodic movement is so closely tied to the rhythm of the Latin words.

> The easy *Sanctus XIII,* with its solid, rock-like acclamations, and the way the music takes flight in the *Benedictus.*

> *Sanctus X,* which smiles like a spring morning.

> *Sanctus I* of Eastertime. It illustrates the distance that separates a simple melody from an acclamation. Its carillon of notes evoke the light of Easter morning.

Of course, those communities that love Gregorian chant may use any other *Sanctus* as an acclamation. There are different sensibilities: a community of older people will not "acclaim" in the same way as a young community. What counts is the joy of the celebrating community: to take into account the nature of the *Sanctus* as envisaged by the council.

What music would be desirable for the *Sanctus* in the future?

The ideal is that the *Sanctus* should be the united acclamation of the community, whether it is sung in Latin or in the vernacular. Once the assembly's full participation is taken for granted, the choir may be able to harmonize with the melody sung by the assembly. Vatican II asked us to be creative. There is still much creative work to be accomplished.

The Text

The text of the *Sanctus* is so familiar to us that we are no longer aware of the difficulties of the present text.

The triple repetition "Holy, holy, holy" is a Hebraism that is normally translated by a superlative or an equivalent phrase: "You are holy indeed" = *Vere sanctus*. In either case this Hebraicism lacks a contemporary expression. No one repeats an adjective three times at the beginning of a phrase, as for example, "Strong, strong, strong is the lion," or "Great, great, great is the Lord." To simply transpose the Hebraicism into the vernacular is not an adequate way of translating the primitive meaning.

The acclamation "Hosanna in the highest" is a particularly inadequate rendering of the Hebrew. Familiarity has made it acceptable to us, even giving it an affective weight. Yet it would be difficult for the faithful to define the meaning of the phrase. No one uses "Hosanna" or "in the highest." The acclamation is found in the Gospel accounts of Jesus' Messianic entry into Jerusalem in Matthew, Mark, and John. Luke judged that his Greek readers would not understand it and therefore that it was of no use to include it in his Gospel account. He simply replaced it with "Glory!"[65]

The question is whether it would not be useful to improve the text of the *Sanctus* or, even better, to envisage the use of other biblical acclamations with a greater theological import than "Hosanna in the highest," ones that are pastorally more suitable. There would then be the choice between using the traditional *Sanctus* or other new formulas.

There is a simple answer. The first Supper, which the Lord celebrated with his disciples, was celebrated in a festive climate, created by the use of the Hallel psalms (Pss 113–18). It would be easy to find acclamations perfectly adapted to the celebration in these psalmic prayers that could be sung in union with Christ Jesus who sang them at the Last Supper.

For example, Psalm 118–from which the acclamation "Hosanna" is taken–could provide an excellent text:

> [Let us] give thanks to the LORD, for he is good;
>   his steadfast love endures forever.
>
> Save us O LORD, we beseech you, O LORD!
>   O LORD, we beseech you, give us success!
> Blessed is the one who comes in the name of the LORD.
>
> [Let us] give thanks to the LORD, for he is good,
>   for his steadfast love endures forever (Ps 118:1, 25-26, 29).

---

[65] Compare Luke 19:38 with Matt 21:9, Mark 11:10, and John 12:13.

Such an acclamation that gives thanks—that is, that "makes eucharist" in celebrating the goodness of the Lord, is in perfect harmony with the movement of the Eucharistic Prayer. It also recounts the praise of Jesus himself at the Last Supper.

The First Song of the Mass

There is a hierarchy among the songs and chants of the Mass. The *Sanctus* is of first importance.

No other song can claim more dignity. The *Gloria* also celebrates the immensity of God's glory, but this is an ecclesiastical composition and is also situated outside of the specifically Eucharistic thanksgiving. It may even be omitted: this is the case in most Masses and does not disturb the harmonious development of the celebration. The *Sanctus,* by contrast, is situated at the heart of the liturgical action. We sing it, united to the angels and all the hosts of heaven, with our sisters and brothers on earth and in heaven and with the entire universe with its millions of galaxies.

Thus, if we must give any song a full musical treatment, it is surely the *Sanctus.* Sometimes on certain occasions the entrance chant is superbly orchestrated and accompanied by the organ and other instruments, while the *Sanctus* is something to get through as quickly and as sparingly as possible. This is a mistake! All and any musical resources should first be used for the *Sanctus,* and only afterwards for other parts of the Mass.

The Anamnesis

The anamnesis is the prayer that comes after the consecration and commemorates (ἀνάμνησις) Christ, especially his death and resurrection. The Church signifies by this anamnesis that it intends to carry out in the Eucharistic celebration the Lord's commandment at the Last Supper: "Do this in memory (εἰς ἀνάμνησιν) of me."[66]

In the ancient liturgies, the anamnesis is directly linked to the words of institution. Thus in the *Apostolic Tradition* of Hippolytus we find:

> Remembering therefore your death
> and your resurrection,

[66] 1 Cor 11:24, 25 and Luke 22:19.

we offer you the bread and the wine,
we thank you for having judged us worthy
to stand before you and serve you.[67]

The Text

The liturgy actually has two anamneses. The first is that of the assembly. It is said immediately after the consecration. Three formulas are given, all referring to the death and resurrection of Jesus, and two of them refer to his future return.

First Formula (a)
> Christ has died,
> Christ is risen,
> Christ will come again.

Second Formula (b)
> Dying you destroyed our death,
> rising you restored our life.
> Lord Jesus, come in glory.

Third Formula (c)
> When we eat this bread and drink this cup,
> we proclaim your death, Lord Jesus.

Fourth Formula (d)
> Lord, by your cross and resurrection
> you have set us free.
> You are the Savior of the world.

The second anamnesis is said by the priest alone, after the anamnesis of the assembly. At the memorial of the passion and resurrection (Eucharistic Prayer II), Eucharistic Prayer I adds "and his ascension into glory"; Eucharistic Prayer III, the hope "to greet him when he comes again"; and Eucharistic Prayer IV, "his descent among the dead." The most complete anamnesis is found in Eucharistic Prayer IV:

> We recall Christ's death, his descent among the dead,
> his resurrection, and his ascension to your right hand;
> and, looking forward to his coming in glory,
> we offer you this body and blood,

---

[67] *Apostolic Tradition* 4, in Deiss, *Springtime,* 131.

the acceptable sacrifice
which brings salvation to the world.

The anamnesis is no simple historical remembering, nor an account of the foundational events of the faith, but praise of the Father for the mysteries in which Jesus came to us and brought us salvation. The liturgy does not commemorate the brute facts of the events but primarily their spiritual significance. It does not remember the passion so much as an ignominious slaughter, but uses the simple phrase "recall the passion" (Eucharistic Prayer I), the passion that led Jesus from the wretchedness of this world to his Father and manifested his love: "He loved [his own] to the end" (John 13:1); not so much the blood that flowed from the heart of the Crucified but the New Covenant sealed in that blood (Luke 22:20); not so much the resurrection from the tomb, marvelous as it was, but the path to God's eternity that Jesus has opened for all of us; not his ascension and seating at the Father's right hand but the place now kept for us there; not even his return on the clouds of heaven but rather the Father's blessing to be sought by the elect.

It is from such a perspective that the most ancient anamnesis–to be found in the Second Letter to Timothy (2:8)–begins with: "Remember Jesus Christ, raised from the dead," and then mentions "the salvation is in Christ Jesus with eternal glory" (2:10). The anamnesis is the loving song in which the Church remembers the history of salvation brought by Jesus and gives thanks to the Father: "We offer you in thanksgiving this holy and living sacrifice" (Eucharistic Prayer III).

Music

The music must adapt itself to the literary genre of each text and its rhythm. It must be appropriate to the context of adoration that follows the consecration.

Further Reflections

The introduction of the singing of the anamnesis by the entire celebrating community was one of the innovations most welcomed in the 1969 Missal.

Yet the duplication of the anamnesis by the priest seems much less welcome. It slows down the rhythm of the celebration. The whole assembly—of which the priest is part—has proclaimed the commemoration of Jesus' death and resurrection, and then the priest, as if he has paid no attention whatever to the proclamation of the community, repeats the same idea: "Calling to mind the death . . . and his glorious resurrection. . . ." As we have already seen, the anaphora of Hippolytus linked up directly with the anamnesis. The ancient Canon does likewise. After having said "Do this in memory of me," the priest continued: "Remembering therefore . . ." *(Unde et memores)*. The rhythm flows perfectly.

The major hesitation concerning this duplication is of a theological nature: it seems to question the understanding of the Prayer as a (con)celebration, in the sense that the whole community is in some way a co-celebrant. The Eucharistic Prayer is the prayer of the whole community, even if it is said by the priest alone. The tradition affirms, in the citation from Guerric d'Igny already cited above (ch. 2, n. 5): "The priest does not sacrifice alone, he does not consecrate alone, but the whole assembly of the assisting faithful consecrates with him, sacrifices with him." Just as the priest no longer—as in former times—has to read the readings privately, which the reader reads before the whole assembly, and to say the *Gloria* and the *Sanctus,* which the whole assembly sings, so he should not have to render an anamnesis alone, which the assembly has already sung. Such repetition does not foster an appreciation of the community as one, unified, celebrating community.

Other texts have been proposed for the anamnesis that would avoid such repetition. Some of them are good literary and theological compositions. We must wait to see if it is possible to integrate them into the liturgy on a long-term basis. Their reception by Christian communities and the consensus gradually established in their regard will decide if they can become part of the official liturgy.[68]

---

[68] See G. King, "Réception consensus et droit ecclésiastique," in *Concilium* 243 (1992) 49–61.

4

The Responsorial Psalm

The restoration of the responsorial psalm is one of the most significant reforms in the new liturgy. It is important not only in the domain of singing, where it totally transforms the character of the Gregorian gradual, restoring its ancient, austere beauty, but also and primarily in the domain of the Word of God, where it enriches the celebration with an additional reading.

The reform put thirteen centuries of "traditions" aside, in order to find the authentic liturgical Tradition for this part of the Mass. Thirteen centuries of tradition have reduced the psalm to an organ piece: only two verses of the psalm survived. But they had been clothed in a thousand Gregorian splendors. The reform weighed Gregorian splendor and the infinite dignity of God's Word in the balance, and opted for the dignity of the Word of God. The restoration of the Word of God demanded by Vatican II–"a more ample, more varied, and more suitable reading"[1]–necessitated a more ample, more varied, and more suitable responsorial psalm. There was no choice: one could have either the delights of the *jubilus,* its beauty but also its fragility, which is part of all created beauty, or the Word of God and its eternity.

Need we say once again that the present liturgy is in no way a criticism of the beauty of the past? The reform of the responsorial psalm does not imply the devaluation of the splendors of Gregorian chant. We admire and appreciate the past. The reform says only that what was done in the past is not necessarily what should be done in

[1] Flannery, op. cit., 12.

today. This is simply the law of all life—things evolve. It is also the law of the liturgy.

The instruction *Musicam Sacram* (1967) underlines the importance of the responsorial psalm:

> The song after the lessons, be it in the form of gradual or responsorial psalm, has a special importance among the songs of the Proper. By its very nature it forms part of the Liturgy of the Word. It should be performed with all seated and listening to it—and what is more, participating in it as far as possible (MS, art. 33).[2]

MINISTERIAL FUNCTION

The responsorial psalm is the response with which the community welcomes the Word that is proclaimed to it. It is certainly true that the essential response to the Word is obedience to God and adoration of his holy will. Such was Mary's response to the angel's words at the Annunciation: "Here I am, the servant of the Lord; let it be with me according to your word" (Luke 1:38). Yet in the liturgical celebration, the responsorial psalm ritualizes the response of the celebrating community.

In the History of the People of God

Far from being a monologue that heaven imposes on the earth, the Word seeks to open a dialogue between human freedom and God's tenderness. The Word calls out to the community, it inserts itself into the hearts of the people, it calls for a choice. Not to respond is one form of response. The person to whom God has spoken can never again be undisturbed, or rather the dialogue can never be interrupted.

In its simplest form, the assembly's response and acceptance of the Word is expressed by Amen. After the proclamation of the Law in the assembly at Shechem, when the people had just crossed the Jordan, they confirmed each precept of the Law by a mighty Amen that echoed between Mount Ebal and Mount Gerizim.[3]

---

[2] Flannery, op. cit., 88.

[3] See Deut 27:15-26 and L. Deiss, "The Responsorial Psalm," *Notitiae* 24 (1966) 365–72, from which we draw for the present chapter. See also L. Deiss, *Celebration of the Word* (Collegeville, Minn.: The Liturgical Press, 1993) ch. 3, 42–53.

This Amen is no literary cliché; it signifies the "Yes" of human beings to God, the acceptance of his Word, and human thanksgiving for his mercy. When God suddenly bursts into a human life, what can one do but kneel down and give thanks? This is illustrated in the accounts of the Yahwistic tradition of Isaac's marriage with Rebekah. On the orders of Abraham, his servant returns to the land of Abraham's ancestors, taking ten camels with him, to find a wife for Isaac. He arrives at Nahor early in the evening, and stops by the well. The women come to draw water. The servant humbly asks God for a sign to distinguish the one marked out for Isaac: the woman whom Yahweh inspires to give the servant a drink and to water the camels will be the designated wife of Isaac. Receiving the sign when pretty Rebekah offers him a drink, he prostrates himself, adores Yahweh, and says:

> "Blessed be the LORD, the God of my master Abraham, who has not forsaken his steadfast love and his faithfulness toward my master" (Gen 24:27).

The servant responds to the Word of God with blessing and praise.

When God's intervention is particularly prodigious and decisive, and a single utterance does not seem enough to express the soul's joy, the thanksgiving of the faithful breaks out into a joyful litany, becoming a "canticle" or a psalm. The biblical examples are numerous:

In the Old Testament

> God delivers the people in the Exodus and leads them through the Red Sea. Moses and the children of Israel respond and sing of God their Savior who stilled the waves in the heart of the sea, made them stand up like a wall, and led his own through the sea to his holy mountain. Miriam accompanied their song with the tambourine, singing of Yahweh: "for he has triumphed gloriously; horse and rider he has thrown into the sea" (Canticles of Moses and Miriam, Exod 15:1-18, 21).

> God delivers his people from the hand of Sisera, who, with his nine hundred iron-girded chariots, had harshly oppressed the children of Israel for twenty years. Deborah and Barak respond to Yahweh, blessing him and remembering him as the hero of past battles: he it was who, in the earthquake and in the shaking of the stars and in the boiling torrent of Kishon, had swept away

the enemy and crushed enemy kings (Canticles of Deborah and of Barak, Judg 5:2-31).

God delivers Hannah from her sterility, making her the mother of Samuel. Hannah responds to God with her canticle: she rejoices greatly in God her Savior, who has given her, the sterile one, such joy as befits having given birth to seven sons (Canticle of Hannah, 1 Sam 2:1-10).

God delivers King Hezekiah from illness just when his life threatens to let itself be carried away like a shepherd's tent in a desert thunderstorm. Hezekiah responds to the God who has snatched him from the jaws of death (Canticle of Hezekiah, Isa 38:10-20).

Jonah also breaks out in a great cry of distress and thanksgiving when, imprisoned in the belly of the whale, he already envisages his deliverance, and composes his response in the midst of the waves (Canticle of Jonah, Jonah 2:3-10).

God delivers old Tobit from his blindness and from the kingdom of shadows; he recovers his sight, sees an angel, and sings of his deliverance (Canticle of Tobit, Tob 13:1-17).

God preserves the three young men, Hananiah, Mishael, and Azariah, from the stain of idolatry and the burning flames. Nebuchadnezzar praises their God in the canticle "Blessed be the God of Shadrach, Meshach, and Abednego, who has sent his angel and delivered his servants, who trusted in him" (Dan 3:26-30).

God delivers his people from the oppression of Holofernes by the hand of Judith, a woman "blessed by the Most High God above all other women on earth" (Jdt 13:18). The community sings of its deliverance (Canticle of Judith, Jdt 16:1-17).

In the New Testament

God carries out his saving plan by the incarnation of Jesus. Mary, daughter of Zion, the purest and most intense expression of the mystery of the Church, sings her *Magnificat* (Luke 1:46-55).

God intervenes in favor of the incredulous Zechariah, and leads Zechariah to renewed faith. Zechariah responds by blessing

God "who has looked favorably upon his people and redeemed them" (Luke 1:68-79).

God reveals himself to Simeon; Simeon takes the child Jesus in his arms and proclaims that his eyes "have seen [God's] salvation" in Jesus (Luke 2:29-32).

It is interesting to note that these canticles, for the most part, do not belong to the stage of the biblical tradition in which they are presented in the written biblical accounts.[4] They originated in different contexts, came from different sources, and ultimately were placed in the mouths of the personages in the written biblical accounts. This fact illustrates how natural it is for human beings in any context to respond to God's saving action with praise and thanksgiving.

This response can be made in different prayer forms; the biblical "blessing," which is thanksgiving for God's marvelous acts, is the form most commonly used. For our purposes, the most significant biblical examples are to be found in the:

Hallel, the great psalm of praise of the Old Testament (Ps 136), in which every wonderful work of God is acclaimed with the praise "For his steadfast love endures forever";

Magnificat of the New Testament, in which Mary exults for joy in God her Savior, Jesus (Yahweh saves), whom she carries in her womb.

In the Liturgical Celebration

The reading of the Word of God in the liturgical assembly is not simply the reading of the archives of the people of God in the Old and New Testaments. It is rather the *actualization* ("Today this scripture has been fulfilled in your hearing"—Luke 4:21), for the benefit of the liturgical assembly, of the events and prophesies that announce and proclaim the advent of Jesus Christ. It is a celebration of the presence of Christ in the Scriptures.

The community responds to this proclamation of Christ in his Word with the responsorial psalm. A parallel may be made between the biblical canticle with which the people of God in the Old Testament

---

[4] Such is surely the case for the canticles of Moses, Hannah, Hezekiah, Hananiah, Mishael, and Azariah.

responded to God's wonderful deeds and the way in which the contemporary liturgical community responds to the Word that commemorates these wonderful deeds with the responsorial psalm. This psalm expresses the community's acceptance of the Word through its praise, thanksgiving, and petition.

In Summary

> In sacred history, the community responds to God's wonderful deeds on its behalf with the biblical canticle.
>
> In the liturgy, the community responds to the proclamation and actualization of these wonderful deeds with the responsorial psalm.

A Meditative Chant?

The responsorial psalm is sometimes presented as a meditative chant.[5] The faithful are encouraged to meditate on the Word of God while they sing or listen to the psalm.

In itself, this suggestion is good. Just as it is desirable that there be a time of personal thanksgiving[6] after receiving the Body and Blood of Christ, so it is desirable that there be a time of meditation after receiving Christ in his Word. We must not, however, exaggerate the frequency and length of this period of silence. The liturgy is primarily celebration and not meditation. When the faithful come together, it is not to enjoy a period of communal silence together: they have the rest of the day or the week to meditate on the Word.

The suggestion of keeping a time of silence is also good if in this way we understand the necessity of interiorizing the Word. This is also true for the other prayers of the Mass. In the encyclical *Mediator Dei,* Pius XII taught that:

> the chief element of divine worship must be interior. For we must always live in Christ and give ourselves to him completely so that in

---

[5] It is possible that "meditative chant" found its origin in the time when the Schola sang the gradual and alleluia alone, and when the people—who had nothing else to do—were encouraged to meditate during this singing.

[6] The instruction *Tres Abhinc annos,* art. 15 (May 4, 1967), suggests a time of silence before the postcommunion prayer, and the instruction *Eucharisticum mysterium,* art. 38 (May 25, 1967), recommends that "those who have been nourished by holy communion should be encouraged to remain for a while in prayer" (after Mass), Flannery, op. cit., 124.

him, with him and through him the heavenly Father may be duly glorified. The sacred liturgy requires, however, that both of these elements [interior and exterior acts of worship] be intimately linked with each other. This recommendation the liturgy itself is careful to repeat, as often as it prescribes an exterior act of worship (art 24).[7]

Yet for all this, the liturgical celebration is not a meditation.

The question asked here is the following: Is it appropriate to consider the responsorial psalm as a meditative song, and therefore to surround the psalm with an atmosphere of recollection in which the community can meditate on the Word?

The answer is undoubtedly "No." At least not necessarily, and certainly not in all cases.

First, there is the reply of common sense. If a psalm proclaims "Clap your hands, all you peoples" (Ps 47:2) or "Praise him with tambourine and dance" (Ps 150:4) or "O come, let us worship and bow down, let us kneel before the LORD, our Maker!" (Ps 95:6), no one has difficulty in understanding that the community is not being invited to recollect itself in meditation, but simply to clap its hands, to dance in God's presence, and to prostrate oneself before him. One can certainly meditate while dancing. Yet dance is not the most conducive path to meditation.

The psalter is a collection of material from almost a thousand years[8] and is made up of many varied literary genres. We can distinguish:

> Liturgies properly speaking, such as Psalm 24, a processional song for the entry of the Ark into Zion, or Psalm 134, a *lucernarium* (song for the evening office).

> Hymns that celebrate the glory of God, such as Psalms 145, 147, 148, 150, and the triumphant litany of the "Great Hallel," Psalm 136.

---

[7] AAS 39 (1947), in Seasoltz, op. cit., 114.

[8] Certain psalmic fragments, such as those of Psalms 18, 29, and 69, may be traced to the period of the Judges (11th–12th c. B.C.E.). Psalm 29 may be the oldest psalm (see H. J. Kraus, *Psalmen*, vol. 1, LVIII. The compilation of the psalter was completed by the middle of the 2nd c. B.C.E. (see O. Eissfeldt, *Einleitung in das Alte Testament*, 3rd ed. (Tübingen: J.C.B. Mohr, 1964) 608. On literary genres, see Manatti (Paris: Desclée de Brouwer, 1966) vol. 1, 41–74; L. Sabourin, *Un classement littéraire des Psaumes* (Paris: Desclée, 1964).

Enthronement psalms, which contain the cry, in effect, "God reigns," such as Psalms 90 to 99.

Royal psalms that celebrate the Davidic monarchy, such as the supplication for the king of Psalm 20 and the long polyphony of Psalm 89.

"Zion" songs, such as Psalm 137: "By the rivers of Babylon."

Wisdom psalms that celebrate the law of the Lord, such as the long Psalm 119.

"Historic" psalms that recall the wonders of salvation history, such as Psalms 78 and 106.

Prophetic exhortations that relay divine oracles, such as Psalm 50.

Thanksgiving psalms, psalms of trust and of supplication.

Undoubtedly, it is not possible to distinguish the categories of each psalm exactly. Genres sometimes overlap. As it develops, a single psalm may use a number of different literary genres. Despite this, however, it is not possible to confuse an enthronement psalm with a lamentation, or a wisdom psalm with a prophetic oracle.

The literary genre of the Responsorial psalm will be exactly the literary genre of the psalm itself. If a psalm is a prayer of supplication, the responsorial psalm will be a supplication. If it is a lamentation, a hymn, or an enthronement psalm, the responsorial psalm will be, respectively, a lamentation, a hymn, or an enthronement psalm. The responsorial psalm may even be a meditation if the psalm itself is originally a meditation, or calls one to meditative reflection. Psalm 119 is a case in point: it meditates on the Word of God for 176 verses.

One might think that the liturgy utilizes the psalms according to its own decided form (which is meditation) and rids a psalm of its original literary genre and flavor.

This may have happened in the past, but it must be avoided today. The original essence, literary genre, and flavor of a psalm, as it comes to us from God's inspiration, is of the utmost importance. We must watch that we do not disfigure psalms by singing those that shout for joy or cry out in pain in a meditative air: "You have turned my mourning into dancing . . . [you have] clothed me with joy" (Ps 30:11), or

"O LORD . . . incline your ear to my cry" (Ps 88:1-2), or "Let the floods clap their hands; let the hills sing together for joy" (Ps 98:8).

To conclude: It is always appropriate to interiorize the Word. Yet it is also essential to respect the authenticity of the psalm by respecting its literary genre.

THE TEXT OF THE RESPONSORIAL PSALM

The Text of the Psalm

The responsorial psalm is usually chosen in relation to the reading before it. The revision of the Lectionary leads therefore naturally to the revision of the responsorial psalm. To assure the harmony between the Word and the psalm, the Lectionary gives the following rules:

1. When the first reading cites a psalm, this psalm is used as the responsorial psalm. Thus, on Easter Monday, Peter's discourse cites Psalm 16. The responsorial psalm for the day is Psalm 16.

2. When the Gospel cites a psalm, the Lectionary uses this psalm as the responsorial psalm, like an anticipated response to the gospel. Thus on the First Sunday of Lent, Year C, Psalm 91, which is cited in the Gospel account of the Temptation of Jesus, is used as the responsorial psalm.

3. The Lectionary chooses responsorial psalms that have a literary connection with the first reading. Thus a reading from the prophet Jeremiah leads naturally to a responsorial psalm which is said to be from Jeremiah,[9] and which uses the same phrases and terminology as the first reading. In the reading for the Nativity of John the Baptist, June 24, the consecration of Jeremiah as a prophet in his mother's womb (Jer 1:5) leads to the use of Psalm 71 as Responsorial psalm, a psalm that speaks of having a particular vocation since the time of being in the maternal womb (Ps 71:5-6).

4. The Lectionary also uses the psalm that will best help illuminate the meaning of the proclaimed Word, even if there is no

[9] See P. Bonnard, *Le Psautier selon Jérémie,* Coll. Lectio Divina 26 (Paris: Cerf, 1959).

literary link. Thus on Good Shepherd Sunday (Third Sunday of Easter), Psalm 23, the Good Shepherd psalm, is used.

5. During the major seasons of the Liturgical Year—Advent, Christmastime, Lent, and Easter—the reformers decided to use certain psalms which had become traditional for each season, and which had formed the Christian consciousness during these seasons for centuries. Thus we find:

> For Advent, Psalms 25, 80, and 85.
> For the week of Christmas, the Enthronement psalms, 96, 97, and 98.
> For the Epiphany cycle, Psalm 72.
> For Lent, Psalms 26, 51, 91, and 130.
> For Holy Week, Psalm 22.
> For Eastertide, Psalms 66 and 118.
> For Pentecost, Psalm 104.

6. When no other rule takes precedence, the Lectionary chooses to use the psalms that have not been chosen under another title, so as to familiarize the Christian community with the entire psalter.

The Refrain or Antiphon

The assembly usually participates in the singing of the responsorial psalm by a short refrain, according to St. Augustine's words: "to the reader [i.e., the psalmist], we replied by singing."[10] The tradition insisted on the importance of this participation. St. John Chrysostom explains:

> If you sing "Like a deer that yearns for running streams, so my soul is yearning for you my God," you conclude a pact with God; you sign a pact with him, without ink or paper. Your voice proclaims that you love him above all things, that you prefer nothing to him, that you burn with love for him. . . .
> Do not chant the refrains out of habit, but take them up like a staff for the journey. Each verse is able to teach us much wisdom. . . .
> Even if you are poor, even if you are too poor to buy books, even if you have books, but have no time to read, at least remember the psalm refrains that you have sung, not once, twice, or three times, but

---

[10] *In Psalmum 40 Enarratio, Sermo ad plebem,* 1, *Corpus christianorum,* vol. 38, 447. PL 36.453.

so often, and you will gain great consolation from them. See what an immense treasure the psalm refrains open to us! . . .

I exhort you not to leave here with empty hands but to gather up the refrains as though gathering pearls, to keep them always with you, to meditate on them, to sing them all to your friends and your wives. And if anxiety invades your soul, if cupidity, anger, or any other passion troubles your soul, sing them assiduously. Thus we shall rejoice in great peace in this life, and we shall obtain eternal rewards in the next, through the grace and love of our Lord Jesus Christ.[11]

Our communities know well those refrains sung "routinely" and others that shine "like stars." The creation of an antiphonary that would constitute "an immense treasure" has hardly begun. Much time and effort will be needed to grow from "Minute Antiphons"– those that are learned in a minute and forgotten the next–to the sort of splendor that the old Latin antiphons such as "O magnum mysterium" or "Hodie Christus natus est" displayed. Yet what a joy it would be to work on such a project!

EXECUTION OF THE RESPONSORIAL PSALM

Execution of the Psalm in the Biblical Tradition

Do the psalms themselves tell us something about how they should be prayed? Can we find in the psalter itself the way to use it?

We have only a rough idea of how the psalms were prayed in the Temple or synagogue,[12] or in domestic liturgies (Passover itself was celebrated in the family). But the psalter does give us certain hints.

The responsorial form was certainly used: an antiphon or refrain or a response (this term tended to be used when the antiphon was very short) repeated several times during the praying of the psalm, which thus created the rhythm of the prayer. We find such antiphons in certain psalms.[13] For example, in Psalms 42 and 43, the following antiphon is repeated three times:

---

[11] *Expositio in Psalmum*, 41.5 and 7. PL 55.163.166–67.

[12] See A. Arens, *Die Psalmen im Gottesdienst des Alten Bundes* (Trier: Paulinus-Verlag, 1961).

[13] See: Ps 8, antiphon vv. 2 and 10; Ps 46, antiphon vv. 8 and 12; Ps 49, antiphon vv. 13 and 21; Ps 56, antiphon vv. 5 and 11; Ps 57, antiphon vv. 6 and 12; Ps 62, antiphon vv. 3 and 7; Ps 67, antiphon vv. 4 and 6; Ps 80, antiphon vv. 4, 8, (15?), and 20; Ps 118,

Why are you cast down, O my soul,
    and why are you disquieted within me?
Hope in God; for I shall again praise him,
    my help and my God.

Sometimes the antiphon serves as a prelude which introduces the
psalm and as a conclusion which resumes the essence of its thought.
For example, Psalm 103 cries out "Bless the LORD, O my soul!" (vv.
1, 22) at the recitation of God's marvelous works.

Alternating psalmody must also have been used.[14] The alternation
could be between the soloist and the assembly or between two parts
of the assembly. Such must have been the case for Psalm 121:

First choir or soloist
I lift up my eyes to the hills—
    from where will my help come?

Second choir or soloist
My help comes from the LORD
    who made heaven and earth.

First choir
He will not let your foot be moved;
    he who keeps you will not slumber.

Second choir
He who keeps Israel
    will neither slumber nor sleep.

It is clear that an execution by two choirs brings out to best advantage the literary structure of this psalm. It is hard to imagine a
single soloist praying both "From where will my help come?" and the
response "My help comes from the LORD."

A simple reading of the psalm is the most modest way of praying
it. Such a reading is to be chosen when there is "nothing to sing," for
example, in the historical psalms in which the reader simply proclaims the facts of Israel's history.[15] Yet normally, the psalms are to be

antiphon vv. 1 and 29; Ps 136, antiphon is repeated after each verse; Pss 146–50, the
Alleluia psalms: each psalm begins and ends with an Alleluia.

[14] A. Szörényi, *Psalmen und Kult im Alten Testament* (Budapest: Sankt Stephan Gesell-
schaft, 1961) 358–86, discusses the question of the dialogues in the cultic psalms.

[15] General Instruction of the Liturgy of the Hours, 279, notes that "it may be better
to read the sapiential and historical psalms. . . ." *The Liturgy of the Hours* I (New York:
Catholic Book Publishing Co., 1975) 96–97.

sung, or at least monotoned or cantillated. How could one not sing "O sing to the Lord a new song"? The General Instruction on the Liturgy of the Hours, 103,[16] wisely says:

> The psalms are not readings or prose prayers. They can on occasion be recited as readings, but they are properly called *tehillim* ("songs of praise") in Hebrew and *psalmoi* ("songs to be sung to the lyre") in Greek. In fact, all the psalms have a musical quality which determines their correct style of delivery. When a psalm is recited and not sung, its delivery must still be governed by its musical character.[17]

The Execution of the Psalm in the Liturgical Tradition

Basing itself on the tradition, the Introduction to the Lectionary gives different ways of praying the responsorial psalm:

> The responsorial psalm is normally sung. Two ways of singing the psalm after the first reading are to be noted: the responsorial form or the direct form.
>
> In the *responsorial form*, which is to be preferred as far as possible, the psalmist or reader proclaims the verses of the Psalm. The community responds with the response.
>
> In the *direct form*, the psalm is sung without the community's response. The psalm is sung either by the psalmist or cantor while the community listens, or by everyone together.[18]

These indications given by the Lectionary are most valuable. They trace a wise path.

We may note that "normally" singing and "as far as possible" the responsorial form are to be preferred. The psalmist should be encouraged to sing the psalm and the community to sing the antiphon. Blessed are those communities that achieve this ideal execution of the

---

[16] Hereafter GILH.

[17] *Liturgy of the Hours* I, 56.

[18] *Ordo Lectionum Missae, Praenotanda*, 20. Original Latin text is to be found in *Notitiae*, 180–83 (1981) 369. The text given above is the *Ordo Lectionum Missae*, 2nd ed., January 21, 1981. This edition modifies the first considerably, and presents an excellent theology of the celebration of the Word.

The GILH also speaks of different ways of executing the psalms: The psalms are sung or said in one of three ways, according to the different usages established in tradition or experience: as a single unit without a break *(in directum)*, or with two choirs or sections of the congregation singing alternate verses or strophes, or responsorially (art. 122). *Liturgy of the Hours* I, 63.

psalm, when the beauty of the music brings out the splendor of God's Word. The Lectionary counsels "insofar as possible" the avoidance of a simple reading of the psalm or antiphon. Often at many weekday Masses—and even sometimes on Sunday—the reader, who has just finished the first reading, also reads the psalm, and the community half-heartedly mumbles the antiphon in a flat and lifeless tone as a response. The Lectionary encourages communities to commit themselves, "insofar as possible," to an authentic celebration of the psalm.

The direct form, in which the psalmist or the community sings the whole psalm, is rarely used. We lack melodies that allow the psalm to be sung without several repetitions of the same psalm formula. For the whole community to sing or read the psalm, they need to be provided with psalters, or at least with the text of the psalm. We have a long way to go before communities know a certain number of psalms by heart. Two thousand years separate us from the time when the community sang the hymns (that is, the psalms of the Easter liturgy): the community of the Twelve, at the time of Jesus, did so.[19] In an oral society in which memory often served in place of a book, we might expect that the people whom God had created for his praise (Isa 43:21) would be able to use the psalms to praise him without needing a written text.

The Lectionary gives the option of singing the psalm as a solo and encourages it. It is not always easy, however, to execute this psalm with the dignity appropriate to the liturgical celebration. Moderation rather than excess should be the prevalent usage. The soloist's voice should be so beautiful that the community is caught up and captivated by the Word of God. The soloist's voice must not call attention to itself but should rather make the community forget the one who is singing. It is a real blessing if a community possesses such a psalmist. If it does not have such a person, let the community remember that a clear and intelligent proclamation is also a grace, and that such a proclamation is greatly preferable to a psalm sung in mediocre fashion. There is no place in music for mediocrity.

We need to remember, too, that "those who pray the psalms in the liturgy . . . do so not so much in their own name as in the name of the entire Body of Christ."[20] All ministries are at the service of the entire church. Yet that of the psalmist, like that of the reader, is tied more

[19] Matt 26:30; Mark 14:26.
[20] GILH 108.

closely to the mystery of Christ. The Word of God is the epiphany of Christ. The psalmist actualizes this epiphany.

FURTHER REFLECTIONS

The restoration of the responsorial psalm has enriched the celebration of the Word. Can we hope for even further progress without wanting to reform the reform? We can always dream, and here are two for thought.

The first dream concerns the texts of the responsorial psalms. These psalms have been chosen, as the Lectionary affirms, according to their *congruentia*[21] (suitability) in relation to the readings, and especially in regard to the first reading. In fact, this affirmation is only successfully supported in a small number of cases when the chosen psalm is particularly short. In all other cases the psalm has not been retained in its integrity but only through selection of a few verses. This selection is well chosen, but it does not always show the character of any particular psalm to best advantage, i.e., as it is found in its original biblical context.

We understand why a psalm is often reduced to a few verses: the time allowed for the celebration must not be endlessly lengthened. This idea may be valuable in some urban parishes where there are consecutive Sunday Masses. It may also be that the psalm itself is not a single, solid, literary structure: we can then reduce the number of verses without destroying the structure of the psalm (e.g., the interminable 176-verse-long litany of Psalm 119 regarding the Word of God). But it is hard to determine when these conditions are present. Our communities do not know the poignant story of the poor person of Psalm 22, who flounders about in the throes of distress crying out "My God, my God, why have you forsaken me?" (v. 1), who after having slept in the dust of death (v. 15), finds himself saved from the lion's mouth (v. 21), and recounts his deliverance not only to his brothers (v. 22), but to the entire earth and the generations yet to come (v. 30). Yet it is important to know this story in its entirety: it is the story of Jesus himself. Our communities are likewise ignorant of the story of the forgiven and healed sinner of Psalm 103, whom God crowns with love and tenderness (v. 4) and who discovers in God's forgiveness the name

---

[21] *Ordo Lectionum Missae* 24.

of the Lord of mercy and grace (v. 8). Yet here, too, this story is sublime because it is one with the revelation of Sinai: the revelation of "a God merciful and gracious" (Exod 34:6). We can only begin to tell it by blessing the holy name of the Lord: "Bless the Lord O my soul, and all that is within me bless his holy name" (v. 1), and conclude it by taking up the blessing again: "Bless the Lord O my soul" (v. 22).

We can continue to cite other psalms in the same way. In the past, each psalm the faithful of the Old Covenant prayed pointed forward to the prayer of Jesus. Today, in the time of the New Covenant, each psalm that we pray is a continuation of the prayer of the Lord. Did Jesus shorten the psalms when he prayed them? We also should not shorten the psalms.

What, then, should we do? What can we reasonably suggest? Simply to pray each psalm in its entirety whenever this is at all possible.

Are communities ready to make the psalter the prayerbook of the covenant community, as it was in the time of Jesus? Will they agree to exchange the few verses that are given in the Lectionary—the result of human choice—for the entire psalm given by the Holy Spirit? Are they ready to pay the price—a few more minutes of authentic prayer—to receive such riches?

The second remark concerns the manner of praying the responsorial psalm. The ideal of many communities is a calm and peaceful rendering of the psalm, an attentive listening to the soloist, with a gentle antiphonal response without much rhythmic verve. It is perfectly suitable for many of the psalms.

But not all. Nor for all communities. No other prayer invites the community so often to associate body and soul in prayer: prostrating oneself, lifting one's hands, moving forward with cries of joy, processing around the altar. At least we affirm in the psalms that we do these. Should we really perform such actions? At least whenever possible? Can we really pray "Lift up your hands" without ever dreaming of lifting up our hands as a sign of our prayer? Or "Clap your hands, all you peoples; shout to God with loud songs of joy," without ever clapping our hands in unison with "all the peoples"? Or perhaps would it be irreverent to clap and shout for joy in God's presence? Can we really affirm that we have seen the divine processions, "the singers in front, the musicians last, between them girls playing tambourines" (Ps 68:25), without dreaming of organizing similar processions? Or must the liturgy of the New Covenant be less joyful than that of the Old Covenant? What can we say of a community that, when it hears the invitation offered to it by the psalmist, "Let us worship and bow down, let us kneel before the LORD, our Maker!" (Ps 95:6), rests tranquilly seated, eyes closed in meditation, as if the psalm had nothing to do with them? Can we say: "Let them praise his name with dancing" (Ps 149:3) without ever dreaming of expressing our love by dancing? Are not music and dance also God's creations, created to celebrate the marvels of his love? Is our body not the temple of the Holy Spirit in which Jesus celebrates the adoration of the Father? Where are the harps and lyres, the stringed instruments and flutes, the triumphant cymbals, the trumpet blasts and tambourines to accompany the Alleluia dance of which Psalm 150 speaks? Some of the psalms in which Israel cried out its joy or lamented its distress are as incandescent as hot lava. They must shine like the sun in the Liturgy of the Word as the summit of the people's participation. Alas! Often sung in an anemic melody of three or four notes, they become dimmed lanterns, islands of weariness. Some communities, to rid themselves of this dreary singing, have even dared to replace the psalms by songs that they judged more "alive" (as if the Word of God could be replaced by a song!).

It is possible to dream of communities in which prayer is not reduced to an intellectual activity but which engages the whole person, body and soul; in which each psalm is celebrated according to its particular genre, not simply as a response to a reading, as if to heighten the value of the first reading but for its own worth and for what it truly is: the Word of God and revelation of Jesus Christ. Each psalm is an icon of Christ that reflects his mystery. Divine prayer, but also human prayer, spiritual but also bodily, intellectual but also of the senses was Jesus' prayer in which he sang and danced the psalms, like all the children of Israel, while remaining at the same time, the beloved Son of the Father.

It is not for anyone to tell another how to pray or how to put into practice the recommendation of the Apostle: "[Sing] psalms and hymns and spiritual songs among yourselves, singing and making melody to the Lord in your hearts, giving thanks to God the Father at all times and for everything in the name of our Lord Jesus Christ" (Eph 5:19).

The communities that are peacefully and happily secure in their liturgical practice continue to celebrate the responsorial psalm as in the past. When the psalmist invites them to lift up their hands or to kneel, they prefer to lift up their hands only in spirit and kneel spiritually. They think this is preferable to physically lifting their hands and kneeling.

Other communities—some of them in the Third World or in mission countries—find that the prayer of the body, far from hindering that of the soul, supports it. Since the Spirit invented the prayer of the psalms, and since the Spirit inspires prayer today, they prefer to pray, as much as possible, as the Spirit recommends.

Each community must see to what extent it can integrate dance or other forms of gesture into its liturgy, recognizing and honoring its own cultural sensitivities. The ideal is not to sing better or to dance more but to pray better, following the Spirit's leadings. Such praying communities are building tomorrow's liturgy.[22]

Conclusion: The Importance of the Responsorial Psalm

In his last instructions to his disciples after his resurrection, Jesus speaks of what has been written about him "in the law of Moses, the prophets, and the psalms . . ." (Luke 24:44). The story of Jesus is to be found, then, not only in the law—the Pentateuch—and the prophets but also in the psalms. The responsorial psalm sings of this story of Jesus.

In each psalm there is the face of Christ Jesus revealed to the believing community, an image of praise and blessing of the Father when, in the *hymnic psalms,* he unites his song with that of all his sisters and brothers and joins them to his own praise:

O magnify the LORD with me,
    and let us exalt his name together (Ps 34:3).

It is an image of humble, trustful supplication in the *psalms of supplication.* Walking at the head of an immense caravan of those poor who ask for God's love, he joins them to his prayer to the Father and implores with them:

Turn, O LORD, save my life;
    deliver me for the sake of your steadfast love (Ps 6:5).

It is the image of the man of sorrows in the *lamentation psalms,* in which he implores with all those agonizing in their suffering:

---

[22] On dance in the liturgy, see L. Deiss and G. Weyman, *Liturgical Dance* (Phoenix: NALR, 1984) and *Louez Dieu par la danse* (Paris–Montreal: Ed. du Levain, 1981).

> For my soul is full of troubles,
> > and my life draws near to Sheol.
> I am counted among those who go down into the Pit;
> > I am like those who have no help . . . (Ps 88:3-4).

It is an image of thanksgiving in the *thanksgiving psalms,* in which he thanks God for delivering the poor:

> I will bless the LORD at all times;
> > his praise shall continually be in my mouth . . .
> This poor soul cried, and was heard by the LORD,
> > and was saved from every trouble (Ps 34:1, 6).

It is an image of the royal Son of David in the *royal psalms,* in which God promises to establish the king's dynasty forever, in an eternity of love:

> Forever I will keep my steadfast love for him;
> > and my covenant with him shall stand firm (Ps 89:28).

It is the image of the risen One, in the *enthronement psalms,* who triumphs over the forces of evil and inaugurates the eternal reign of his Father:

> Say among the nations, "The Lord is King! . . .
> > He will judge the peoples with equity."
> Let the heavens be glad, and let the earth rejoice . . . (Ps 96:10-11).

It is an image of the teacher of wisdom in the *wisdom psalms:*

> The mouths of the righteous utter wisdom . . .
> > The law of their God is in their hearts (Ps 37:30-31).

It is an image of the Word of God in the *prophetic exhortations* the Word proclaims:

> Let me hear what God the LORD will speak,
> > for he will speak peace to his people,
> > to his faithful, to those who turn to him in their hearts (Ps 85:8).

It is an image of Emmanuel, who reigns in the heart of his Church in the *Songs of Zion:*

> The LORD of hosts is with us;
> > the God of Jacob is our refuge (Ps 46:7, 11).

It is an image of the ruler of history, who holds our lives in his hands in the *historical psalms:*

> Blessed be the Lord, the God of Israel,
>   from everlasting to everlasting (Ps 106:48).

The New Testament "christianizes" a number of the psalms when it applies them to Christ.[23] The liturgy christianizes them all, considering them either as Christ's prayer or as prayer to Christ.

In the responsorial psalm, it is truly the face of Christ Jesus that presents itself to the community.

It is the image of the *Son of Man,* in which each member of the faithful can recognize the traits of his or her own face. This immense symphony of psalms in which innumerable voices cry out in joy or pain is unified in a single song: the prayer of Christ Jesus.

It is the image, too, of the *Son of God.* For the Son of Man "was declared to be Son of God with power according to the spirit of holiness by resurrection from the dead . . ." (Rom 1:4). All members of the faithful may recognize in Christ's transfigured face the prophecy of their own destiny, their own vocation to share the glory of heaven with the Christ of the psalms.

The weight of the responsorial psalm is summed up in the prayer of Psalm 4:7:

> "Let the light of your face shine on us, O LORD!" (Ps 4:6).

---

[23] The New Testament cites the psalms fifty-seven times. See M. Gourgue, *Les Psaumes et Jésus–Jésus et les Psaumes,* Cahiers Evangile 25 (1978).

Introduction to the Processional Songs

The Mass of the Roman Rite has four processions:

The entrance procession

The gospel procession

The presentation of the gifts procession

The communion procession

Each of these processions is accompanied by a song called a processional.

These processions highlight the mystery of Christ by underlining his presence. *Sacrosanctum Concilium* 7 recalls the three modes of Christ's presence in the liturgical celebration:

> Christ is present in the celebrating community, as he promised: "For where two or three are gathered together in my name, I am there among them" (Matt 18:20).

> He is present in his Word, for it is he who speaks when the holy Scriptures are read in the church.

> He is present in the Eucharistic species.

These presences are "real." The presence of Christ in the Eucharistic elements is called real "because he is substantially present there through that conversion of bread and wine which, as the Council of Trent tells us, is most aptly named transubstantiation."[1]

---

[1] Instruction *Eucharisticum Mysterium* 9. See Flannery, op. cit., 104. This Instruction cites the Paul VI encyclical *Mysterium fidei*, AAS 57 (1965) 764.

Each of these modes of presence is signified in a rite that is accompanied by a song.

1. *The Presence of Christ in the Community*
This presence is realized more particularly when a crowd of Christians becomes a hierarchically structured assembly at the beginning of the liturgical celebration.

The rite that signifies this mystery is the entrance of the presider, who represents Jesus in the midst of the community.

The song that accompanies this rite is the entrance song.

2. *The Presence of Christ in the Word*
This presence is realized in the first two readings and in the responsorial psalm. But it finds its culmination in the proclamation of the gospel. The *Ordo Lectionum Missae, Praenotanda* (13) says: "The reading of the gospel constitutes the summit of the Liturgy of the Word." It is here that the affirmation of *Sacrosanctum Concilium* (33) is most clearly manifested: "For in the liturgy God speaks to his people, and Christ is still proclaiming his gospel."[2]

The rite that underlines this presence of Christ is the procession of the Gospel Book.

The song that accompanies this rite is the Alleluia song (or another acclamation of the gospel).

3. *The Presence of Christ in the Eucharistic Species*
This presence is realized by the Eucharistic Prayer, the center of which are the words of institution and the epiclesis.[3]

Different rites, crowned by the elevation and the doxology that concludes the Eucharistic Prayer, underline this presence. Two processions set the pace for the Eucharistic liturgy. The first, at the beginning, brings the bread and wine, which will become the Body and Blood of the Lord, to the altar. The second, toward

---

[2] Flannery, op. cit., 11–12.

[3] The epiclesis (Greek *epiklesis:* invocation = *klesis,* to call; *epi* = on) is the prayer that invokes the coming of the Spirit on the bread and wine so that they might be transubstantiated into the Body and Blood of Christ.

the end of the Eucharistic liturgy, is that of the communion procession. It leads the faithful to the altar to receive the bread and wine that have been made Eucharist.

The songs that accompany these two processions are those of the presentation of the gifts and the communion song.

5

The Entrance Processional

SIGNIFICANCE

What is the significance of the entrance song? What mystery does it emphasize?

The Coming of Christ

Sacrosanctum Concilium 33 states that the priest "in the person of Christ, presides over the community."[4] When he joins himself to the community in the entrance procession, the liturgical community organizes itself hierarchically and becomes an epiphany of Christ. In its heart, the heart of the Church beats. This assembly is not a part that, when joined to thousands of other parts, makes up the people of God. The Church is not a mosaic of individual assemblies. In each particular assembly the fullness of the Church's mystery is incarnated.[5]

The Entrance of the Community

The arrival of the priest determines another mystery: the entrance of the celebrating community. For the community has an entrance to make too. We are not speaking here of an entrance procession in which the whole community participates. Communities that are able to enjoy

[4] Flannery, op. cit., 12.
[5] *Sacrosanctum Concilium* 42: "[Parishes] . . . in some way . . . represent the visible Church constituted throughout the world." Flannery, op. cit., 15.

121

such a luxury may do so freely; there is nothing wrong with this. If the community likes it, there is no reason to deprive it of this procession.[6] But this procession is important in another way: it is the entrance of the people into a state of celebration, into the celebration itself.

While Peter and Paul and Lucy and Catherine are outside the church, they remain isolated Christians in their individuality and are part of the worldly domain. When they gather in front of the church, they exchange the kind of normal greetings that all ordinary people exchange: "Hi! How are you?" But once they cross the threshold of the church, they enter into sacred space, their conversation stops, and it is replaced by the entrance song. Once apart, they were linked by the invisible mystery of the communion of saints. Gathered in the ecclesial community, this link is now visibly signified by the constitution of the assembly. The Church's song has nothing to do with the kind of entrances made by stage artists or the ovations that greet sports figures at the beginning of a match. Rather, it manifests visibly the mystery of the Church itself.

Perhaps it is the entrance song that most immediately illustrates the unifying power of song, which, as we have seen,[7] is one of the ministerial functions of song. The faithful coming to church are a crowd, sometimes even an unruly one. In the church, they are juxtaposed units. Singing together, they express their unity for the first time. John Chrysostom explains:

> As soon as the singing of the psalm begins, it regroups the dispersed voices in unity, it gathers them all together in a harmonious canticle. Young and old, rich and poor, women and men, slaves and free, we all sing a single melody. The musician plucks the different strings of his lyre, but he plays a single melody. How surprising that the power of the psalm and of the inspired canticle produces the same result! . . . The prophet speaks, we all respond, together we form a single choir. Here there is neither slave nor free, neither rich nor poor, neither master nor servant. The inequality that exists in the world is laid aside, all form a single choir, all voices are of equal worth, earth imitates heaven. Such is the noble quality of the Church![8]

---

[6] A procession is not authentic unless it is liturgically useful: the community must move from one place to another. Such is the case in the celebration of the Easter Vigil: the community gathers first to bless the new fire outside the church, and then processes into the church following Christ, who is symbolized in the paschal candle.

[7] See chapter 2.

[8] *Homilia* V, *De studio praesentium* 2; PG 63, 486–87.

It is because of the need to express this unity of the assembly that a rite will always be necessary at the beginning of the celebration. It would be contrary to the laws of celebration, as well as to the laws of group psychology to begin *ex abrupto,* without having offered the community a chance to express its common soul. Of course, song is not the only way of manifesting the unity of the assembly. On Good Friday, when the community celebrates the passion of the Lord, it begins with a prostration before the altar as a sign that it humbles itself in silence and adoration. Other rites are possible, like the common recitation of a prayer. Yet among the traditional ways of expressing unity, song is the simplest and the most immediately effective.

These thoughts about the coming of Christ in the person of the presiding priest, and of the gathering of the community and its entry into the celebration, allow us to resolve in a simple way the question of how long the entrance song should be.

This was not a question in the past; it was regulated by the rubrics. The entrance song lasted the length of time it took to sing or intone the official text. But today, such a rubrical approach has been superseded.

Today some think that the entrance song should last for as long as it takes the priest to reach the altar. "In any case, it is over when the priest arrives at his chair."[9] But such a judgment reveals a strictly clerical vision of the liturgy. It is not for the community to regulate itself according to what its presider does, but rather for the presider—who is at the service of the community—to regulate his own actions in accord with those of the community. The celebration is the act of the whole community, of which the priest is a part.

To remain liturgically authentic, we must affirm that the entrance song performs a ministerial function. It must, therefore, last as long as necessary for it to perform that function, that is, all the time it takes for the community to gather spiritually as one and acclaim Christ. If a single verse is sufficient, a single verse should be sung. If five or six are needed, even if the priest has only two steps to take to arrive at the altar, five or six should be sung—whatever time is necessary to create a celebrating community.

---

[9] See A. Rozier, *Eglise qui chante,* 79–80 (1967) 27.

The Text

Along with the music, the text is the path that leads the faithful into the heart of the liturgical celebration.

Before the reform of Vatican II, the liturgy had no concern about the entrance song: it was obligatory to use the text set forth in the Missal. Can the past give us some indications of what would be fitting for the present?

If the feast being celebrated possessed a strong liturgical "personality," the liturgy chose biblical texts that highlighted the mystery being celebrated. In the wonderful introit for Christmas, the path toward the Lord's crib was easy to find when the community was able to sing the text of Isaiah 9:6:

> For a child has been born for us,
>   a son given to us.

In several instances, tradition did not hesitate to adapt the text to the community, sometimes risking the possibility of dismissing its literal sense. The old introit for the Sunday of the Octave of Christmas is a well-known example:

> When peaceful silence lay over all, and night had run half of her swift course, your all-powerful word, O Lord, leaped down from heaven, from the royal throne . . . .

This text would be wonderful if the following verses were not "bounded, a fierce warrior, into the doomed land, bearing the sharp sword of your inexorable decree" (Wis 18:14-16). The "word" in the passage is, in fact, that which punished the Egyptians at the time of the Exodus.[10] There is a dismissal of the literal, primitive sense, which is intolerable because it is the Word of God and because it is used in the liturgy.

Outside of liturgically strong times, that is, on the Sundays after Pentecost, the tradition was not very creative, and took refuge in the psalter. Are there not valid sentiments of adoration, praise, thanksgiving, and supplication to be found there? The choir director used to follow the numerical order of the psalms, beginning with the first and finishing with the last. This was the rule not only for the introit but also for the Alleluia chant, the offertory, and the communion chant.

---

[10] It is regrettable that the new Missal has retained this text as the antiphon for the opening of the Mass of the Second Sunday after Christmas.

This use of the psalms as processional songs is very ancient: it was solidly implanted in the liturgy before the middle of the sixth century. It is explained above all by the fact that the text of the psalms was used as a protection against the hymns produced by the Gnostics, Manichees, and other heretics of every shade and color, who inundated the market of religious songs and threatened the purity of the Christian faith.

Tradition also utilized ecclesial compositions, for example, the *Salve Sancta Parens,* the text of which is taken from the *Carmen Paschale* of Sedulius (5th c.),[11] and whose melody can be traced in that of the introit *Ecce advenit* of the Mass of Epiphany. It would therefore be in full conformity with tradition not to simply take up the ancient texts again but to compose new texts. The patristic and medieval periods have left us with some 30,000 hymns.[12] This shows us that each age sang of Christ in its own particular way and spirit, each showing a different image of Jesus. Each age thus paid him its "tribute of praise."[13] Our age must also not fail to do its duty.

This diversity of tradition contains a rich teaching. The question is not whether we should take psalm texts or other biblical texts or ancient or modern ecclesiastical texts. That question resolves itself before the priority of ministerial function: we must take—or invent— the text that is best for the celebrating community, the text that is the most joyful way for the community to enter into the celebration.

We need popular and vibrant texts, without theological or metaphysical complexity, that reflect the splendor of the Word. When they encounter Christ at the beginning of the celebration, the faithful must encounter the radiant and liberating joy that Jesus' contemporaries encountered when they met the Lord on the paths of Galilee. This first contact with the Lord, this beginning of the gathering of the children of God in the Church, must radiate peace and joy. The entrance song must radiate the gentle face of the risen One to the community.

The establishment of a quality repertoire in vernacular languages is the ideal toward which all linguistic communities tend. Sometimes we think of accelerating the pace of the creation of such a repertoire by producing song selections that are more or less official. These selections

---

[11] See J. Gajard, in H. du Manoir, *Maria,* vol. II (Paris: Beauchesne, 1952) 370.

[12] See P. Salmon, "La prière des heures," in A. G. Martimort, *L'Eglise en Prière,* 3rd ed. (Paris: Desclée, 1965) 848.

[13] "To glorify the day of your birth, we offer you the tribute of praise," Hymn *Jesu Redemptor omnium,* Christmas vespers.

provide incontestable service to communities by providing them with quality songs. They also have their drawbacks: they have a tendency to become clichés, and they render a somewhat static liturgical scene for perhaps a generation. But the liturgy is in continual evolution: what is modern today will be ancient tomorrow, perhaps even obsolete. These selections also represent the tastes of those who produce them: even if they are of excellent taste, do they reflect the tastes of the communities that use them? These selections also discourage the creation of new songs: new songs, created by new composers, are excluded definitively from certain books, even if they are better than the old songs.

We must remember that no popular liturgy has ever been created from random selections, however excellent. History proves otherwise. The liturgy has always come from being "lived" in the celebrating assembly. The best way of improving the repertoire is to offer texts that are so outstanding that communities will spontaneously want to adopt them.

Finally, let it be said that it is easier to reclaim texts of value than to create them, and easier to ask for music that is radiant with beauty than to compose it. The Gregorian repertoire that we love so much took centuries to develop. Undoubtedly, at the present time we need a great deal of patience.

The Music

Festive Music

The first requirement for the music of the entrance song is that it be festive. It must transport the faithful from the profane world and place them in a festive world, that of celebration. This is not the negation of the everyday world that surrounds us with its ties of tenderness, joy, and sorrow. It is rather the entry of this world into the presence of the Father, of our tears and our smiles "into the kingdom of his beloved Son" (Col 1:13). More than in the other processional songs—those of the gospel, the presentation of the gifts, or the communion—the music must be responsible for a certain detachment from the profane and who we are, and a certain attachment to the divine and who we wish we were. It is a path to God. And its function is all the more important to the degree that our hearts are heavy and have not yet been lifted up by the Word of God that will soon be proclaimed. If I am walking in the street and someone suddenly begins to sing, I say to myself that something has just happened to him or her. To the Christian who suddenly begins to sing with his sisters and brothers, something has happened: he or she just met Jesus Christ. And so they sing.

Suitable Music

Suitability is the second requirement for the entrance song. It must be functional, that is, it must fulfill its own ministerial function.

First, it must be *suitable for the particular community* that celebrates in particular circumstances. Celebrating communities are very diverse. Their liturgical personalities must be respected, that is, their particular manner of loving Christ and of expressing this love in song. To express the incomparable riches of Christ, there are a thousand different musical possibilities offered to communities, whether they are North American, African, South American, Indian, Chinese, etc. As *Sacrosanctum Concilium* 40 states, the ecclesiastical authority must "carefully and prudently consider which elements from the traditions and cultures of individual peoples might appropriately be admitted into divine worship."[14] The "prudence" of which the Constitution speaks will serve to open the doors of the liturgy as wide as possible to all worthy forms of music in use among the people. The music of each nation is, in effect, invited to kneel before Jesus Christ and sing his glory.

When we see the extraordinary explosion of new musical creations that have multiplied in mission countries, we may affirm that the "prudence" of creating songs that are suitable for these communities has been fully respected.

The music must also be suitable to the *celebration* itself. The community not only enters into a state of celebration but into a particular celebration. Culture and musical formation will suggest apt solutions. Here, as elsewhere, we should observe Paul's principle in regard to charismatic manifestations in the primitive Church: "Do not quench the Spirit. Do not despise the words of prophets, but *test everything; hold fast to what is good*" (1 Thess 5:19-21).

It would be a pity, after having rid ourselves of the wandering demons of rubrical convention, to be seduced by a new rubricism and to sing under the pretext of having to sing. We must remember

[14] Flannery, op. cit., 14.

that the best song is not that which is the best selection in the song-book, but that which is best for the particular celebrating community.

The Participants

It is normal for the entire celebrating community to sing the entrance song, perhaps with the choir's help.

Through this song, the community signifies that it is has become an ecclesial community and that it acclaims Christ's presence in its midst. This mystery is lived by all the faithful. All the faithful, therefore, express this mystery by joining in singing the entrance song.

The Form

Different forms are possible. They are even desirable, when one considers the diverse communities that exist in the Church.

The Traditional Form of Gregorian Chant

Communities that love chant and its tradition may, of course, always use it if it helps them.

Note that the opening antiphon given by the Missal is normally an adaptation of the text of the Gregorian introit. It does not replace the entrance song. The Missal simply notes: "If there is no singing for the entrance, the antiphon in the Missal is recited either by the faithful, by some of them, or by the priest after the greeting."[15]

Versed Song

The German *Kirchenlied,* the English chorale, and hymns, in general, are examples of versed song.

It is sometimes affirmed that this is a "closed form," each verse being, in a certain way, an entity in itself; the whole song is created by the juxtaposition of autonomous elements. This form would therefore be good to use as a processional. Such an opinion does not appear immediately evident. One remembers the old Lutheran chorales that Bach reused so masterfully in his cantatas, which brim with vitality.

As the *text* develops meaning as it progresses, so the song develops from verse to verse. Magical incantation shows us how repetition can be used to create a tension that resolves itself fully in the last verse.

---

[15] GIRM 26.

We may think that "closed" *melodies* exist: they try to lift themselves to wider horizons but, in fact, fall back on themselves without breaking out of their confines. How does this happen? From the melodic makeup itself. If the resources of modulation are ignored, and if the melody settles on the tonic at the end of every verse, it will never take flight. Other melodies can take flight because they are built with greater magnanimity, lyricism, and more inspiration. Who could say that the hymn *Vexilla Regis*, which is written in verse form, is a closed melody, when each verse calls forth the next? Let us just say that there are good and bad, open or closed melodies.

The Troparion

In the liturgies of the East, the troparion is a song that actualizes the mystery of the feast celebrated in the liturgy. It is usually composed of:

- a long antiphon (stanza) coming at the beginning and at the end of the song;

- a refrain, sung by the whole community, and linked up with the stanza;

- one or more verses taken from the psalms or inspired by other biblical or liturgical texts. The refrain is sung after each verse.

The troparion has come into its own in some countries with the reform of liturgical song. Its literary flexibility frees it from the constraints of versed song. It is therefore more able to express the nuances of the mystery celebrated by the liturgy. Here, as an example, is a troparion for the feast of Epiphany:

A new star has risen.
They set out in the night
on the path traveled through generations
to adore the King.
He opens his arms
to the whole world.

R/. Joy to the whole universe!
Behold the dawning of the kingdom!

Let us worship
before the Lord of lords,
the Creator of the stars.

Let us offer our lives
to the Prince of peace,
the Rising Sun who comes to visit us.

Let us proclaim this wonder
to the people dwelling in darkness:
Proclaim our God who is Light.[16]

Full Form

In most communities, there are three possible ways of singing the entrance song.

The assembly sings the song.

The choir sings the song.

The soloist sings the song.

Each of these ways fulfills a precise function:

When the assembly sings, the participation of the whole community is assured.

When the choir sings, it adds solemnity to the entrance song through harmony.

When the soloist sings, the text that the whole community must hear and understand is clearly proclaimed.

Here, as an example, is the song *Without Seeing You, We Love You*[17] arranged for all three ways of singing:

Assembly + choir (Antiphon)
Without seeing you, we love you,
Without seeing you, we believe,
And we sing, Lord, in joy your glory.
You are our Savior.
We believe in you!

---

[16] Translated from Commission Francophone Cistercienne, *Tropaires des Dimanches,* Le Livre d'Heures d'En-Calcat (1980) 15.

[17] *Biblical Hymns & Psalms,* vol. II (Chicago: World Library Publications, 1970).

Soloist (Verse)
Blessed are those who will listen to your word;
They shall truly never see death,
For by you, they are heir to a new life.

Choir
O Lord, to whom shall we go?
You alone have the words of eternal life!

The acclamation of the choir comes after each verse sung by the soloist, and musically calls forth the repetition of the antiphon by the whole assembly.

Let us not forget what enrichment the organ can bring to a celebration. The organ may be used to announce the beginning of the celebration. A festive opening is truly a grace for a community. The organist bears a large responsibility for how the people sing, not only when the organist accompanies the people but also in introducing and concluding their song.

The Psalm with an Antiphon

A psalm with an antiphon may also be used, as was customary in the usage of the Roman liturgy. This psalm may be executed either antiphonally or responsorially.

In the responsorial form, the soloist or choir sings a verse, and the people respond with the antiphon.

In the antiphonal form, the soloist or choir sings a verse, the assembly takes up the second verse, and everyone sings the antiphon.

To sing a psalm is evidently less musically burdensome: the soloist dialogues with the assembly. This way of singing can be used for most celebrations. Yet it is not without problems. Some communities use the psalms exclusively for processionals: there is a psalm for the entrance song, a psalm for the preparation of the gifts procession, and a psalm for the communion procession, without counting the responsorial psalm. Such a multiplication, which fails to register the unique function and meaning of each song in the celebration, is the surest way of devaluing the psalms, in general, and the responsorial psalm, the most important psalm of the Mass, in particular.

"The Weight of the Opening Songs": The Introit, Kyrie, and Gloria

We cannot consider the question of the entrance song without speaking of the *Kyrie* and the *Gloria:* There are three songs at the beginning of the celebration. It is not without reason, therefore, that one has spoken of "the weight of the opening songs."

This weight is revealed particularly in the vernacular, when the Mass is celebrated as called for in *Musicam Sacram* 6: "The meaning and proper nature of each part and of each song [must] be carefully observed."[18]

The entrance song has its own function to fulfill: uniting the entire assembly, introducing the feast, and fostering a festive atmosphere. When it has fulfilled this function, the *Kyrie* and the *Gloria* cannot fulfill it again. Not only can they not do this, but they even serve to distract the attention and upset the assembly's prayer. The faithful have just entered spiritually into the celebration when they are torn away by the supplications of the *Kyrie,* which transports them into a totally different atmosphere; no sooner are they established in the spirit of the *Kyrie* than they are dragged away once again and transported into a context of praise and thanksgiving. Which of the faithful is capable of retaining peace of soul and the joy of the celebration during these pious gymnastics?

Over the centuries, the Christian community has created a defense against such aggression. It has transformed the prayer of the entrance song, the penitential rite of the *Kyrie,* and the praise of the *Gloria* into . . . songs. Three prayers, which should always be transformed by song, are sometimes reduced to the level of three rites.

During the reform of the Mass after Vatican II, the reformers did not dare to lighten the rites at the beginning of Mass, undoubtedly because of the excessive attachment of some to the former way of celebrating. They should have been inspired by the simplicity of Christian origins in this domain,[19] and proposed one single rite or single song. The present-day rubrics, however, prompt a few suggestions.

If the entrance song really fulfills its ministerial function of introducing the community into the atmosphere of the feast and

---

[18] Flannery, op. cit., 82.

[19] At the time of St. Augustine (354–430), the Mass began with the presider's greeting to the assembly, and was followed immediately by the Liturgy of the Word. See *City of God,* XXII. 8, 22.

the nature of the particular celebration, the *Kyrie* and the *Gloria* should be played down as much as possible.

In the penitential seasons of Advent and Lent, the *Kyrie* and its penitential character may be accentuated.

It is sometimes possible to make a link between the entrance song and the *Kyrie*. This was done by some ancient German chorales in which every verse finished with a *Kyrie eleison*, as in the chorale *Jesus Christus, unser Heiland*, which uses a text by Luther: Jesus, our Savior, who has conquered death, is risen, and has triumphed over sin. *Kyrie eleison.*

It would be good to create similar songs that could serve as both entrance song and the penitential prayer of the *Kyrie*.

During the Christmas cycle, the *Gloria* may be highlighted, and may be used as the entrance song.

6

The Alleluia or Gospel Processional

SIGNIFICANCE

"The reading of the gospel constitutes the summit of the Liturgy of the Word" according to the *Ordo Lectionum Missae 13*. It is this reading of the gospel that the affirmation of Vatican II, as expressed in *Sacrosanctum Concilium 7*, is most clearly shown: "[Christ] is present in his Word since it is he himself who speaks when the holy Scriptures are read in the church."[1] The whole Bible possesses the supreme dignity of the Word of God, yet the biblical writings point toward the Christ of the Gospels. It is therefore to be expected that the liturgy surrounds the proclamation of the gospel with a number of rites that underline its particular importance.

The Book of the Gospels is first of all placed on the altar,[2] the practical equivalent of "enthroning" it. It confers an exceptional honor. The altar is, as the instruction *Eucharisticum Mysterium 24* says, "the sign of Christ himself, the place at which the saving mysteries are carried out, and the center of the assembly, to which the greatest reverence is due."[3] Until the ninth and tenth centuries, only the Gospel Book and the Eucharist had the privilege of being placed on the altar. According to the ancient rituals for the consecration of an altar, the bishop placed

---

[1] Flannery, op. cit., 5.

[2] See L. Deiss, *Celebration of the Word*, in which we discuss the rites that surround the proclamation of the gospel.

[3] Flannery, op. cit., 116.

the beginning of the four Gospels with the relics of the martyrs in the altar. We also know that during the holding of Church councils, the Gospel Book was solemnly exposed on the altar, as though to signify that Christ himself presided in person in the assembly gathered in his name. Vatican II happily took up again the rite of enthroning the gospel.

The meaning of these rites is clear: when the deacon takes the Gospel Book from the altar, in order to proclaim the gospel at the ambo, the rite has already signified in advance that, as *Sacrosanctum Concilium 33* says: "For in the liturgy God speaks to his people, and Christ is still proclaiming his gospel."[4]

There are prayers that accompany the one who proclaims the gospel:

> *A prayer for purification* that the priest says: "Almighty God, cleanse my heart and my lips that I may worthily proclaim your gospel."[5]

> *A blessing* that the priest pronounces over the deacon who reads the gospel, and a *commission:* "The Lord be in your heart and on your lips that you may worthily proclaim the gospel. In the name of the Father, and of the Son, and of the Holy Spirit." An ancient prayer formula was even more significant: "May the Holy Spirit rest upon you that you may announce the good news to the poor.[6]

There is the solemn procession from the altar to the ambo. The Missal, GIRM 93–94, expresses it thus:

> During the singing of the *Alleluia* or other chant . . . with hands joined [the priest] bows before the altar and inaudibly says the prayer, "Almighty God, cleanse my heart." If the Book of the Gospels is on the altar, he takes it and goes to the lectern, the servers, who may carry the censer and candles, walking ahead of him.[7]

We know that in antiquity, before the institution of the procession of the Blessed Sacrament, the procession of the Gospel Book was more solemn. According to the ancient Gallican liturgical *Ordo* of the

---

[4] Flannery, op. cit., 11–12.
[5] *The Sacramentary,* 412.
[6] Bobbio Missal (10th–11th c.) cited in Jungmann, op. cit., vol. 2, 225.
[7] See also GIRM 131 for the same rites for a deacon.

sixth century, the clergy used to sing: "Gates, lift up your lintels!
Eternal gates raise high your doors, that the King of glory may
enter!" The *Ordo* explains: "Behold, the procession of the holy gospel
advances, [the procession of] the power of Christ triumphant over
death."[8] We may also think of the splendor of the Little Entrance in
the Byzantine liturgy: the deacon traces the sign of the cross with the
uplifted Gospel Book and proclaims: "Wisdom! Attend!," and the
choir responds: "Come let us adore the Lord, let us bow down before him."[9] The enthronement of the Gospel Book is often accompanied by the singing of the Trisagion.[10]

These honors paid to the Gospel Book by the candles and the incense remind us of the royal dignity of the Lord, as does the whole
community that stands to welcome the Word. The splendor of the
ancient gospel books, which were often covered sumptuously and
decorated with gold, pearls, and ivory, gave witness to the same veneration. The gospel books of the Church in the East are the richest
treasure of the Byzantine churches.

There are, finally, the acclamations, *Glory to you, Lord,* and *Praise to
you, Lord Jesus Christ,* which are addressed directly to Christ.

All of these rites converge toward the same meaning: the proclamation of the Word, and especially of the gospel, cannot be reduced
to a simple reading of the history of the people of God in the Old and
New Testaments, nor to a simple memory of past events. The proclamation of the Word is a real celebration of Christ. It is really him we
acclaim and not the Lectionary when we cry "Glory to you, Lord!"

The *Alleluia* (or the chant that replaces it in Lent) is the processional song of this gospel reverence.

THE TEXT

Alleluia

Alleluia is the transcription of two Hebrew words: *hallelu* = "praise,"
and *Yah,* an abbreviation of Yahweh. Alleluia therefore means "Praise
Yahweh."

---

[8] Gamber, *Ordo Antiquus Gallicanus. Der gallikanische Messritus des 6 Jahrhunderts,* coll.
Textus Patristici et Liturgici (Regensburg: Pustet, 1965) 18.

[9] See P. Evdokimov, *La Prière de l'Eglise d'Orient* (Mulhouse: Salvator, 1966) 113.

[10] See, for example, the Coptic liturgy in F. E. Brightman and C. E. Hammond,
Liturgies Eastern and Western, vol. I (Oxford: Clarendon Press, 1896) 155.

Alleluia is found in the psalms that are called "Alleluia psalms" as a liturgical acclamation: Psalms 105–7, 111–14, 116–18, 135–36, and 146–50. They are essentially psalms of praise and thanksgiving. The group 113–18 constitute the *Hallel*. They were sung by Christ at the Last Supper (Matt 26:30). Thus, the Alleluia, as well as the acclamation "Blessed is the one who comes in the name of the LORD" (Ps 118:26) are among the most ancient songs of the Eucharistic celebration.

By its joyous and triumphant character, the Alleluia evokes the song of the redeemed Church. In the unhappy deportation to Nineveh, old Tobit does not cease to dream of a Jerusalem in which even the houses will cry out "Alleluia!":

> The gates of Jerusalem will sing hymns of joy.
>> and all her houses will cry Alleluia!
> Blessed be the God of Israel" (Tob 13:17).

In the New Testament, the acclamation is found only in the Book of Revelation. The period is one that marks the downfall of the great Whore of Babylon, and the victory of the redeemed:

> After this I heard what seemed to be the loud voice of a great multitude in heaven, saying,
>> "Alleluia!
> Salvation and glory and power to our God,
>> for his judgments . . .
>> "Alleluia!" . . .
> And the twenty-four elders and the four living creatures fell down and worshiped God who is seated on the throne, saying,
>> "Amen, Alleluia!"
> And from the throne came a voice saying,
>> "Praise our God,
>> all you his servants,
> and all who fear him,
>> small and great."
> Then I heard what seemed to be the voice of a great multitude, like the sound of many waters and like the sound of mighty thunderpeals, crying out,
>> "Alleluia!
> For the Lord our God
>> the almighty reigns.
> Let us rejoice and exult
>> and give him glory,
> for the marriage of the Lamb has come . . ." (Rev 19:1-7).

The song of the heavenly liturgy in the Book of Revelation is divided into three choirs. The first choir, which sings Alleluia, is that of all the heavenly beings; it apologizes for the divine judgment that allowed all the deaths of the martyrs slain for the Word. The second is that of the twenty-four elders and the four living creatures: they are no doubt the angels who form the divine court and who watch over the government of the world.[11] The third choir is that of the great multitude of the redeemed who, by its Alleluia, celebrates the inauguration of God's reign.

There is a fourth choir, that of all the faithful who, during the Eucharistic celebration, acclaim the presence of Christ in his Word by their Alleluia. It is in the context of the heavenly liturgy that our earthly liturgy finds itself.

During Lent the Alleluia is replaced by another acclamation of praise, such as "Praise to you, Lord Jesus Christ, king of endless glory!"

This substitution does not signify a diminution of praise. Both texts mean the same thing. It is simply a little rubrical playing about to mark the penitential time of Lent.[12] It presumes that "Praise to you, Lord Jesus Christ," is less joyful than the acclamation "Alleluia." But this is not the place to debate such liturgical curiosities.

The Verses

The verses that the new Lectionary sets forth introduce the gospel. The reform of the Lectionary has been particularly successful in this area: some of the texts are splendid, both from a biblical or a pastoral point of view. The verses are of two kinds:

Verses that can be used at any time are centered on the mystery of the Word. Here are a few examples:

"Speak Lord, for your servant is listening" (1 Sam 3:9).
"You have the words of eternal life" (John 6:69).
"Sanctify them in the truth; your word is truth" (John 17:17).

[11] See E. Corsini, *L'Apocalypse maintenant* (Paris: Seuil, 1980) 120.

[12] A certain folklore surrounds the period from Mardi Gras until Holy Saturday. In the Middle Ages, on the Saturday before Septuagesima Sunday, the Alleluia was "buried" with great pomp; incense, candles, holy water, and lamentations around a catafalque were usual (according to the Ordo of the church of Toul 15th c.; see J. Brinktrine, *Die Heilige Messe* (Paderborn: Schöningh, 1950) 103–4. Futile pieties that were, if not for edification, at least for the pleasure of our ancestors!

Other verses, given for a particular Sunday, are taken from the gospel of the day. The series for the Sundays of Lent, Cycle A, are particularly good. On the first Sunday, before the gospel of the temptation of the Lord, we are given:

> One does not live by bread alone;
> but by every word that comes from the mouth of God (Matt 4:4).

On the second Sunday, the transfiguration of the Lord, we find:

> From the shining cloud the Father's voice is heard:
> this is my beloved Son; hear him (Matt 17:5).

On the third Sunday, that of the discourse with the Samaritan woman, we have:

> Lord, you are truly the Savior of the World;
> give me living water, that I may never thirst again (John 4:42; 15).

On the fourth Sunday, which celebrates the healing of the man born blind, we find:

> I am the light of the world.
> Whoever follows me will have the light of life (John 8:12).

On the fifth Sunday, that of the resurrection of Lazarus, we have:

> I am the resurrection and the life. Those who believe in me, even
> though they die, will live . . . (John 11:25-26).

THE MUSIC

Music clothes the biblical words with splendor.

In his *Epistola* 77 (PL 22.697), Saint Jerome recounts that at the funeral of his friend Fabiola, the Alleluia resounded so strongly that it shook(!) the roof of the church. We can hope that the music of our alleluias are festive and joyful without doing any damage to the church.

In singing the verses, a joyous well-rhythmed rendition is needed, not the psalmic genre that links up the syllables in a rather somber melody. Multi-voice harmony is certainly possible, insofar as it underlines the meaning of the text.

Plainchant teaches us about beauty when it comes to the Alleluia verses. In its golden age, it deployed the best of its resources in the *jubilus* (the melody that decorates the syllable "ia" of the Allelu-ia). Certain compositions—for example, the Alleluias of the Easter season—are pure marvels in the way the vocalization bubbles and flows, endlessly joyful in its praise of the divine name of Yahweh. These pieces are undoubtedly some of the best creations in the realm of vocal composition. In order to create the equivalent in the vernacular, much time and much genius is necessary. But is not genius sometimes the equivalent of infinite patience?

For the musician considering the *jubilus* merely as a collection of notes, it does not have any precise spiritual significance; it is simply admired as one might admire the beauty of a rose or the song of the nightingale. But Christian antiquity gave it a more precise spiritual significance. St. Augustine explains:

> Those who sing, whether at the wheat harvest or the grape gathering, or in any other invigorating occupation, begin to express their joy in the words of a song. But when they are filled with a joy so great that it cannot be expressed in words, they leave words aside and begin to "rejoice." When we sing the *jubilus,* it is as if the heart is laboring under the weight of not being able to express itself. And who is the cause of this jubilation, if not the unspeakable God. Unspeakable is something that cannot be put into words. If then, you cannot put it into words, and yet, on the other hand, you must not be silent, what else remains to you except to "rejoice"? Thus the heart rejoices without words and the immensity of its joy is not limited by words.[13]

The aim of singing is not only to proclaim an intelligible message. Song also addresses itself to human feelings; it creates an atmosphere of beauty. Thus it can attain an effectiveness beyond the domain of discursive reasoning, and penetrate to the deepest realm of the heart, having an impact on the whole person. If the communication of a message needs words, the expression of a feeling needs no words, but art. The *jubilus* is to music what a smile is to joy and what tears are to sadness. As St. Augustine says, it is a "joy without words."[14]

Plainchant thus teaches us by means of the *jubilus* that the liturgy has need not only of concentrated texts and good literary structures but also of beautiful melodies. Certain notes may seem useless, which are nevertheless extremely necessary on a lyrical level. Only mediocre notes, or notes executed in a mediocre fashion, are useless.

[13] *Enarratio in Ps.,* 32:8; PL 36.283.
[14] "Sonus quidam est laetitiae sine verbis," *Enarratio in Ps.,* 99:4; PL 37.1272.

THE PARTICIPANTS

Because the Alleluia is an acclamation of Christ present in his Word, it is sung by the whole assembly.[15]

Preferably, the verses should be sung by the choir rather than a soloist, especially if a soloist has sung the responsorial psalm. There is nothing to stop the full assembly from singing the verses if the assembly knows the texts and the melodies.

THE FORM

It is preferable to double or even triple the Alleluia of the acclamation: this gives it a better musical rhythm and allows it to be better appreciated.

Often the Alleluia verse can be divided into two parts, with the Alleluia sung after each. A more festive climate is thus created during the procession of the Gospel Book. For example, the Alleluia verse, "Speak Lord, for your servant is listening. You have the words of eternal life" can be treated in the following way:

Choir (or soloist):	Alleluia, alleluia!
All:	Alleluia, alleluia!
Choir (and assembly):	Speak Lord, for your servant is listening.
All:	Alleluia, alleluia!
Choir (and assembly):	You have the words of eternal life.
All:	Alleluia, alleluia!

It is normal for the choir, according to its skill, to enrich the Alleluia acclamation and its verse through harmonization.

The Missal envisages (GIRM 95) that "after the acclamation of the people, [the priest] proclaims the gospel. . . ." As already mentioned, Msgr. Adam, bishop of Libreville, testifies that a liturgical community in Gabon welcomed the gospel, after it had been proclaimed with the words: "Bravo, Jesus, you have spoken well!" Our

---

[15] *Ordo lectionum Missae, Praenotanda 13* [New American Version] affirms: "The *Alleluia* or the verse before the gospel must be sung and during it all stand. It is not to be sung only by the cantor who intones it or by the choir, but by the whole congregation together."

European communities have not found similar formulas. This is still an area to explore. For the present, the simplest method is to take up the Alleluia acclamation several times, with a verse from the gospel of the day.

CONCLUSION

The success of a song—in this case the Alleluia—is measured by the perfection with which it accomplishes its ministerial function.

In the case of the Alleluia, different elements, in addition to the simple song, enter into consideration. Let us simply mention the following :

A procession worthy of the gospel—not merely a movement to the ambo.

A fixed ambo, worthy of the altar, that highlights and illustrates a theology of the two tables, that of the Word and the Eucharist—not simply a moveable lectern called an ambo.

A Gospel Book worthy of representing Christ, that can be venerated by incensing it and by kissing it, and that can be proudly shown to the assembly in the acclamation of Christ—not merely a pocket Missal.

Many communities have enthusiastically produced gospel books that are truly worthy of their celebrations. Others are still on the way. Some seem not even to know what is fitting. We must hope that the celebrations of vibrant communities will eventually awaken those that remain asleep.

As for the texts of the Alleluia verse, it should be noted that they do not produce exactly the biblical text. There is a certain space to freely create texts, biblical or otherwise, that fulfill well their ministerial function. There is room for experimentation.

On the musical level, there is also an area of legitimate experimentation. When the choir is used, there remains the problem of how to integrate the assembly's singing in unison and in harmony with the choir.

The procession of the gospel and the Alleluia song must be the summit of the celebration of the Liturgy of the Word, a summit of joy and beauty. We can admire those attempts that work: they are many. We can hope that their joy and beauty will finally enlighten all our celebrations.

7

The "Offertory" or
Presentation of the Gifts

PRESENTATION OF THE GIFTS OR OFFERTORY

First a question of vocabulary: Before the reform, we used to speak of the "offertory." The prayers that accompanied the old offertory spoke of offering "this immaculate host" (the prayer *Suscipe, sancte Pater*), "the chalice of salvation" (the prayer *Offerimus tibi Domine*). By doing this, they wrongly anticipated the great Eucharistic Prayer. There was a certain incoherence in presenting the bread and wine and offering them as though they were already consecrated.

The new Missal has eliminated these prayers of the old Missal. It has also rightly abandoned the title "offertory" and substituted that of the *Preparatio donorum,* the preparation of the gifts.[1]

This is a happy change of vocabulary. It invites us to avoid theological falsities that were sometimes made in regard to the meaning of this part of the Mass.[2] It is regrettable that a more detailed revision was not carried out. Was it by affection for the past that such phrases as "offertory song"[3] were retained, even when there is no longer an offertory, and when Masses no longer supply a text for this song?

The prayer that accompanies the presentation of the bread and wine also suffers from a certain ambiguity. The Latin text reads: *quem*

---

[1] GIRM 48, 49.

[2] See L. Deiss, *The Lord's Supper: Eucharist of Christians* (Glasgow: Collins, 1980) 91–92.

[3] See *Ordo Missae* 17; GIRM 50; *Ritus servandus in concelebratione Missae* 7.

tibi offerimus, that is, "which we offer to you." The English language Missals translate the letter of the Latin: "We have this bread—this wine—to offer," but the French, Italian, German, and Spanish Missals, faithful to the spirit of the reform, translate: "We have this bread—this wine—to present." It would be vain to be amazed at these incoherences of vocabulary. Who could pretend that the liturgical reform was perfect in every point?

We might well prefer the title "presentation of the gifts" to "preparation of the gifts," for there is scarcely any preparation: the bread is already prepared and the wine has only to be poured into the chalice, if this has not already been done before the beginning of Mass.[4]

MEANING

The Missal, GIRM 49, states:

> At the beginning of the Liturgy of the Eucharist the gifts, which will become Christ's body and blood, are brought to the altar.

It is not fitting to place the paten with the hosts or the chalice with the wine on the altar at the beginning of the Mass, but to bring them to the altar at the beginning of the Eucharistic Liturgy. This is the norm for all Masses, including the most simply celebrated weekday Masses.

This bringing up of the gifts for the Eucharist is done by the faithful. The GIRM says:

> It is desirable for the faithful to present the bread and wine . . . . Even though the faithful no longer, as in the past, bring the bread and wine for the liturgy from their homes, the rite of carrying up the gifts retains the same spiritual value and meaning.

Other gifts may also be brought up, such as the collection or the offerings for the poor. These gifts must not be placed on the altar, which is "the table of the Lord, the central point of the whole Eucharistic Liturgy."[5] "These are to be put in a suitable place but not on the altar" (GIRM 49). The collection may be placed in front of

---

[4] See GIRM 49 (1970 edition).

[5] Ibid., quoting the instruction *Inter Oecumenici* 95, and the instruction *Eucharisticum Mysterium* 24.

the altar. The gifts of food for the poor are assembled at the entrance to the sanctuary in certain Third World countries.

The processional song that accompanies the presentation of the gifts is the song that accompanies the bringing up of the gifts to the altar. GIRM 50 says that it "continues at least until the gifts have been placed on the altar." As the rite is very popular, the procession and the song that accompanies it sometimes take on a certain importance in Third World countries that we in the West judge excessive. But does our cultural sensitivity allow us to judge what is fitting for other communities?

REALIZATIONS

The Processional Song

The simplest solution is that the community should be in dialogue with the choir in the processional song. This song must express the meaning of what the community is doing.

The biblical background of extraordinary richness must inspire fresh and simple texts. Here, for example, is the song *With a Joyful Heart*.[6] The antiphon and verse 3 taken from 1 Chronicles (29:14 and 17), admirably underline the nature of Christian offering: we give back to God what he has first given us. We do it with a simple and joyful heart:

> *Antiphon*
> With a joyful heart, O Lord, my God,
> I give all to you.
>
> *Verses*
> Behold, O Lord, this bread
> which we now carry to your altar.
> This bread will become your body.
>
> Behold, O Lord, this wine;
> accept and bless it for our gladness.
> This wine will become your blood.

---

[6] *Biblical Hymns & Psalms,* vol. II (Chicago: World Library Publications, 1970).

We come to you, O Lord;
We bring the gifts that you have made,
the gifts we return to you.

Here, O Lord, is the wine
which has matured for our joy:
May it become your holy blood.

All comes from you, O Lord,
And now we offer you
What your hand has given us.

It is not necessary that a community's repertoire of such processional songs be large. If these simple songs are well adapted to their ministerial function, they will wear well. The entire community will eventually be able to sing them by heart as they now sing the *Sanctus* or the *Agnus Dei*.

The Choir's Song

Another possibility is to let the choir sing alone. It can execute one of the treasures of the polyphonic or Gregorian repertoire. The community can then rest a little after having given its full attention to the celebration of the Word. The ancient Gregorian "offertories" were based on the psalms taken in numerical order, and were not, properly speaking, offertory hymns but rather pieces that were sung during the offertory. They were sung, even the best of them, to fill gaps in the celebration. They fulfilled their ministerial function insofar as they created zones of silence and peace in the souls of those who heard them.

An Organ Piece

The organ may also be used. The organist may provide a processional song without words through solo playing during the bringing of the gifts. To do this implies that both the organ and the organist are good, and that the latter participates fully in the prayer of the liturgy. Music will flow from the organist's prayer, which will support the assembly's silence and clothe its prayer in beauty. Some organists have a real gift for knowing exactly what will help the community's prayer. Blessed are those communities that have such an organist.

It is clear that there must be a close interchange between priest and organist. If it is disastrous for communities to have organists who interrupt the rhythm of the celebration with their organ playing, it is equally disastrous if the priest interrupts the playing of the organist. A deep, mutual understanding must be always present between the altar and the organ. Such mutual sympathy must reign throughout the assembly. A Eucharistic celebration can only be built on the mutual understanding that comes from authentic love.

There are limits to the use of the organ at this point. The limits are of a cultural nature. The organ is unknown in the East, unsuitable in tropical countries by reason of climate, and unwanted in mission countries that have their own culture. Yet in those restricted regions where the organ is "at home," we need organists who can infuse a "soul" into the instrument.

THE TEACHING OF THE EASTERN LITURGIES: FURTHER PERSPECTIVES

Certain Eastern liturgies have solemnized the transfer of the gifts to the altar by a majestic procession called the Great Entrance. Preceded by candles and incense, the deacon and the priest begin from the table where the gifts have been prepared, and process around the nave to the altar. This procession, which probably dates from the seventh century,[7] recalls Jesus' entry into Jerusalem before his death and resurrection. In the Mass, it symbolizes Christ's entry into the community that is about to celebrate the memorial of this death and resurrection. It is accompanied by the song of the cherubim, the *cherubikon:*

> We who mystically represent the cherubim,
> and who sing to the life-giving Trinity
> the thrice holy hymn,
> Let us lay aside all worldly care
> so as to welcome the King of the universe,
> invisibly escorted by the angelic hosts.
> Alleluia![8]

---

[7] See Cabié, op. cit., 96–97.
[8] See Brightman and Hammond, op. cit., vol. 2, 222.

We may ask if the Latin liturgy, always so proud of its Roman sobriety, cannot learn something from contact with the Eastern liturgies. Our ancient offertory was encumbered with too many prayers and, while beautiful, had obscured the primitive meaning of the rite. The liturgical reform cleaned up the space, but with such thoroughness that no beauty or poetry was left. All is functional: the bread and wine are brought to the altar, but that is all. Where is the joy of a people who approach the altar in hopeful expectation? Where is the joy of the entry into Jerusalem, the joy of the Church today who prepares itself to celebrate the glorious Pasch of the Lord?

How will the procession for the presentation of the gifts develop in the future? Will it come from those who do not appreciate Roman sobriety but instead bring the action to life with joyfulness and exultant dancing?

Who dares play the prophet when it comes to theorizing about the future of the liturgy?

8

The Communion Processional

HISTORY AND MINISTERIAL FUNCTION

From the *Apostolic Constitutions,* which transmit to us the form of the
Syrian liturgy of about the year 380, we learn that the communion
rite was carried out in a festive atmosphere, like that of a Christian
family gathered around Christ:

> The bishop then addresses the people with these words: "Holy things
> to the holy!"

> The people answer:
> "One only Holy One, one only Lord,
> Jesus Christ, who is blessed for ever,
> to the glory of the Father! Amen.

> "Glory to God in the highest heaven,
> on earth, peace,
> among men, good will (of God)" (Luke 2:14).

> "Hosanna to the Son of David,
> Blessed be he who comes in the name of the Lord."
> God the Father has shown himself among us.
> "Hosanna in the highest heaven" (Matt 21:9).[1]

The Jerusalem Church must have known the practice of the
Syrian Churches. The *Mystagogical Catechesis,*[2] attributed to Cyril of

---

[1] *Apostolic Constitutions,* VIII, 13. 12–13, in Deiss, *Springtime,* 237–38.
[2] In Deiss, *Springtime,* 288.

Jerusalem (d. 387), tells us that the bishop of Jerusalem said the same thing: "Holy things to the holy," and that after this came, as in Syria, "One alone is holy. . . ." The *Catechesis* goes on to speak of the communion song:

> Then you hear the cantor inviting you, in a divine song, to communion in the holy mysteries; he says: "Taste and see how good the Lord is" (Ps 34:9).[3]

The text of the "divine canticle" is from verse 9 of Psalm 34 (Ps 33 according to the numbering of the Greek translation). This psalm has been used frequently in both Eastern—as in the Jerusalem and Armenian liturgies[4]—and in the West, as Ambrose[5] (339–397), Augustine[6] (354–430), and Jerome[7] indicate.

The history of the communion song has been directly linked with changing communion practice through the centuries. During the first centuries, people received communion regularly at every Mass. Hippolytus of Rome, in the *Apostolic Tradition* 36–37, tells us that Christians even used to take the communion bread home so that they could take communion each day. But from the fourth century, the practice of receiving communion declined very rapidly in some Churches. We learn from Ambrose that in some of the Eastern Churches people only took communion once a year: Ambrose recommends that the faithful receive every day and not imitate the Greeks.[8] In Gaul, the Synod of Agde (506) decreed that the faithful who did not receive communion at least three times a year could no longer consider themselves Catholics.[9] The Lateran Council (1215) decreed that the faithful receive communion at least once a year.[10]

Several factors contributed to the decline in Eucharistic practice.[11] The most important was undoubtedly the reaction against Arianism, which denied the divinity of Christ; this led the Church to place an emphasis on the *mysterium tremendum* of Christ's divinity. It was judged necessary to receive the sacrament of "confession" in order to purify

---

[3] Ibid., 288.
[4] See Brightman and Hammond, vol. 1, 449–50.
[5] *The Mysteries,* 58, SC 25 bis (1961) 191.
[6] *Sermon,* 225.4; PL 38, 1098.
[7] *Commentary on Isaiah,* II.5.20; PL 24.86D.
[8] *On the Sacraments,* V.25; SC 25 bis (1961) 132.
[9] See Jungmann, *Missarum Solemnia,* vol. III, 292–93.
[10] Denzinger, 812.
[11] See Jungmann, ibid., 293–98.

oneself before receiving communion. The position of the priest was ill-conceived: the faithful thought that the priest received communion for them, and that they received communion by this substitution. In said Masses the priest also substituted for the choir by reading the texts the choir should have sung, and by reading the texts the reader should have read. This substitution not only threatened the integrity of the liturgical celebration but also the spiritual health of the faithful. If one finds another to replace him or her at meals, and does not eat except when substituting for that person, they will not have long to live!

This historical data explains how the communion song, in the absence of the communion of the faithful, became a song that was sung after the priest's communion. It was begun—the rubrics were very exact on this point—when the priest began the ablutions. In such conditions the song no longer fulfilled a ministerial function in the communion rite. It created an atmosphere of beauty if the text, its Gregorian melody, and its execution were good.

The Council of Trent encouraged frequent communion,[12] but the success of this recommendation was limited. Pius X encouraged daily communion.[13] Yet the practice of frequent communion, particularly at High Mass, developed quite slowly. It was accelerated by the Liturgical Movement, especially from 1940 (we need to distinguish at this time, however, between the Low Mass, where communion was usually received before Mass, and High Mass, where the people did not receive communion. Taking communion at High Mass became a common practice after Vatican II. The fact that the prayers are now prayed in the vernacular and that they presume explicitly that the faithful will take communion has meant that we can no longer imagine a Mass without communion.

The fact that the people receive communion at every Mass has opened the door to the restoration of the communion processional. It is no longer a song *after* communion but a song *of* communion. The 1969 Missal, GIRM 56i., testifies well to this restoration:

> [The communion song's] function is to express outwardly the communicants' union in spirit by means of the unity of their voices, to give evidence of joy of heart, and to make the procession . . . more fully an act of community.

---

[12] Council of Trent, *Decretum de Sanctissima Eucharistia* (1551); see Denzinger, 1649.
[13] Decree *Sacra Tridentina* (1905); see Denzinger, 1649.

The Missal gives the possibility of using a psalm with the antiphon of the gradual, the antiphon alone, or another song.

The Psalms

Tradition has it that two psalms refer especially to the Eucharist. Psalm 34, already mentioned. In the Greek Septuagint and the Latin Vulgate, verses 6 and 9 are as follows:

> Draw near to him (the Lord)
> and his light will shine upon you (v. 6).
> Taste and see that the Lord is good (v. 9).

Verse 9 offered the possibility of a play on words between *Christos* = Christ, and *chrestos* = good, which was pronounced as *christos:* Taste and see that the *Christos* is *chrestos*.

Psalm 145 (144). According to the testimony of John Chrysostom[14] (354–407), the neophytes used to take up verse 15 repeatedly during the celebration of communion:

> The eyes of all look to you,
> and you give them their food in due season.

In addition to these two psalms, the tradition and the liturgy have often given a Eucharistic meaning to the verses of the following psalms. Psalm 23 (22)–the psalm of the good shepherd–verse 5:

> You prepare a table before me
> in the presence of my enemies. . . .

Psalm 42 (41)–the psalm of the deer–verse 1:

> As a deer longs for flowing streams,
> so my soul longs for you, O God.

Psalm 43 (42), verse 4:

> Then I will go to the altar of God,
> to God my exceeding joy.

Psalm 84 (83), verses 1-2:

> How lovely is your dwelling place,
> O LORD of hosts!

---

[14] *Commentary on the Psalms,* 144.1; PG 55.454.

My soul longs, indeed it faints
        for the courts of the LORD;
my heart and my flesh sing for joy
        to the living God.

Psalm 104 (103), verses 14-15, 28:

You cause the grass to grow for the cattle,
        and plants for people to use,
to bring forth food from the earth,
        and wine to gladden the human heart . . .
when you give to them, they gather it up;
        when you open your hand,
                they are filled with good things.

Psalm 116 (115), verses 12-13:

What shall I return to the LORD
        for all his bounty to me?
I will lift up the cup of salvation
        and call on the name of the LORD.

This psalm belongs to the group of the Hallel psalms (Pss 113–18) and was recited by Christ at the Last Supper. The verses quoted entered into the Mass rites in the eleventh century[15] as the prayer before communion of the chalice. They disappeared in the reform of 1969.

Psalm 128 (127), verse 3:

your children will be like olive shoots
        around your table.

Psalm 136 (135)–the Great Hallel–verse 25:

who gives food to all flesh,
        for his steadfast love endures forever.

Psalm 147 (146), verses 12, 14:

Praise the LORD , O Jerusalem!
        Praise your God, O Zion! . . .
        he fills you with the finest of wheat.

A literal exegesis of these texts would not find in them explicit allusions to the Eucharist. Yet the Christian insight that comes from

---

[15] See Jungmann, *Missarum Solemnia*, vol. III, 284.

praying the psalms recognized that the thanksgiving found in the psalms could be welcomed and used in the Eucharist, the summit of the Church's thanksgiving.

The Missal also says that "a psalm" may be used, without specifying further.[16] For pastoral reasons, psalms classed as communal or individual thanksgivings and hymns should be chosen. It would also be fitting to use the psalms, from which the Missal gives excerpts, in the communion antiphons.

The Communion Antiphon

The Missal (GIRM 56i) gives the communion antiphon as a second option for the communion song, and usually gives two texts. The second is taken from the biblical readings of the same Mass.

Let us note the liturgical richness that this second text provides. The Mass is made up of the Liturgy of the Word and the Liturgy of the Eucharist. These two parts, as *Sacrosanctum Concilium 56* states, "are so closely connected with each other that they form but one single act of worship."[17] This single act takes up the pattern of the cultic assemblies of the Old Testament:

God gathers his people and gives them his Word.
God seals his covenant with the people in a communion meal.[18]

At each Mass God again gathers his people around his Word and seals the covenant with them in the body and blood of his Son. The liturgy signifies the unity of the Mass by actualizing the Word in the communion antiphon, that is, at the very moment in which the faithful participate in the covenant meal by receiving the bread of heaven and by drinking from the cup of the "Blood of the New Covenant."

Here, as an example, is the Gospel for Epiphany:

The community welcomes the Gospel account of the wise men who came from the East, and recognizes that it too must go in search of the Child to adore him.

---

[16] GIRM 56i. We have already mentioned that in the past it was customary to take and use the psalms in their numerical order. This practice is found at Rome in the sixth century for the Sundays after Pentecost and for the weekdays of Lent; see Jungmann, *Missarum Solemnia,* vol. III, 334.

[17] Flannery, op. cit., 19.

[18] See L. Deiss, *Celebration of the Word,* 27–35.

Then the community seals the covenant, singing the communion antiphon: "We [too] have seen his star, and have come with presents to adore the Lord."

Let us note that these antiphons do not prohibit the singing of the psalms. On the contrary, they can be integrated with them, whether they are used as the antiphon of the psalm or, if the text is more important, as a troparion. In this latter case, the troparion serves as a prelude and a conclusion to the psalm, and the psalm is sung with a brief antiphon.

An Appropriate Song

As a third option the Missal (GIRM 56i.) proposes the use of a "suitable song approved by the conference of bishops." These "suitable songs" are normally canticles or hymns. They may be versed songs or songs with refrain or antiphon.

The versed song is one without a refrain. This works well when the community knows the text and the music by heart (as is normally the case in the German *Kirchenlieder*). Otherwise, the community is obliged to accept the inconvenience of carrying hymnbooks with them during communion.

A song accompanied by an antiphon or refrain seems to be best adapted to accompany the community as they move forward to receive communion. The following rule can be taken as a norm: when the text changes completely with each verse, the community must not be moving. When the community does not move, the text is able to change at each verse. The Missal envisages that there can be a hymn after communion. A versed hymn is perhaps the most appropriate form at this point.

Other Possibilities

There are other possibilities that remain open to enrich the communion rite.

When the distribution of communion lasts for a certain length, the organ may play a piece after the communion song, which in some way continues the song by paraphrasing it musically.

The organ may play during the song by playing a verse solo every two or three verses. This will be like a "commentary" on the antiphon or verse, and will be done in a way that supports the lyric atmosphere already created. The optimal length of these "commentaries" will be the time it takes to sing a verse, and their frequency must be measured (after two or three verses, for example). A single, long intervention upsets the rhythm created by the song.

The choir may also enrich the communion rite by singing a Gregorian or polyphonic piece from tradition.

In the same spirit, it is possible to read a short and rich text from the Gospel of the day after every two or three verses of the song. The community may thus interiorize the Word of God at the moment in which they receive the Word become flesh and the blood of Jesus Christ.

All this should be done with ease, freedom, and joy. Nothing is more detrimental to true devotion than the accumulation of rites, words, and songs. When the faithful exhaust themselves in singing, devotion never profits.

These interventions cannot be improvised. They must be prepared with the agreement of the liturgical team, the organist, the choir director, and the commentator.

MUSIC AND PERFORMERS

Music

The entrance processional is colored by the atmosphere of the liturgical time in which it is sung; the communion processional, on the contrary, simply requires an atmosphere of praise and thanksgiving. It is more independent of the liturgical cycle.

The entrance processional has the role of "breaking the ice": it must overcome the profane climate in which the faithful find themselves and draw them into a state of celebration. It may be presumed that by the time of communion this job has already been done! While remaining festive and joyful, the music can be more discreet at communion.

GIRM 56i. leaves great liberty to the participants in the communion processional: "It is sung by the choir alone or by the choir or cantor with the congregation."

FURTHER REFLECTIONS

How should the communion processional ideally be executed? How should it evolve in the future?

For communities lucky enough to be musically rich, the treasures of tradition—whether Gregorian chant, a motet by Josquin des Près or Palestrina, or an organ piece by Bach—remain fully valid. The only requirement is that the work be executed with the perfection that a masterpiece demands—which is not to demand little. Beauty is the daughter of technical perfection. May the perfection of execution increase so that beauty may also increase, for beauty is a path to Christ. Happy those communities that can provide such beauty for their members!

But the great majority of communities—in long established Christian communities and those of the Third World and of mission countries—do not have the technical means to exploit the treasure. Their knowledge of Gregorian chant or classical polyphony is poor and sometimes nonexistent, and they do not always have a good organ at their disposal. Their faith and the fervor of their love are their only riches. What can we envision as an ideal evolution in their regard? Is this ideal also valid for communities that are musically rich?

In regard to the music itself that has been created since Vatican II: it expresses itself in a wonderful variety of cultures and a joyous diversity of communities. May it incarnate itself more and more into each culture, that it may be able to carry the prayer of each community ever more perfectly.

In regard to the words alone, no one really knows what the future may bring.

There was a musical explosion of sorts during the 1950s in the singing of psalms with refrain or antiphon. The psalms were used as entrance song, responsorial psalm, "offertory," and communion processional. They practically eliminated the singing of traditional songs, so heady was the discovery of the beauty of God's Word. There was a second explosion, that of the new canticles. Some of these songs, rooted in biblical thought, are very beautiful and seem ageless. This second explosion first marginalized, then did away with, the singing of the psalms. Even the responsorial psalm, which belongs to the celebration of the Word of God, was sometimes replaced by a meditative song. As regards the communion processional, the majority of parish communities (all of them?) choose to sing a song, whether as a processional or as a hymn after communion.

This practice, insofar as it eliminates the psalm as a communion song, does not seem a good practice; it leads to a certain impoverishment in the expression of the faith. Just as the best bread in the world cannot replace the Eucharistic bread, the bread of heaven, so the most beautiful song in all the world cannot replace the psalm, the Word of God.

It is true that these songs are often inspired by the Word of God. They reflect it, sometimes beautifully, yet always through the prism of their authors. This is true for all the texts composed for the liturgy. The question is always: Does a community prefer to thank God with human words rather than with the Word of God? To drink from the poet's cup or from the living spring of God's Word?

There is a great amount of work yet to be done, on the one hand, of choosing the most fitting psalm texts and freeing them from unworthy melodic ditties by creating simple and joyful melodies; and on the other, of composing antiphons from the biblical texts, especially from the Gospels,[19] and of clothing them in music worthy of a gospel.

The New Testament (Titus 1:13; 2:2) speaks of the health of faith. This health is the source of life and joy, but it has a price: loving service of the Word of God.

---

[19] The form of the troparion furnishes an interesting model; see in French, for example, *Tropaires des Dimanches,* the Office Book of the Benedictine Monastery of Encalcat (1980), which gives some good examples—sometimes, perhaps, a little too far from the original biblical texts.

Introduction to the Litanies

The term "litany" is from the Greek *litaneia,* which means prayer, supplication. By litany we mean the group of supplications that normally end with the same invocation.

Among the litanic prayers of the Mass are the *Kyrie eleison,* the prayer of the faithful or universal prayer, the anaphoric intercessions, and the *Agnus Dei.*

9

The Kyrie Eleison

THE TRADITION

The origin of the *Kyrie* in the Roman Mass is controversial. The testimonies are sparse and the texts not very forthcoming.[1]

In the East

The first testimony that we possess about the *Kyrie* comes from the pilgrim Egeria. In her *Diary of a Pilgrim*[2] (which dates from the years 381–384), she recounts with awe the form of the prayer in the church of the Anastasis (the resurrection) in Jerusalem at the office of the lucernarium: "Amidst the unending light" of the candles, the deacon gives the intentions and a great number of children respond *Kyrie eleison,* which means, she translates, "Lord have mercy." She adds: "Their voices create an unending murmur."

The use of the *Kyrie eleison* in the prayer of the faithful is confirmed by the witness of the *Apostolic Constitutions*[3] (which date from the same era, about 380):

---

[1] The principal works in this field are by E. Bishop (1918), Dom Capelle (1939), A. Chavasse (1960), and P. de Clerck (1970). A review of these findings can be found in the excellent work of P. de Clerck, *La Prière universelle dans les liturgies latines anciennes,* Coll. Liturgiewissenschaftliche Quellen und Forschungen, (Munster Westfalen: Aschendorf, 1977) 282–95.

[2] *Diary of a Pilgrim,* 24, 4, in Source chrétiennes 296 (Paris: Cerf, 1982) 238–40.

[3] *Apostolic Constitutions,* VIII, 6, 6, 9, in Deiss, *Springtime,* 223.

All the faithful then pray for the catechumens with all their heart, saying *Kyrie eleison!* . . .

To all the intentions the deacon proclaims, the people, and especially the children, respond, as we have already said: *Kyrie eleison.*

We may also note that the Mass, according to the *Apostolic Constitutions,* has not one litanic prayer but four. This may simply be a reference to the wide use of this form or a witness to the beginning of its devaluation.

We have, therefore, two testimonies in the East concerning the use of the *Kyrie,* one at the evening office, the other at Mass. Both date from the end of the fourth century. This does not mean that the *Kyrie* was not used earlier but simply that we do not possess any proof.

In the West

The most ancient witness seems to be that of the *Divinae pacis* prayer of the Milanese liturgy. This is a litanic prayer where the intentions are concluded by *Domine, miserere* (Lord have mercy). This prayer, which undoubtedly dates from the first half of the fifth century,[4] is found at the beginning of the Mass after the greeting of the priest and the opening prayer. At the end of the litanic prayer, there is a triple *Kyrie eleison,* as if to make a more insistent request.

The litanic prayer of Pope Gelasius I (492–496), called *Deprecatio Gelasii,* is a crucial document for discussion about the *Kyrie.* It used to be thought that the pope had suppressed the ancient prayer of the faithful and had placed his *Deprecatio* in the place of the *Kyrie.* This is not unlikely. Yet a number of questions remain unanswered. It is certain that the Roman Mass no longer had the prayer of the faithful after Gelasius' predecessor, Pope Felix III (483–492). It is also certain that the *Deprecatio Gelasii* is from Gelasius' hand. But it is not certain that this prayer had the *Kyrie eleison* as the response of the people, nor can the link with the *Kyrie* be proved.[5]

The regional Council of Vaison (Vaucluse) in 529, at which Caesarius of Arles presided, introduced, at matins, Mass, and vespers, the use of the *Quirieleison* (sic) into the churches of Provence. This was already used in Rome: the council speaks of it as a sweet and salutary

[4] See De Clerck, 165. Text of the *Divinae pacis,* 156–58.
[5] See De Clerck, 286. On this council, see 284–86.

custom. We are not told at which place in the liturgy the *Kyrie eleison* was introduced. We may imagine that it was "a song that seemed much appreciated at the time."[6]

In the *Rule of St. Benedict,* which dates from the same time,[7] lauds and vespers finish with a litanic prayer *(litania),*[8] while matins, prime, and the Little Hours, as well as compline, finish with the *Quirie eleison.*[9] The *Kyrie eleison,* therefore, existed as an independent song at the office.

A letter from Gregory the Great to John of Syracuse shows us that the invocation was used in the Roman Mass with that of *Christe eleison.*[10] The letter dates from 598.

At this time, the *Kyrie eleison* was a very popular acclamation. St. Gregory of Tours describes how during a procession prescribed by Gregory the Great in 590, at the time of an epidemic, the faithful of Rome, coming from seven different churches, gathered together in St. Mary Major: "They all cried out into the squares of the city: '*Kyrie eleison.*'"[11]

Under the pressure of the anti-Arian struggles, the first three *Kyrie* were addressed to the Father, the three *Christe* to the Son, and the last three *Kyrie* to the Holy Spirit, thus giving the whole a trinitarian reference. Amalarius (before 850) is a witness to this interpretation, which lasted throughout the Middle Ages[12] and, in fact, until the contemporary reform of the Mass.[13] Bach used this trinitarian theme in his Dogmatic Chorales. In the Missal of Paul VI, the *Kyrie* is addressed entirely to Christ.

Let us pause here to clarify the data of the tradition. The story of the *Kyrie* in the Mass remains obscured by the mists of history. What seems certain is that the *Kyrie* appeared in the Mass before the Council of Vaison in 529, and that the prayer of the faithful disappeared from the Mass in the sixth century. We also know that the *Kyrie* was used as a response to a litanic prayer or as an independent

---

[6] Ibid., 166–87.

[7] According to A. de Vogüé and J. Neufville, "the Benedictine rule was written not far from Rome in the years after 530," SC 181 (1972) 172.

[8] *Rule,* 12.4; 17.4, 5.

[9] Ibid., 9.10; 17.4, 5, 10. For matins, the Rule speaks of *supplicatio litaniae id est quirie eleison:* the supplication of the litany is thus reduced to the *Kyrie eleison.*

[10] *Ep.* 9.26; PL 77.956.

[11] *Historia Francorum* X.1; PL 71.529.

[12] *De officiis ecclesiasticis* III.6; PL 105.1113f.

[13] J. Brinktrine, *Die heilige Messe,* 3rd ed. (Paderborn: Ed. Schoningh, 1950) 72, considers the *Kyrie* a "true song of praise to the Trinity, like a kind of doxology."

prayer. But we do not know how it was introduced into the entrance rites of the Mass.

All this to show that it is wise not to lean too heavily on tradition in order to understand the meaning of the *Kyrie* in the contemporary Mass.

BIBLICAL SIGNIFICANCE

Kyrie is the vocative form of *Κύριος,* which means "Lord." In the Old Testament, *Kyrios* regularly translated the ineffable name of God, Yahweh. In the New Testament, *Kyrios* evokes the resurrection of Christ: the Father has raised his Son, Jesus, and thus established him as "Lord *(Κύριος)* and Christ," having given him the name "that is above every name" (Phil 2:9-11). *Christe* is the vocative of *Χριστός,* which means *Oint,* Messiah. *Eleison* transcribes the Greek *ἐλέησον,* which is the imperative form of the verb *eleein,* to have pity, mercy.

In the supplication of the *Kyrie eleison,* the Church therefore implores the mercy *(ἔλεος)* of the Lord *(Kyrios).* The term *eleos,* which in the Septuagint regularly translates the Hebrew *hesed,* is at the heart of revelation. It designates the merciful goodness, the faithful pity with which God surrounds his people in virtue of the covenant. Since the revelation of Sinai, Yahweh defined himself as "a God merciful and gracious, slow to anger, and abounding in steadfast love and faithfulness, keeping steadfast love for the thousandth generation" (Exod 34:6). The covenant is the mysterious betrothal union, both tender and joyful, that God concludes with his people "in mercy and in love" (Hos 2:21; cf. Jer 31:3). In imploring the Lord's mercy, the Church proclaims, even in its supplications, the essential message that it celebrates: "God is love" (1 John 4:8, 16).

The supreme manifestation of the mercy of God was reserved for the time of the Messiah. It burst into the world with the coming of the Lord Jesus (Titus 2:11; 3:5). It is he whom the poor in the Gospel seek with their *Kyrie eleison,* as a litany of wretchedness, or as a cry of hope that resounds unceasingly in the Gospels: it is the cry of the two blind men imploring the light (Matt 9:27), the unrestrained cry of Bartimaeus (Mark 10:47-48; Matt 20:31; Luke 18:39), or the audacious prayer of the Canaanite woman (Matt 15:22). The *Kyrie eleison* of the Gospels draws all the misery of humanity to itself, a humanity in search of Christ's mercy. In taking up this litany of the poor of the

Gospels, the Church holds out its hand to the Lord; the Church knows that it cannot truly listen to his Word and celebrate his Eucharist unless God "manifests his pity in its regard," as he did to Elizabeth at the beginning of Luke's Gospel (1:48).

Like the Eucharist itself, the *Kyrie* possesses an eschatological dimension. It is prayed to the Lord "until he comes"; "May the Lord grant that [the Church] will find mercy from the Lord on that day!" (cf. 2 Tim 1:18). Thus the Father "who is rich in mercy" will make the Church for eternity to become the people who "have received mercy" (Eph 2:4; 1 Pet 2:10). Then the supplication of the *Kyrie* will be changed into jubilation that will praise and magnify God's glory (cf. Eph 1:12).

MINISTERIAL FUNCTION

In the Missal of Paul VI, the *Kyrie eleison* appears twice.

It first appears in the *actus paenitentialis* (penitential rite) after the opening greeting.

Three forms are given for this rite in the *Ordo missae cum populo 4* (cf. GIRM 30):

A form of general confession according to the old *Confiteor* in abbreviated form.

Two verses of dialogue between priest and assembly, inspired by Psalm 85:8.

The *Kyrie eleison* with "brief troparion" that may be inserted between the invocation *Kyrie* and the petition, *eleison*.

The *Kyrie eleison* is thus placed in a penitential context. In addition, these three penitential formulas are preceded by the following monition of the priest: "As we prepare to celebrate the mystery of Christ's love, let us acknowledge our failures and ask the Lord for pardon and strength." The formulas are followed by the general absolution: "May Almighty God have mercy on us, forgive us our sins, and bring us to everlasting life."

The second time the *Kyrie* appears, it is in its simplest form: two *Kyrie*, two *Christe*, and two *Kyrie*. These *Kyrie* and *Christe* are called "invocations" in the Missal. They are omitted if they have already been used in the third form of the penitential rite. They are also omitted if the penitential rite is replaced by the aspersion of the assembly with holy water.

GIRM 30 reads:

> Then the *Kyrie* begins, unless it has already been included as part of the penitential rite. Since it is a song by which the faithful praise the Lord and implore his mercy, it is ordinarily prayed by all. . . .

Each acclamation is normally said twice, but this does not exclude the possibility of repeating it more often, or of inserting a brief troparion, according to the idioms of different languages and music.

The liturgy, therefore, gives different ministerial functions to the *Kyrie*. It is:

An acclamation of Christ (GIRM)

The imploring of his mercy (GIRM)

An invocation (*Ordo Missae* and GIRM)

A song, but a song that may also be recited and may also be omitted when the aspersion of the assembly with holy water is performed.

This diversity of ministerial functions is part of the richness of the *Kyrie*. But it also produces a certain lack of clarity. It appears that the "mists of history" that obscure the origins of the *Kyrie* continue to obscure the Missal of Paul VI.

TEXT

The Greek Text

The waves resulting from the use of vernacular after Vatican II have been so strong that they have swept away almost all of the dead-language texts that were part of the liturgy, leaving only tiny "islands" like the Hebrew *Amen, Alleluia,* or *Hosanna.* This may be explained as a reaction against the Latin that dominated in the past, to the detriment of vernacular languages. We need to remember that *Kyrie eleison* has no connection with any Latin text, and that, in our opinion, it is worth keeping in the liturgy. This text, in the sacred language of the Gospels, symbolically represents the prayer of the Eastern Churches in our Western liturgy. It is the only Greek prayer the people know. On both accounts, it may be kept and used, at least in some celebrations.

We realize that this argument is affective rather than liturgical. We can just as well pray in union with our Eastern sisters and brothers in English. Yet, in the ecumenical domain, the affective dimension has its own weight and place.

An Enriched *Kyrie*

The text of the *Kyrie* may be enriched by the interpolation of a "short verse (trope)." The Missal itself gives several examples.

It is always fitting to use the Word of God for these brief text insertions. If the *Kyrie* is celebrated as an invocation of Christ, the titles that proclaim him in the Word of God used for the Mass readings can be used. If the *Kyrie* is used to implore God's mercy, the penitential dimension may be highlighted.[14]

However, we should avoid making the short insertions an anticipation of the readings as a whole or, even worse, of the homily. We should also avoid creating a double prayer of the faithful: this would devalue both.

PARTICIPANTS AND MUSICAL FORMS

Participants

GIRM 30 explains:

Since [the *Kyrie*] is a song by which the faithful praise the Lord and implore his mercy, it is ordinarily prayed by all, that is, alternately by the congregation and the choir or cantor.

Musical Forms

We can distinguish the litanic form that is undoubtedly the best for the ministerial function of the *Kyrie,* the strophic or versed form, and various more elaborate or decorated forms.

The Litanic Form

Gregorian chant provides excellent examples of these supplications that best bring out the function of the litanic form of the *Kyrie.* For example:

14 See L. Deiss, *Reflections of His Word,* Sunday Prayers, Cycles A, B, and C (Chicago: World Library Publications, 1980, 1981, 1982).

The *Kyrie* of the litany of the saints.

Kyrie XVI, In feriis per annum (note that the melodic change on the ninth *Kyrie* does not exert its influence unduly).

Kyrie XVIII, In feriis Adventus and *Quadragesimae.*

The *Kyrie* formulas for the litany of the Virgin Mary.

The "Gallican" *Kyrie,* which has one of the simplest but one of the most beautiful formulas.

These melodies, which are very discreet and perfectly fulfill their function, certainly remain usable in today's liturgy.

When the *Kyrie* is sung in the vernacular, the melodic forms are either supplications or acclamations.

If a two-part structure is used, there is an alternation between the soloist (or choir) and the assembly: two *Kyrie,* two *Christe,* two *Kyrie.* This way of singing the *Kyrie* is undoubtedly the easiest and the most popular.

If a three-part structure is used, the following are possible:

Soloist(s), choir, assembly and choir.

Soloist(s), assembly, assembly and choir.

The second is easier to use than the first. Usually the people are not made to wait until the third *Kyrie* to join in the singing; the assembly spontaneously feels called to respond to the soloist. The choir may take up the third *Kyrie* with the assembly, and enrich the singing by its harmonization.

The Strophic or Versed Form

The *Kyrie* is regarded as a canticle or hymn with three verses and is treated musically as such. In this case the assembly sings the whole *Kyrie,* without any alternation.

The Decorated Form

Most of the Gregorian Masses have decorated *Kyrie*s. The supplication of the prayer is treated like the *jubilus* of a chant, so much so that in about the eighth century, the expression *kyrieleisare* was almost synonymous with *jubilare.* The syllables themselves are cut short and become *Kyrieleis, Kyryoleis, Chrisleis,* etc.[15] The Gregorian creations of the tenth and following centuries are often melodic marvels. If one thinks, for example, of the supplication of *Kyrie V,* the tenderness of *Kyrie X* that is sung on the feasts of Our Lady, or of the solemnity of *Kyrie I* of Eastertime.

No one would think of casting doubt on the musical magnificence of these pieces. For those who have used them, they are unforgettable. Yet we must simply recognize that they do not fulfill well the ministerial function of the *Kyrie.* The texts are drowned in the marvels of vocalization.

What has been said of the Gregorian *Kyries* can also be said for the *Kyrie* of the polyphonic Masses of classical or romantic genius. For example, the *Kyries* of Palestrina or Roland de Lassus use the text simply to support the musical harmonies. The words may be continually repeated, and for as long as the music or harmony requires[16] (as already mentioned above, the melody of the sopranos in the first choir in Bach's B-minor Mass takes up the *Kyrie* fifteen times and the *eleison* forty-nine times—divine!). This is wonderful music. It is simply that its place is not the *Kyrie* of the Mass.

There is no universal solution that will successfully serve every community. The official rubric says that the *Kyrie* is "ordinarily prayed by all." This means that there can be exceptions. Each community must see how it can "ordinarily" do what the liturgical rubrics require.

FURTHER REFLECTIONS

The *actus penitentialis* in the opening rites was welcomed by liturgists with some reservations.[17] Today, it is still felt that there is a certain heaviness hanging over this part of the Mass.[18]

It is not the recognition of our condition as sinners that makes the opening of the Mass so heavy but rather the frequency of the

---

[15] See Sefani, *L'acclamation de tout un peuple,* Coll. Kinnor (Paris: Fleurus, 1967) 68.

[16] Sometimes the same melodic theme continues in all the pieces of the Mass; in the Gregorian Masses, the same melody is used for the *Kyrie* and for the *Ite missa est*—the beauty of the music comes before the ministerial function of these *Kyries.*

[17] See R. Cabié, "Le nouvel 'Ordo missae,'" in *La Maison-Dieu* 100 (1969) 26; B. Botte, *Le mouvement liturgique* (Paris: Desclée, 1973) 180, 186.

[18] See J. Baldovin, "Kyrie eleison and the Entrance Rite of the Roman Eucharist," in *Worship* 60 (1986) 334–47.

penitential formulas that break the rhythm of the prayer. The priest invites the people to recognize that they are sinners, the people respond and make a general confession, the priest gives the general absolution—and then, as if the community forgets that it has just received God's forgiveness, it launches into the *Kyrie,* asking once more for forgiveness! This penitential cloud arises again amidst the jubilation of the *Gloria,* in which we pray "Lamb of God, you take away the sin of the world: have mercy on us." There are further penitential prayers: the priest cannot wash his hands without praying "Lord, wash away my iniquity; cleanse me from my sin." In the Lord's Prayer we pray "Forgive us our trespasses as we forgive those who trespass against us"; there is another penitential cloud just before communion: "Lamb of God, you take away the sins of the world: have mercy on us." *Sacrosanctum Concilium 34,* however, had demanded that the reformed rites should "be short, clear, and free of useless repetitions." Why, then, did its authors not follow their own recommendations?! Thus the penitential action is reduced to a mere ritual, for one cannot pray repeatedly the same prayer with the same intensity and authenticity.

In approving the *actus penitentialis* of the reformed Mass, Paul VI wanted to underline the necessity of repentance in the Christian life. He had already reminded the faithful of this necessity in his Apostolic Constitution *Paenitemini,* written in 1966, just after the end of the council. In a world that refuses to recognize the reality of sin, and thus God's forgiveness and the liberality of his love, in a Christian community that no longer avails itself regularly—if at all—of the sacrament of reconciliation with individual confession, this teaching is salutary. On the other hand, for those communities that remember with nostalgia and regret the loss of the old prayers at the foot of the altar, with the *Confiteor,* the penitential preparation of the reformed Mass can seem like a restoration. But the necessity of repentance and penance in our lives is quite different from its presence in every celebration.[19]

It remains for each community to negotiate with prudence the problem of the *actus penitentialis* in its liturgical celebrations.

To arrive at a noticeable brevity and to avoid "useless repetitions," we may first decide not to lengthen the penitential rite. This may be done by integrating the *Kyrie* into the penitential rite, as the Missal suggests. In this way the experience of having a penitential celebration

---

[19] Ibid., 346–47.

with one of the three formulas, followed by a general absolution and then a second penitential celebration with the *Kyrie,* will be avoided.

In those Masses in which we wish to emphasize the penitential aspect of the celebration, for example, in the Lenten Masses, the *Kyrie* may be given a certain amplitude and may be used as the entrance song.

The most suitable musical form is undoubtedly the litanic form. The most ample text is one enriched by additional insertions *(tropes/ troparion).* The best source for these interpolations is the Word of God.

These interpolations may be phrases asking for forgiveness or acclamations of Christ. The two are closely linked: the best form of the "confession" of sins is "confession," that is, the recognition of Christ's forgiveness and the acclamation of his love that forgives our sins.

It seems best to always sing the *Kyrie,* thus giving it a certain liturgical consistency. If it is simply recited, it lasts only ten to fifteen seconds: can it fulfill any ministerial function in so short a time or is it reduced simply to a rubric? Rubrics must be observed to serve the community's prayer–not prayer serving the rubrics.

A final remark. The heart of the celebration of forgiveness is not the penitential preparation but rather the celebration of the Eucharist itself. God's forgiveness is proclaimed to us in the very words of the consecration, since the blood of the new covenant, as Jesus tells us, is poured out "for all, so that sins may be forgiven." The penitential preparation is not a kind of mat on which we wipe our feet before entering God's holy sanctuary. To search out and bewail our sins in a sort of massive self-accusation is of little worth: it is God we must search out, and his mercy and love that we must celebrate.

10

The Prayer of the Faithful

The Constitution on the Sacred Liturgy of 1963 asked for the restoration of the ancient prayer of the faithful, or universal prayer, after a gap of more than a thousand years:

> The "common prayer" or "prayer of the faithful" is to be restored after the gospel and homily, especially on Sundays and holidays of obligation. By this prayer in which the people are to take part, intercession will be made for holy Church, for the civil authorities, for those oppressed by various needs, for all mankind, and for the salvation of the entire world.[1]

The council for the implementation of the Constitution on the Liturgy opened the path of this restoration in 1965 by publishing a sort of "Directory" called *Common Prayer or the Prayer of the Faithful*.[2] After some practical comments, the Directory gives fifty-four examples of the universal prayer: the texts are excellent, even if they are a little too divorced from history by reason of their generality. The Directory adds a brief historical outline.

GIRM 45 (1969) sealed this restoration. It called this prayer *oratio universalis seu oratio fidelium*, *universal prayer* or *prayer of the faithful*. In the English-speaking world, prayer of the faithful has become the more normal term.

---

[1] Art. 53, in Flannery, op. cit., 18. See the article of P. de Clerck cited above, and the remarks of P. M. Gy in *La Maison-Dieu* 129 (1977) 150.

[2] *De Oratione communi seu fidelium*, April 17, 1966 (new edition).

The *Ordo Lectionum 30,* of 1981, which keeps the two titles, says that this prayer flows from the Word of God that has just been proclaimed. There was, then, from the start, a certain fluidity of vocabulary. This fluidity revealed the richness of this new rite that had been integrated into the ancient Mass. The Church confided to the most humble and youngest of its members its intercession for the whole world: this is why it is called the universal prayer. On the other hand, this prayer is the prayer of those who by their baptism have become a royal priesthood (Rev 1:6) whose vocation is to intercede with God for the whole of humanity: thus it is called the prayer of the faithful, that is, of the baptized. This prayer is placed after the Liturgy of the Word and before the Eucharistic Liturgy, where, in the past, the catechumens were sent out of the assembly, so that only the faithful remained.[3]

In itself this prayer is not new; the faithful did not have to wait until Vatican II in order to learn to pray for the intentions of the universal Church: the whole Mass is a universal prayer, and the prayer of all the faithful. Yet the liturgical form in which this prayer is expressed is new.

THE TRADITION

Sacrosanctum Concilium 53 gives 1 Timothy 2:1-2 as the scriptural basis of the universal prayer; 1 Timothy 2:1-4 is relevant:

> First of all, then, I urge that supplications, prayers, intercessions, and thanksgivings be made for everyone, for kings and all who are in high positions, so that we may lead a quiet and peaceable life in all godliness and dignity. This is right and is acceptable in the sight of God our Savior, who desires everyone to be saved and to come to the knowledge of the truth.

This text strongly affirms the universality of Christian prayer. It joins itself to the will of God that wants all people to be saved. It prolongs the Jewish tradition when it intercedes for those in authority.[4] It also echoes Jesus' teaching when he demands that his disciples pray even for their enemies and persecutors, and so become true sons and

---

[3] See, for example, *Apostolic Constitutions,* VIII, 6.1–14, in Deiss, *Springtime,* 222–24.
[4] See C. Spicq, *Les Epîtres Pastorales,* coll. Etudes bibliques (Paris: Gabalda et Cie, 1969) 360.

daughters of their Father in heaven who "makes his sun rise on the evil and on the good, and sends rain on the righteous and on the unrighteous" (Matt 5:45).

1 Timothy 2:1-4 does not explain the presence of the universal prayer in the reformed Mass,[5] but it shows that it fits well with the scriptural tradition.

The first explicit witness to the universal prayer in the Mass is found in Justin's (d. ca. 165 C.E.) *First Apology 65* (written about 150 C.E.). He describes the prayer that takes place just before the Eucharistic celebration of the baptismal Mass:

> We offer prayers in common for ourselves, for all people who have just been enlightened, and for all everywhere. It is our desire, now that we have come to know the truth, to be found worthy of doing good deeds and obeying the commandments, and thus to obtain eternal salvation.[6]

He then *(First Apology 67)* describes the Sunday Mass:

> On the day named after the sun, all who live in city or countryside assemble.
>
> *(Reading of the Word)*
> Then the memoirs of the apostles (= Gospels) or the writings of the prophets are read for as long as time allows.
>
> *(Homily)*
> When the lector has finished, the president addresses us and exhorts us to imitate the splendid things we have heard.
>
> *(Universal Prayer)*
> Then we all stand and pray.
>
> *(Celebration of the Eucharist)*
> As we said earlier, when we have finished praying, bread, wine, and water are brought up. The president then prays and gives thanks according to his ability, and the people give their assent with an "Amen!"

Justin's testimony allows us to conclude that there was a prayer placed after the readings and before the bread and wine were brought

---

[5] We do not know the date of this text, nor are we sure of its Pauline authenticity: different commentators place it between 65 and the beginning of the second century, or even 58 C.E. We do not know what the structure of the Eucharistic celebration was like at this date.

[6] In Deiss, *Springtime*, 92.

in. We also know the intentions of this prayer: Christians prayed for the community, for the neophytes, and for the faithful throughout the world.

We also know that later a number of litanic prayers were current. They proliferated above all in the Eastern liturgies, sometimes in an excessive manner, or at least to our Western sensitivity.[7] Yet the history of the universal prayer or prayer of the faithful, properly speaking, is lost on the many paths it traveled in both the Eastern and Western liturgies. Paul de Clerck proceeds with a wise caution:

> Yes, the early Church knew of the universal prayer, but perhaps not everywhere, nor from its origins, nor during all of the first five centuries. It probably owes its origin more to the command given in 1 Timothy 2:1-2 than to the influences of Jewish liturgy.[8]

As far as the Church of Rome is concerned, the solemn prayers of Good Friday, of which there are 250–300, can be mentioned (prayers that in the beginning consisted solely of invitatories). The introduction of a litanic prayer into the Roman liturgy is usually attributed to Pope Gelasius I (492–496). This prayer, called the *Deprecatio papae Gelasii* sometimes had *Kyrie eleison* as its response. It remained in the Mass until the middle of the sixth century, then disappeared.

We do not know what link could have existed between the universal prayer and the *Kyrie* at the beginning of the Mass, or the anaphoric intercessions after the consecration.

There are traces of the universal prayer in the last part of the Litany of the Saints, as well as in the prayers of the prone that the priest used to pray when standing before the sanctuary (from the Greek, *pro-naos,* pro-ne), and which were in the form of a dialogue until the fifteenth century.[9]

The restoration of the universal prayer or prayer of the faithful has been one of the greatest successes of Vatican II. R. Cabié describes the situation well when he writes:

---

[7] Thus in the *Apostolic Constitutions* there is a litanic prayer for the catechumens, another for the faithful, and, after the consecration, a litanic prayer made by the bishop and another made by the deacon. See Deiss, *Springtime,* 92.

[8] De Clerck, op. cit., 110.

[9] See P. Jounel, *La Messe hier et aujourd'hui* (Paris: Ed. O.E.I.L., 1986) 102. Certain German-speaking dioceses knew the *Allgemeines Gebet* (common prayer) or the *Fürbitten* (intercessions) that were recited at all Masses after the gospel or homily; see also J. Gulden, W. Muschick, *Fürbitten* (Freiburg im Breisgau: Christophorus-Verlag, 1965) 5.

The universal prayer seems like the end of the whole Liturgy of the Word and the threshold of the Eucharist properly speaking. Placed after the sending away of the catechumens, it is the privilege of the faithful, which underlines its priestly character. We may say that it is the reverse side of evangelization: speaking to human beings about God cannot be disassociated from talking to God about human beings.[10]

PRESENT-DAY NEEDS

The universal prayer is linked organically to the celebration of the Word. It thus lifts up its voice as an echo of God's voice in the voice of the assembly. This is the normal rhythm of prayer:

God speaks to human beings revealing to them his mystery.

Human beings respond to God in opening their hearts to him.

Let us note well that it is not the only response to the Word of God. The essential response to the Word of God is the celebration of the Eucharist, properly speaking. A response of praise, blessing, thanksgiving. A response that is linked so organically to the Word that according to the teaching of Vatican II, "the two parts . . . the Liturgy of the Word and the Eucharistic liturgy, are so closely connected with each other that they form but one single act of worship." And this single act of worship is the celebration of the covenant.[11] But the universal prayer presents this response in the form of petition in the context of the Mass. It may also present it in the form of thanksgiving in the Sunday celebrations in the absence of a priest.

There are two qualities of the universal prayer or prayer of the faithful that should be emphasized: its biblical nature and its universality.

A Biblical Prayer

By this name we mean to say that the petitions of this prayer are usually rooted in the Word of God that has just been celebrated, or

---

[10] Cabié, "L'Eucharistie," in A. G. Martimort, *L'Eglise en Prière,* vol. II (Paris: Desclée, 1983) 92.

[11] *Sacrosanctum Concilium* 56, in Flannery, op. cit., 19. See also L. Deiss, *Vivre la Parole en communauté* (Paris: Desclée, 1974) 297–308.

that they celebrate the Word in the form of petitions. The Word in some way sows itself in the community. The seed of the Word grows up in the form of prayer.

This rooting of the prayer of the faithful in the Word is not universally perceived. Some authors think that the prayer must keep its autonomy. In analyzing the most ancient prayer formulas, they say that there was no link between the readings and the prayer of the faithful.

We may think, however, that the absence of a clear link between the readings and the prayer is due to the fixed nature of ancient liturgical formulas: ancient formulas were not changed, especially if they were cast in gracious literary form. It was this unchangeability no doubt, that caused the rapid decline of the prayer and the reason for its disappearance from the Roman liturgy in the sixth century.

In any case the past history of the prayer of the faithful cannot be the sole criterion for its use in the present, and certainly not an absolute criterion. If the homily is the actualization of the Word of God, the universal prayer or prayer of the faithful is a central part of this actualization. The *Ordo Lectionum 30* makes a comment that is full of good liturgical sense when it affirms:

> In the universal prayer, the assembly of the faithful, in the light of the Word of God, responds to it. . . .[12]

As an example, let us suppose that the Gospel quotes the words of Jesus in Luke 6:36: "Be merciful, just as your Father is merciful." If the homily actualizes this word by affirming that "today this scripture has been fulfilled in your hearing," and the Lord today commands us to be merciful, how can the universal prayer not make the link and ask: "Give us the grace to be merciful as your Son Jesus commands us today?"

Our prayer always needs to be evangelized. It must be in harmony with the heart of God so that the Holy Spirit, who is the heart of our prayer, will be able to make the words of our heart his own. It will be more profoundly in harmony with God's heart insofar as it reflects the Word of God that gave it birth.

A Universal Prayer

The prayer of the Catholic Church is universal by definition (*katholicos* in classical Greek = universal). If this is not so, it degenerates into

[12] See, however, the comments of P. de Clerck in *La Maison-Dieu* 153 (1983) 126–30, where he draws the limits of this assertion.

the prayer of a sect. It is catholic not only because it intercedes for all humanity but, even more, because it intercedes in the name of all the faithful. It is called prayer of the faithful because "the people, exercising their priestly function, intercede for all humanity" (GIRM 45).

The liturgy must teach us to pray in the plural. No one has the right to say: "My Father in heaven, give me today my daily bread." No one, except Christ alone is able to say in all truth: "My Father and your Father" (John 20:17). Prayer and the contemplation of God are also the concern of the human family, a memorial, so to speak, of all humanity. It is universal because each community, whether the largest or the smallest, bears the joy and sorrow of the whole of humanity.

Each particular church must "represent the universal Church as perfectly as possible," according to the Decree on the Church's Missionary Activity, *Ad Gentes 20*.[13] Sign of the universal church, each community is also a sign of the Church's universal prayer. The future of the Church, and thus the future of the whole of humanity, rests on the shoulders of each particular local church, even if this church is reduced to a few faithful. Each community intercedes in God's presence for several billion people.

This prayer is called universal not because it takes to itself the intentions of all the members of the community but because all the members of the community take to themselves the intentions of the universal Church. It does not limit itself to presenting its wounds to God so that all the members of the Church may be healed. It is rather the prayer of the priestly people who by their baptism have become intercessors for the whole world. Between God and the nations God has placed the intercession of this community.

The Four Series of Intentions

Sacrosanctum Concilium 53 gives four groups of intentions. The universal prayer intercedes for:

> The holy Church
> Those in authority
> Those weighed down by diverse necessities
> All humanity and the salvation of the whole world

---

[13] Flannery, op. cit., 836.

These four groups or series of intentions may be regarded as the rubrical framework in which the community expresses its prayer with a "wise freedom" *(sapienti libertate)* as the *Ordo Lectionum* puts it. This form does not wish to crush creativity or prevent new prayer forms, it seeks rather to channel creativity positively. To repeat the same formulas at every Mass would be precisely to crush creativity: "Let us pray for the Church. . . . Let us pray for those in authority. . . . Let us pray for the poor. . . . Let us pray for the world." These formulas correspond perfectly to the four series of "official" intentions but are perfectly death-dealing. To protect ourselves from the routine of repetitive formulas, as we said above, the universal prayer must be inspired by the Word of God that is new every morning; just as the homily discerns new horizons every day in which to actualize the Word, so the universal prayer must blossom each day with new intentions inspired by the Spirit of God. We may add this: We must accept with goodwill the particular intentions that are sometimes proposed, even when they do not seem to have any link with any of the four "official" series of intentions, nor even with the readings that have just been read. These intentions sometimes refer to various things that have happened in the locality: the most insignificant happening can become an occasion to turn toward God. There is a certain greatness in this way of praying as well as a certain pettiness. The greatness is the trust in God that is heard. God's ear is infinitely and finely tuned so that he can discern the deep intentions of the heart in the most banal petitions addressed to him, and hear in the midst of the human tumult the humble cry of those who scarcely dare whisper their distress and who hide their face. Yet there is also a certain smallness, even pettiness, on our part: we mix the God of sublime glory with our small little histories. The most astonishing thing is that God accepts to be touched by our distress. God hears all sorts of miserable prayers! Such is God's infinite tenderness.

> The LORD is near to all who call on him
> to all who call on him in truth (Ps 145:18).

It is enough that we present our distress to God for God to turn toward us. This is what Hezekiah did in Isaiah's time: when he received Sennacherib's letter announcing that the Assyrians would burn Jerusalem and put its inhabitants to the sword, he went to the Temple, opened up the letter before Yahweh, and said to him: "Open your eyes, O LORD, and see" (Isa 37:17). This is what each community must do:

present itself before God, open its heart to the Lord, and say: "Lord, open your eyes and see!"

Silence

It is normal that there be a period of silence within the prayer of the faithful. Neither the "official" intentions nor the intentions based on the biblical readings can cover every petition of the community. Certain intentions cannot be said publicly. We carry them as a joyous treasure, as a ray of light, or as a burden that weighs on the heart. A time of silence in which everyone can present before God the letter of their hearts, as Hezekiah did, is highly desirable. We sometimes criticize celebrations for being too wordy, of eating up all the silences by filling them with words. Such a criticism cannot be made if the celebration is well ordered, and if it knows how to provide spaces of silence and interiority within its prayer.

STRUCTURE

The universal prayer is composed of:

An introduction presented by the priest

Prayer intentions, followed by the response of the assembly

A concluding prayer said by the priest

Each of these elements may perhaps be given in a general formula valuable for all Masses and for all communities. Yet it may also be built on the particular Word of God heard by the assembly and in the context of the needs and desire of that particular community.

Introduction

The importance of this introduction to the universal prayer lies in the following: the priest has a few seconds—no more—the time of a phrase!—to gain the attention of the faithful and open their hearts to the Lord. In these moments the priest seeks to realize what Lydia, that amiable seller of purple dye in Thyatira, experienced: "The Lord opened her heart to listen eagerly to what was said by Paul" (Acts

16:14). Here, too, there are hearts to open so that they will "listen eagerly" to the words of the prayer. We must therefore find the right words to unlock the door.

General Formula

The formulas proposed by the Directory are normally more than adequate. Here is Formula 1, inspired by 1 Timothy 2:4:

> Let us direct our prayers with all our heart,
> beloved brothers and sisters,
> toward God the Almighty Father,
> who wishes *all people to be saved and come to the knowledge of the truth.*

We may also think of much shorter formulas, such as: "Let us pray for the universal church." It is always appropriate to respect the following rule: If there is nothing special to say, it is best to be quiet. It is a common-sense rule.

Particular Formula

The introduction may also vary according to each celebration, taking into account the liturgical time or theme of the feast, or the life of the saint who is being commemorated, and linking the introduction to the prayer that follows.[14] Once the introduction is personalized in this way, it acquires a strikingly powerful force, harpooning, as it were, the attention of the faithful, especially when it takes its inspiration from the Word of God. Here is Formula 5 for Christmas; it takes its inspiration from Titus 3:4-5, which is from the epistle of the Second Mass of Christmas:

> *On this day,* beloved sisters and brothers,
> *when the goodness and love of God our Savior for humanity is manifested,*
> let us put our trust *not in our own meritorious actions but in his mercy,*
> let us pray humbly to God.[15]

Here is Formula 11 for Palm Sunday; it takes its inspiration from Hebrews 5:7, and is part of the second reading:

> In the time of his Passion,
> *when Christ offered prayers and supplications to his Father,*

[14] Ibid., art 7, p. 9.
[15] Ibid., 33.

with loud cries and tears,
let us implore God that in his goodness,
he will hear our prayers
because of the devotion of his Son.[16]

Here is Formula 18 for the feast of Pentecost; it takes its inspiration from Romans 8:15:

Since, beloved sisters and brothers.
We have received the Spirit of sons and daughters
through whom we cry out: "Abba, Father,"
let us direct our prayers with filial and daughterly feeling
toward the Almighty Father.[17]

A Wise Liberty

We have already mentioned the four official series of intentions, and have spoken of them as a legal framework. The Directory reveals the necessity of adapting this prayer to the celebrating community:

In order that the common prayer express the authentic prayer of the Church, universal, certainly, but adapted to each place and time, it is desirable that the freedom to vary the formulas and to adapt them to the mentality of regions and peoples be left open.[18]

This wise liberty is especially apt in the case of ritual Masses:

If a votive Mass is celebrated, as for marriages, funerals, etc., a greater place is to be given to the votive intention, yet without ever totally abandoning the universal intentions.[19]

In these cases it would be preferable to reverse the order of the four series of intentions and to begin with the intentions for which the community has come together,[20] which is the fourth series in the official series. At a Nuptial Mass, for example, the assembly might pray first for the newlyweds, for the joy and tranquillity of their love, rather than for the well-being of the country's president (second series of intentions).

---

[16] Ibid., 47.
[17] Ibid., 63.
[18] Ibid., art. 15, p. 11.
[19] Ibid., art. 10, p. 10.
[20] Ibid., 13.

Forms

The Directory gives three possible forms:[21]

The complete form, in which one announces the person or situation for which one prays, and the grace for which one asks in their regard.

Let us pray for the holy church of the living God,
That God may keep it unified.

The partial form 1, in which one enunciates immediately the grace that is being asked, mentioning the person or situation for whom or which one prays in a single word:

Let us pray that God will keep the Church unified.

The partial form 2, in which one announces only the intention for which one prays:

Let us pray for the Church.

The lines that separate these forms are permeable. The essential is not in the form of prayer but in the prayer itself.

Attention should be paid to the literary form of the prayers so that they possess a certain literary perfection. Prayer is never indifferent to beauty, which requires simplicity and nobility if a text is to be proclaimed before an assembly.

The Response of the Assembly

This response can be very general, for example, "Lord, graciously hear our prayer," which can be used during any liturgical season or situation, or, more particularly, adapted to a particular liturgical season or feast. This adaptation is very desirable, especially for the major liturgical seasons. It is clear, for example, that the invocation "Emmanuel, come and save us," for Advent, or "O Risen Christ, hear us," for Eastertime, speaks more forcibly than a simple "Graciously hear us." It is for each community to see how it can avoid the pitfall of routine and can, as it were, seduce the attention of its members.

In order that the intentions arise from out of the community with a certain spontaneity, this response must be "summoned." A successful way of achieving this is to use the same clause at the end of every

---

[21] Ibid., art. 11, p. 10.

intention. The assembly feels safe with such a cue and knows clearly where it should come in.

Concluding Prayer

In the concluding prayer the priest "asks God to listen to the prayers with benevolence." This prayer is not meant in one way or another to echo the collect of the day. In votive celebrations, however, if the greater number of the prayers are concerned with a particular intention, the priest may take up the intention in the concluding prayer.[22]

It is always good to construct prayers based on the Word of God just read, and to let the prayers take their inspiration from the traditional schema of ancient prayers:

> *Invocation:* God . . .
> *Thanksgiving:* Who . . .
> *Petition:* Gives . . .
> *Conclusion:* Through Christ . . .

If the universal prayer has been done well, this prayer can be very short, sometimes even reduced to a simple conclusion: "We ask you this through Christ our Lord."

MUSIC AND SINGING

Intentions

If the intentions are sung, the singing should be submitted to the general laws of cantillation.

The Directory does not hide its preference for singing the intentions: *optabile est* = "it is desirable."[23] This can perhaps be contested in certain cases. It depends on the literary makeup of the text. It is only desirable to sing a text if the text is "singable," if it possesses a certain interior rhythm in the grouping of words and phrases.

It also depends on who sings. The Directory justly notes:

> When the intentions are sung, as is desirable, it is necessary that the minister or the one who sings them knows how to sing well.[24]

[22] Ibid., art. 14, p. 11.
[23] Ibid., art. 8, p. 9.
[24] Ibid.

This is a wise reflection. The singing must be of such quality that it brings a positive element to the celebration: it must make the intercessions more accessible, the prayer more loving, the faithful more eager to pray. It is not a question of singing or of not singing, but of facilitating the prayer.

When all these elements are present: a good literary form for the prayers, a pleasant and sober recitative, a prayerful, harmonious voice—then singing will help the celebration by facilitating the prayer.

When the intentions are simply read, it sometimes happens that they are supported by a musical background, whether by the organ or another instrument, such as the guitar. The aim of this support is to embellish the prayer—which is highly desirable. Yet in practice, this is difficult to do: the music tends to overwhelm the prayer. We may think that the ideal is also the simplest way of doing things: neither singing the intentions nor accompanying them with a background of music but proclaiming them intelligently and clearly before the assembly.

The Response of the Assembly

The invocations of the assembly are normally sung. One of the ministerial functions of song is to gather voices together and so to express the unity of the assembly in a common prayer. Without the rhythm of the singing and the harnessing of the words to a melody, the response can easily lose consistency and disintegrate into an agglomeration of confused murmuring.

The choir can support the assembly's response by clothing it in the rich cloak of harmony.

The Universal Prayer of Each Celebration

The Missal, GIRM 45, affirms that "It is appropriate that this prayer be included in all Masses celebrated with a congregation. . . ." It is not necessary that the people be numerous in order to constitute a true celebrating assembly. Two or three of the faithful suffice: "For where two or three are gathered in my name, I am there among them" (Matt 18:20).

It should not be so difficult in each celebration of the Word of God to contemplate Jesus who speaks to the community: this is the homily's task. Likewise, it should not be so difficult to implore Jesus' mercy, such as it is revealed in each reading of the Mass: this is the task of the universal prayer. In practice, the universal prayer or prayer of the faithful is an integral part of each celebration, the same level as the homily.

FURTHER REFLECTIONS

The restoration of the universal prayer was one of the most successful accomplishments of the liturgical reform, as we have already said. How has it developed? What should we hope for in the future?

In general terms, it has been perfectly integrated into our celebrations and remains very much alive and well. We may, however, note a certain erosion, not in the prayer itself but in the four series of intentions that have sometimes been forgotten as the wind of renewal swept the Church. This is especially true for communities that, well before the council, had the longstanding custom of making these prayers—for example, certain German dioceses[25]—and who have kept the formulas forged by their own tradition and ways of praying.

In some celebrations the members of the faithful present their own intentions. This is possible when the community is small and this prayer can express the rich diversity of persons. Yet it can also wander off along a path of great poverty: improvisation—which seeks to renew everything—can easily end up in the most deplorable banalities.

This improvised prayer often bases itself on the very immediate events of the present or on strictly personal intentions. Then it is the priest's task to keep the prayer open to the universal dimensions of the Church and world.

Some communities replace this prayer by a time of silence or by another sort of prayer.

Some sleepy communities have not yet realized the necessity of the universal prayer at every celebration. These are usually the same communities as those that have not seen the need for a homily to actualize the Word just proclaimed.

What development is desirable? How can we help this prayer keep its liturgical freshness and save it from slipping into banalities?

The reform placed the universal prayer or prayer of the faithful after the proclamation of the gospel and the homily. It is therefore situated in the light of the Word, as a response to this Word.[26]

---

[25] See Gulen, Muschick.
[26] *Ordo Lectionum Missae* 30.

The quality of the universal prayer is rooted in the quality of the homily that actualizes the Word. And the quality of the homily depends on the quality of the celebration of the Word.

The future of the universal prayer is thus linked to the future of the celebration of the Word.

Nothing has been completely played out.[27] Anything is still possible. We may hope for a marvelous prayer that springs up from its source—the Word. We may also fear a prayer that has become routine and becomes simply another additional prayer to weigh down the celebration. This is to say that the future of the universal prayer or prayer of the faithful is in the hands of each community.

NOTE: THE ANAPHORIC INTERCESSIONS

The anaphoric intercessions are those that are integrated into the anaphora or Eucharistic Prayers. These prayers are often in the form of litanies.

The Tradition

The ancient Jewish or Judeo-Christian blessings served as skeletons for the first Christian anaphora. These blessings normally ended with prayers of intercession. The "Eucharistic" prayer of the *Didache*[28] concludes the thanksgiving with the following petitions:

> Lord, remember your Church,
> and deliver it from all evil;
> make it perfect in your love
> and gather it from the four winds,
> this sanctified Church,
> into your kingdom which you have prepared for it
> for power and glory are yours through all the ages!

---

[27] A. Greeley affirms that the greatest problem in the Church in the United States is the poverty of the homilies given (in L. B. Cateura, *Catholic USA* [New York: William Morrow and Co., 1989] 326–27). It is possible that this problem has always existed in every country and at all times. This is to say that the problem of the universal prayer is a universal problem.

[28] *Didache*, 10.5; see Deiss, *Springtime*, 74–76.

The movement that goes from thanksgiving to petition is a natural one. After having lifted their hands to God in praise and blessing, the early Christians then held them out in petition.[29]

We find these intercessions in the ancient anaphora. Except for the early third-century anaphora of the *Apostolic Tradition* of Hippolytus, which is strongly influenced by its author, all the later Eucharistic Prayers follow Jewish and Judeo-Christian tradition and have prayers of intercession.[30] They are sometimes very long. Thus, at the end of the fourth century, the *Apostolic Constitutions*[31] give two litanic prayers after the communion epiclesis, one for the bishop, with twelve intentions, and one for the deacon, with nine. These prayers are the equivalent of the universal prayer. In the Coptic liturgy, the petitions are detailed: during the sowing season (October 7 to January 5), they pray about the sowing of the harvest; during the fruit season (January 6 to June 6), about the fruit; and from October 6 to June 7, for a good rising of the Nile.

The Present Eucharistic Prayers

Eucharistic Prayer I, which more or less takes up the ancient Roman Canon, has kept the intercessions in their ancient place, that is, both before and after the consecration. The new Eucharistic Prayers, II, III, and IV, have placed them after the communion epiclesis and before the final doxology, in conformity with tradition.

If we desire to highlight these intercessions and support the participation of the whole community in the prayer the priest offers, we could easily treat them as litanic prayers. For example, in Eucharistic Prayer II, the community could join in by singing: "Lord remember [us]!":

> Lord, remember your church throughout the world;
> *Lord remember [us]!–*
> make us grow in love
> together with *N.* our Pope,
> *N.* our bishop,
> and all the clergy.
> Lord remember [us]!

---

[29] The same movement from praise and thanksgiving to petition is found in the Pauline corpus; see L. Bouyer, *Eucharistie* (Paris: Desclée, 1990) 109–16.

[30] See E. Lanne, "Liturgie eucharistique en Orient et en Occident (1er–4me siècles)," in *Dictionnaire de Spiritualité*, vol. 9, col. 897.

[31] VIII, 12.40–51; 13.1–9; see Deiss, *Springtime*, 235–36.

And in Eucharistic Prayer IV:

> Remember those who have died in the peace of Christ
> and all the dead whose faith is known to you alone
> *Lord remember [us]!*
> Father, in your mercy grant also to us, your children,
> to enter into our heavenly inheritance
> in the company of the Virgin Mary, the Mother of God,
> and your apostles and saints.
> *Lord remember [us]!*

Theological Significance

However venerable and traditional the anaphoric intercessions may be, they nevertheless slow down the tendency of the thanksgiving to move naturally toward the final doxology, "Through him, with him, and in him, in the unity of the Holy Spirit. . . . They also risk appearing like doublets of the universal prayer, especially if this latter is not based on the Word of God. They do, however, have an intense theological significance.

In placing the intercession for the members of the celebrating community, for the whole church—the pope, bishops, priests, deacons, and all the holy people at the very heart of the Eucharistic Prayer, the liturgy affirms that its prayer of praise becomes intercession for the world. The walls of the church may enfold those who pray, but their prayer reaches out to all humanity.

Our sisters and brothers who have left the earthly Church also belong to the universal Church. They are alive and live with God. The liturgy also intercedes for them:

> Remember, Lord, those who have died
> and have gone before us marked with the sign of faith,
> especially those for whom we now pray, *N.* and *N.* (Eucharistic Prayer I).

Our prayer concerns them. They are part of the family. We are "fellow citizens with the saints"—συμπολῖται (Eph 2:19), members of the same town, so to speak. We are united with them in a common prayer.

This Church of earth and of heaven remains in communion "with Mary, the virgin Mother of God, with the apostles and with all the saints . . . throughout the ages" (Eucharistic Prayer II). Universal in space, the Church's prayer is also universal in time. The universality of the anaphoric intercessions in some way, therefore, responds to the universality of the praise in the preface and in the *Sanctus*. There we sing the glory of God with all the saints and angels. Here we pray with them in order to form, in eternity, a single community of praise.

11

The Agnus Dei

THE BIBLICAL TRADITION

The liturgical text of the *Agnus Dei* is taken from the witness that John the Baptist gave to Jesus at the time of his baptism:

> The next day he saw Jesus coming toward him and declared, "Here is the Lamb of God who takes away the sins of the world" (John 1:29).

While the preaching of the Baptist, according to the Synoptics, is full of threats in regard to the "brood of vipers" who did not know how to flee the anger that would come upon them if they did not repent (Matt 3:7-8; Luke 3:7-8), that which the fourth Gospel presents is the peaceful contemplation of the mystery of Christ the Redeemer. As John the Baptist said, Jesus "takes away the sins of the world," and to signify this mystery, he presents Jesus as the Lamb of God.

The image of the Lamb of God is very rich on a biblical level. Different readings and interpretations are possible. We may ask what John the Baptist actually said, for the text remains open to different interpretations (for example, we may ask how John saw the Spirit descend on Jesus and give testimony that he was the Chosen One of God (John 1:32, 34), and then ask Jesus, through his disciples, "Are you the one who is to come?" (Matt 11:3; Luke 7:19). We may also ask how the primitive community interpreted the image of the Lamb of God after the passion and resurrection, and how the later Johannine traditions interpreted it.

On the exegetical level, three interpretations are generally suggested: that of the Servant of Yahweh, that of the Paschal Lamb, and that of the conquering Lamb of the visions in the Book of Revelation.

The Servant of Yahweh

The image of the Lamb of God recalls the Servant of Yahweh in the fourth Servant Song in Isaiah:[1]

> He was oppressed, and he was afflicted,
>   yet he did not open his mouth;
> like a lamb that is led to the slaughter,
>   and like a sheep that before its shearers is silent,
> so he did not open his mouth. . . .
>   Out of his anguish he shall see light . . .
> The righteous one, my servant, shall make many righteous,
>   and he shall bear their iniquities (Isa 53:7, 11).

The primitive Christian community saw in the sufferings of the Servant of Yahweh, and in his glorification, the prophecy of the story of Jesus. Thus in the Book of Acts (8:32-33 = Isa 53:7-8), the deacon Philip announces the good news of Jesus to the queen of Candace's eunuch, basing himself on the fourth Servant Song:

> "Like a sheep he was led to the slaughter,
>   and like a lamb silent before its shearer,
>   so he does not open his mouth.
> In his humiliation justice was denied him.
>   Who can describe his generation?
>   For his life is taken away from the earth."

It is clear that the primitive community liked to apply the title "Servant"[2] to Jesus, a title that may also be translated "child" or "son." This represents exactly the history of Jesus: Jesus was the "holy servant" of God (Acts 4:27-30), humiliated in his passion but constituted "Son of God with power . . . by resurrection from the dead" (Rom 1:4).

The holy Servant is compared to a lamb, and in Aramaic the word *talya,* which we translate as "lamb," can also mean "son." There

---

[1] See the articles of J. Jeremias in *Theologisches Wörterbuch zum Neuen Testament,* art. *amnos,* vol. 1 (Stuttgart: Kohlhammer, 1957) 342–45, and *pais,* vol. 5 (1954) 653–713.

[2] On the use of the Servant of Yahweh prophecies in the Gospels see L. Deiss, *Synopse* (Paris: Desclée, 1991) 412.

was, then, in the consciousness of the primitive community, a super-imposition of the two meanings. The lowliness of the title *Servant* could have led to its replacement by *Lamb*. John the Baptist could have designated Christ:

> "Here is the Servant of God
> who takes away the sins of the world."

After the resurrection, the primitive community preferred to say:

> "Here is the Lamb of God
> who takes away the sin of the world."

Such an evolution is at one with the evolution of the text of Jesus' Baptism. The primitive text of Mark 1:11, which cites the first Servant Song (Isa 42:1), could have read: "You are my Servant . . ."; but after the resurrection it was read and understood as: "You are my Son."[3]

The Paschal Lamb

The image of the Lamb of God also evokes the theme of the Paschal Lamb.

The connection is implicitly suggested by the historical circumstances of the Lord's death: Jesus dies at the moment when the lamb for the Jewish Passover is sacrificed. Paul clarifies this connection when he writes, ca. 54 C.E.:

> For our paschal lamb, Christ, has been sacrificed (1 Cor 5:7).

John takes up this interpretation in the account of the passion. He states that the soldiers did not break Jesus' legs as they did those of the two thieves crucified with him, so that "the scripture might be fulfilled" (John 19:36). He thus cites the proscription of Exodus 12:46, which refers to the Paschal Lamb:

> You shall not break any of its bones.

The First Letter of Peter also seems to make an allusion to the Paschal Lamb:

---

[3] M.-E. Boismard and A. Lamouille think that the title Lamb of God could also have evoked the figure of Moses: Jesus is called the Lamb of God as the New Moses; see Deiss, *Synopse,* vol. III (Paris: Cerf, 1977) 92; vol. II (1972) 79–80.

You know that you were ransomed from the futile ways inherited from your ancestors . . . with the precious blood of Christ, like that of a lamb without defect or blemish (1 Pet 1:18-19).

In thus speaking of Christ, the author recalls the Jewish Passover rubric according to which the paschal lamb had to be without stain or blemish (Exod 12:5).

The Conquering Lamb in the Book of Revelation

The Book of Revelation is particularly fond of the image of the conquering Lamb: the word "lamb" is used twenty-nine times (in the form of *arnion,* which is, significantly, the diminutive, "little lamb"[4]). The image seems to come from apocalyptic circles in Judaism;[5] it has been adapted to Christian tradition and applied to Christ who, in taking away the sins of the world, would establish a kingdom of holiness.

In the Book of Revelation the image is very much a two-sided one. At one time it carries echoes of the One whose eyes exude flames of fire (Rev 19:13) and casts terror among the mighty ones of the earth in the great day of his anger (6:15-17); at another, the image is softened with echoes of the loving Husband who tenderly welcomes his Bride to the "feast of the Lamb" (19:7). These oppositions complement each other and provide a fuller picture. An angel announces "the Lion of the tribe of Judah, the Root of David," in the splendor of his glorious victory, but a "lamb [looking] as if it had been slaughtered" appears, standing near the throne (5:6). It still carries the traces of the knife on its neck; its wounds, which do not heal, can be touched, for in the blood that flows from them those "who have come out of the great ordeal" have washed their robes and made them white again (7:14). The risen One will carry eternally the scars of his martyrdom.

This slain lamb is "the Lord of lords and King of kings" (17:14). It is the Lord whom the myriads of angels acclaim in the heavenly liturgy, in seven terms that signify the fullness of God's glory:

---

[4] To express Lamb of God, the Gospel of John does not use the word ἀρνίον but ἀμνός, a word never used in the Book of Revelation. In the Gospel, ἀρνίον is found only once, in 21:15 (which is usually thought to be an addition to John's original text). In the biblical language of the LXX, the difference between the two words is unimportant (see Jeremias, vol. 1, 344). We may simply recognize that the authors of the Gospel and Revelation were different, even if they came from the same Johannine circles, and that the Gospel image of the Lamb of God does not have the same meaning as the Lamb in Revelation.

[5] See A. Jaubert, *Approches de l'Evangile de Jean* (Paris: Seuil, 1976) 137–39.

"Worthy is the Lamb that was slaughtered
to receive power and wealth and wisdom and might
and honor and glory and blessing!" (5:12).

It is God who breaks open the seven seals (5:9), who executes judgment, and condemns those who adore the Beast and makes them drink the cup of his wrath (14:10).

Alternating with these images of fire is the gentle image of the lamb who is also the shepherd who leads his flock:

> for the Lamb at the center of the throne will be their shepherd,
>   and he will guide them to springs of the water of life,
> and God will wipe away every tear from their eyes" (7:17).

In about the year 95, at the time when the Johannine tradition was putting the last touches to the final redaction of the Book of Revelation, the Lamb had become one of the privileged titles of Christ. An image of weakness itself, the Lamb, conqueror of all the powers hostile to God, had become the symbol for the Paschal Mystery of Christ.

Lamb-Servant of Yahweh according to Isaiah, Passover Lamb of the New Covenant, Conquering Lamb in the visions of Revelation: Do we need to choose between these images, as if one excludes the others? From the beginning of Jesus' public ministry, when John first met the Lord, until the end of the first century, the date of the final Johannine writings, the theme of Jesus as Lamb developed in different directions. The image was not thereby degraded but rather enriched by the mutual complementarity of images.

From the richness of this imagery, we may recall:

The humility and patience of Christ-Servant, suffering like a lamb led to the slaughter.

The expiatory character of his death opening up into the triumph of his resurrection. He is the Servant crushed by suffering and the Son glorified by his resurrection.

The memorial of the Paschal Mystery. While the ancient Passover concerned only the people of Israel, the new Passover concerns the whole of humanity: the Lamb of God takes away "the sins of the world."

The final triumph of the Lamb over every power hostile to God.

THE LITURGICAL TRADITION

The first witness we have to the *Agnus Dei* chant in the Roman liturgy dates from the seventh century. The *Liber Pontificalis*[6] states that Pope Sergius I (687–701) prescribed that "during the time of the breaking of the Body of the Lord, the clergy and the people must sing: "Lamb of God, you take away the sin of the world, have mercy on us." Even if this witness can be contested—the redactor may have shown himself overly generous to Sergius—it is certain that this song was imported from the East (Sergius was himself from the East). We do not know if the Roman liturgy possessed another song before this time for the breaking of the bread. In Rome at this time all of the presbyters were involved in the breaking of the bread. The pope broke the bread on the paten, and the other priests put the pieces into bags that acolytes handed to them.

The rite has a twofold meaning in the Christian tradition.

A Single Loaf

The first meaning is biblical in origin.

The Eucharist renews the Lord's action, and is carried out according to his commandment: "Do this in remembrance of me." All the four traditions (Matt 26:26; Mark 14:22; 1 Cor 11:24 and Luke 22:19, which is part of the same tradition) that recount the institution of the Supper mention the breaking of the bread: Jesus takes bread, gives thanks to the Father, breaks the bread and says: "This is my body." This is a typically Jewish rite. The expression "breaking of the bread," while unknown in secular Greek, designated the beginning of a Jewish meal: the father of the family broke the flat bread and distributed it to those assembled.

In the primitive community, the rite of breaking the bread had considerable importance. The Book of Acts identifies the breaking of bread with the Eucharistic meal:

> They devoted themselves to the apostles' teaching and fellowship, to the *breaking of bread* and the prayers (2:42).

> Day by day, as they spent much time together in the temple, they *broke bread* at home and ate their food with glad and generous hearts (2:46).

---

[6] See J. A. Jungmann, *Missarum Solemnia*, vol. III (Paris: Aubier, 1954) 261.

The action of breaking the bread witnessed graphically to the unity of a single family around a single table sharing a single loaf. Around the year 57, Paul explains in his First Letter to the Corinthians:

> The cup of blessing that we bless, is it not a sharing in the blood of Christ? The bread that we break, is it not a sharing in the body of Christ? Because there is one bread, we who are many are one body, for we all partake of the one bread (1 Cor 10:16-17).

GIRM 56c. retains the idea of unity:

> Breaking of the bread: in apostolic times this gesture of Christ at the Last Supper gave the entire Eucharistic action its name. This rite . . . is a sign that in sharing in the one bread of life which is Christ we who are many are made one body.

Body Given, Blood Outpoured

Since the sixth century, the breaking of the bread has been considered in the East as an evocation of the Lord's sufferings. The East thinks less of the sharing of the bread than of the Body that is *given* for us and the Blood that is *poured out* for us in the passion. In Western Syria the priest recites the following prayer:

> Truly the Word of God suffered in his flesh, was sacrificed and broken on the Cross. . . . His side was opened with a lance, and from it flowed blood and water, a propitiation for the whole world.[7]

Another prayer from the same liturgy evokes the theme of the Lamb of God:

> You are Christ, you are God, you whose side was opened for us on Golgotha, in Jerusalem; you are the Lamb of God who takes away the sin of the world. Forgive us our sins and remit our faults.[8]

This interpretation highlights the prophecy of the Servant of Yahweh in the Book of Isaiah and in John's account of the passion. It appears secondary in the context of the fraction rite, but it is highlighted in the biblical context of the *Lamb of God*.

---

[7] See Brightman, vol. 1, 97.
[8] Ibid., 99.

MUSIC AND FORM

Situated between the Eucharistic Prayer and the communion, between the offering the Church makes of Christ to the Father and the offering the Father makes of Christ to the Church, this liturgical song must be of great solemnity; it must echo the acclamations that the liturgy addresses to the triumphant, slain Lamb. The Lamb of the New Passover, who will become our food, is the center of the heavenly and earthly liturgy, and while the heavenly Church sings hymns of victory to God, the Church on earth, which is still journeying, begs for the forgiveness of its sins, deliverance from servitude to sin, and for peace of soul: Have mercy on us, grant us peace!

No music can express the fullness of these different biblical or liturgical themes. It can only try to suggest one or other of these themes.

As for the form, it is determined, at least partially, by the ministerial function of the song that is to accompany the rite of the breaking of the bread and the mixing of the bread and wine. The GIRM 56c. explicitly envisages that the *Agnus Dei* "may be repeated as often as necessary to accompany the breaking of the bread."[9]

The litanic melody must have a solid internal structure to assure its stability and autonomy, for it must be able to be repeated without becoming frustratingly repetitive. A good example of a melody that has this quality is the Gregorian *Agnus Dei XVIII*. It is a little masterpiece that rests on two major thirds, *fa-la* and *sol-ti*, like a bridge with two arches. Anchored in the granite of G *(sol)*, it can be repeated indefinitely without becoming boring or losing its simple joyfulness.

The three phrases can also be regarded as a musical whole. Carried by the text, these phrases are parallel and echo one another. It is normal that they should be tied in a logical melodic progression, as in every well-conceived work. The *Agnus Dei* that is so treated resembles a short hymn of three verses that develops melodically.

---

[9] The Missal gives no explanation of the rite of the mixing of bread and wine. We are not sure of the origin and signification of this rite; see R. Cabié, "L'Eucharistie," op. cit., 129–31.

The Participants

According to the Instruction *Musicam Sacram* 34, "it is desirable that the people should participate in this song, at least by the final invocation."[10]

Exceptional choirs may sing one of the polyphonic *Agnus Dei* of great musical value, but the choir should sing it as a motet during communion.

FURTHER REFLECTIONS

There is a certain feeling of incompleteness in the *Agnus Dei*. It could be said that it wanders like an orphan, dressed in the clothes of the ancient tradition, without really finding its true home in the new liturgy.

We may ask certain questions about the rite itself, about the text, and about the singing.

The Rite of the Breaking of the Bread

We speak about the breaking of the bread, but so often there is no bread to break except a small host that can be broken in less time than it takes to intone the song. We speak of sharing—but usually there is nothing to share, only little hosts to distribute. We speak of mixing bread and wine, but we do not know the meaning of this rite. GIRM 283 gives the following directives:

> The nature of the sign demands that the material for the Eucharistic celebration truly have the appearance of food. Accordingly, even though unleavened and baked in the traditional shape, the Eucharistic bread should be made in such a way that in a Mass with a congregation the priest is able actually to break the host into parts and distribute them to at least some of the faithful. . . . The action of the breaking of the bread, the simplest term for the Eucharist in apostolic times, will more clearly bring out the force and meaning of the sign of unity of all in the one bread and of their charity, since the one bread is being distributed among the members of one family.

These words are golden. They demand that the host really look like bread, and that this bread is able to be broken and shared by the

---

[10] Flannery, op. cit., 89.

priest and faithful. They also affirm that this action is a sign of unity and charity.

In order that this sign really be authentic, it is necessary that the bread/wafer be such that it can be broken into a number of pieces. This is certainly possible, even when the assembly is very large. In this last case, other wafers or breads can be used along with the wafer to be broken. The gesture of breaking the bread, carried out with a certain grandness of means and spirit, will still manifest its intended meaning.[11]

The Text

The biblical text *Agnus Dei* is very rich, as we have seen. But it is inadequate to illustrate the richness of the breaking of the bread rite.

Other texts could be richer and more suitable, for example the text about the broken bread as a sign of participation in the Body of Christ in 1 Corinthians 10:16-17 cited previously, or the Emmaus account in Luke 24:31, where "their eyes were opened, and they recognized him [in the breaking of the bread]." The phrase "who takes away the sins of the world" of the *Agnus Dei* could be replaced by texts (tropes) that express the graces of unity and charity which the rite signifies.[12]

---

[11] Cabié, 231, justly notes: "The symbolism of the breaking of the bread is sufficiently important in the Church's tradition not to let ourselves be hampered by a few practical inconveniences."

[12] See J. Gelineau, *Dans vos assemblées*, vol. 1 (Paris: Desclée, 1989) 496.

12

The Hymns

The hymn is a poetic composition expressing the Christian mystery, composed to be sung in the liturgical celebration.

POETIC EXPRESSION OF THE CHRISTIAN MYSTERY

The Christian mystery is expressed throughout the celebration of the Mass in the readings, the prayers, the psalms, the homily, the anaphora, the litanies, and in the rites themselves. Yet it is the role of the hymns to clothe the message in poetic beauty and human tenderness, to re-create the feelings of joy, thanksgiving, sadness, and exaltation that the gospel message provokes in the Church with the splendor of art and the magic of the word. The liturgy cannot be content simply to say: "Christ is risen," but it must sing in the *Victimae paschali laudes:*

> *Surrexit Christus, spes mea.*
> *Agnus redemit oves.*
> *Tu nobis victor Rex, miserere!*

> Christ, my hope, is risen.
> The Lamb has redeemed the sheep.
> You, victorious Conqueror, have mercy on us!

The patristic era and the Middle Ages have given us some three thousand hymns that are actually known and published.[1] Each age

[1] See note 12 of chapter 5.

experiences the need to sing to Christ according to its own charism, its own particular vision of the Christian message, and the sentiments that the Spirit awakens. This is to say that to compose hymns is a duty for each age, a duty that must continue until the end of time precisely in order to remain faithful to the tradition and create new traditions. A Christianity that fails to do this would be an agonizing reality because it would have renounced the attempt to present Christ to its time in the words, images, and rhythms of its own epoch. Christ is certainly contemporary to all ages, but the formulas we use to sing to Christ are passing and perishable and must be unceasingly renewed. This variability of forms is dictated by the fickle nature of literary sensitivities and tastes. The Church does not make judgments about such fickleness in public sensitivity, rather it must simply make use of the forms that are used so that each generation, as we have already said above, will be able to place at the feet of the risen One its "tribute of praise." Each generation must verify for itself what Eusebius of Caesarea wrote of the first Christians: "So many psalms and canticles, written by brothers and sisters in the faith since the earliest times, sing to Christ the Word of God and proclaim him God."[2]

If we consider the Christian message in itself, poetic perfection is of little importance. But it is highly desirable when we think of the form in which the message comes to us. Let us remember that poetic beauty is God's creation too. God did not judge it as useless but made use of it in giving us the Word: two-thirds of the Bible is poetry. It is certainly not always a question of seeking the rhythm of words and the splendor of images in themselves in the search of plastic beauty or in the name of artistic creativity, as in certain pages of the Song of Songs, but more often a situation where the message attains its greatest intensity, where the most essential revelations of God[3] are concerned, even those at the root of our knowledge of God and the Christian vision of the world. Let us also remember that the last prayers of Christ on the Cross were "poetry"—the poetry of Psalm 22: "My God, my God, why have you forsaken me?," and of Psalm 31, verse 5: "Into your hands I commend my Spirit."

[2] Eusebius of Caesarea, *Ecclesiastical History*, V.28.5. See Sources chrétiennes 41 (Paris: Cerf, 1955) 74.

[3] In the Bible, poetry is a superior way of expressing history; see G. Von Rad, *Theologie des Alten Testaments*, vol. 1 (München: Kaiser Verlag, 1958) 114–16.

THE MUSICAL EXPRESSION
OF THE CHRISTIAN MYSTERY

The music is as essential to a hymn as the text itself. Without the music, the hymn's poetry would be a body without a soul. The text only becomes a hymn when it is carried by a singing community, illustrating well the principle that a song is only a song when it is sung.

The importance of the hymn's music is not inferior to a processional song. In fact, all things being equal, that is, when the pastoral value of both processional and hymn are the same, the importance of the hymn's music may be even greater. A processional accompanies a rite. Text and music refer to the rite. This assures it of a certain stability in the liturgy: the song is sung each time the rite is performed. This diminishes the autonomy of the processional song: it is sung as an accompaniment to a rite. The hymn, on the contrary, may be sung for its own sake: when we sing the *Gloria,* for example, nothing else happens: we just sing the *Gloria.* This gives the hymn a certain autonomy. It also explains its fragility in the liturgical celebration: it can be moved around easily without disturbing the whole structure of the celebration. It may even be omitted, as often happens to the *Gloria,* without threatening the general lines of the celebration.

It is not possible, however, to omit all the hymns at every celebration. This would be like taking away all the statues and all the stained glass from a church. Human beings do not live by clear concepts alone. They also need a minimum of beauty. Their souls are nourished by poetry and music.

The hymn enriches the equilibrium between the different musical forms of the songs used in the Mass. A celebration in which all the songs were psalms accompanied by an antiphon would die of boredom. It would be just as insufferable if all the songs were hymns. The excess of lyricism would unbalance the equilibrium just as much as its total absence.

The following examines the hymn of the *Gloria,* the hymn that surrounds the gospel, the hymn after communion and the final hymn.

GLORY TO GOD IN THE HIGHEST

The Tradition

The text of the hymn *Glory to God in the Highest* has come to us in a triple recension:

The Syrian text of the Nestorian liturgy;

The Greek text of the *Apostolic Constitutions;*

The Greek text of the *Codex Alexandrinus,* which approximates the actual text in the Roman Missal.

Here is the Syrian text of the Nestorian liturgy.[4] Of the three traditions, it is undoubtedly the most lyrical. It is enriched with numerous scriptural phrases:

> *Glory to God in the highest,*
> *and on earth, peace,*
> *to humankind, goodwill (of God)*–Luke 2:14.
> We bless you, we glorify you, we exalt you,
> You who are from all eternity,
> hidden and of an incomprehensible nature,
> Father, Son, and Holy Spirit,
> *King of kings and Lord of lords,*
> *who live in inaccessible light,*
> *whom no one has seen, nor can see* (1 Tim 6:16),
> who alone is holy, alone powerful, alone immortal.
> We confess you by the *Mediator* of our praises (1 Tim 2:5)
> *Jesus Christ, Savior of the world* (John 4:42)
> and Son of the Most High.
> *Lamb of* the living *God,*
> you *who take away the sins of the world* (John 1:29)
> Have mercy on us.
> *You who are seated at the right hand of the Father* (Col 3:1),
> receive our prayer.
> For you are our God and our Lord.
> You are our King and our Savior,
> It is you who remit sins.
> *The eyes of all are turned towards you* (Ps 145:15), Jesus Christ.

---

[4] Text of J. A. Jungmann, in *Missarum Solemnia,* vol. II, 104–5, somewhat altered.

Glory to God, your Father,
and to you and to the Holy Spirit for eternity. Amen.

Here are the versions of the *Apostolic Constitutions* and the *Codex Alexandrinus* set out in columns:[5]

Apostolic Constitutions (ca. 380)	Codex Alexandrinus (ca. 5th c.)
Glory to God in the highest heaven and on earth peace, to men (God's) good will! (Luke 2:14).	*Glory to God in the highest heaven, and on earth peace, to men, (God's) good will!*
We sing you, we praise you, we bless you, we give you glory, and we adore you through your High Priest, you the only God, who exist from all eternity, the only inaccessible one, for your immense glory.	We sing you, we bless you, we worship you, we glorify you, we give you thanks for your great glory.
Lord, King of heaven, God, the almighty Father!	Lord God, King of heaven, God the Father almighty! Lord, only Son, Jesus Christ, and Holy Spirit!
Lord God, Father of Christ, the spotless Lamb *who takes away the sin of the world,* receive our prayer, *"you who sit above the Cherubim"* (Ps 80:2).	Lord God, *Lamb of God,* Son of the Father, *you who take away the sins of the world,* receive our prayer. *You who are seated at the right hand of the Father,* have pity on us.
For you alone art holy, you alone are Lord Jesus, Messiah of the God of the created universe, and of our King. Through him, glory, honor, and adoration to you.	For you alone are holy, you alone are Lord, Jesus Christ, to the glory of God the Father. Amen.

---

[5] Greek text in F. X. Funk, *Didascalia et Constitutiones Apostolorum*, vol. 1, 454–56, translated in Deiss, *Springtime*, 220–21 and 252–53.

It can be noted that the Syrian tradition and that of the *Apostolic Constitutions* insist on the mediation of the Son, while the *Codex Alexandrinus* underlines the Son's equality of the Father. We may have here Arian corrections insisting on the Son's subordination to the Father on the one hand and, on the other, an anti-Arian reaction that stressed the equality of the two divine persons.[6] Let us note that if we look at these hymns in terms of the trinitarian controversies, none of them gives an adequate text, for none gives equal praise to the Holy Spirit. This shows us that a hymn is not a theological treatise. For our purposes, it is sufficient to see from these texts that the common rule of the New Testament and the ancient prayers was to address praise and supplication to the Father through the Son. We cannot criticize a text for imitating Scripture in this way.

The *Gloria,* like the *Kyrie* or the *Agnus Dei,* was not composed for the liturgy of the Mass. In fact, the Eastern liturgies do not use it at Mass. How did it succeed in being introduced into the Mass in the West?

Along with the *Phos hilaron* and the *Te decet laus,* the *Gloria* is one of the most ancient hymns that the Christian tradition, in continuity with the New Testament tradition, invented to honor Jesus Christ.[7] According to the *Apostolic Constitutions,* it was sung as a morning prayer. *De Virginitate* of St. Athanasius (PG 28.276) also places it as a morning praise with Psalm 63 (62) and the Canticle of the Three Young Men (Dan 3:57-88). It was introduced into the Roman Mass by way of Christmas because of its reference to the song of the angels at Bethlehem. In the *Liber Pontificalis,* Pope Symmachus (498–514) extended its use to Masses celebrated by the bishop on Sundays and on feasts of the martyrs. It was normal—and so human—that priests wanted to imitate the bishops by having the right to sing the *Gloria* at their own Masses! According to the *Ordo of Saint-Amand,* they had the right to do so on Easter night and at the first Mass at which they presided in their titular church. Toward the end of the eleventh century, they had obtained the right to recite the *Gloria* at every Mass with a festive character.

---

[6] On the considerable influence that the Arian and anti-Arian struggles had on the liturgy and its formulas, see J. A. Jungmann, *Tradition liturgique et problèmes actuels de Pastorale* (Le Puy: Mappus, 1962) 15–86.

[7] Basil of Caesarea already considered the *Phos hilaron* as an ancient hymn, *On the Holy Spirit,* 29:73, Sources chrétiennes 17 bis (Paris: Cerf, 1968) 508–10—Greek text in R. de Journel, *Enchiridium Patristicum* (Friburgi-Barinone: Herder, 1956) n. 108.

Biblical and Liturgical Meaning

The beginning of the *Gloria* is taken from the hymn of the angels
at Bethlehem. Two translations are possible according to the demands of textual criticism. The first is retained by the Roman Missal:

> Glory to God in the highest
> and peace to his people on earth.

The "people" of his peace are those upon whom the good will of
God rests. The translation "to his people on earth" expresses the sense
of the biblical text perfectly. On the contrary, "to men of good will,"
despite its venerable use, does not express the message of the Word of
God. Peace is a Messianic gift that in biblical thought is essentially the
fruit of God's good will. People can only receive it and use it well.

The second tradition is used in certain Eastern liturgies. It is used
in an extremely powerful way:

> Glory to God in the highest,
> and on earth peace,
> to men, goodwill (of God).

The text recalls the joyful acclamation that the disciples addressed
to Jesus during his Messianic entry into Jerusalem:

> Blessed is the king
> who comes in the name of the Lord!
> Peace in heaven,
> and glory in the highest heaven (Luke 19:37).

These last acclamations of the *Gloria* are found in the Eastern
liturgies in the communion rite. To the bishop who presents the Body
of Christ to the assembly, the assembly replies:

> One alone [is] holy, one alone [is] Lord,
> Jesus Christ, who is blessed for ever,
> to the glory of God the Father! Amen (*Apostolic Constitutions*, VIII, 13.11).

We can see from this that the *Gloria* gathers together very different elements of Christian prayer in a pleasing but disordered literary
form: we adore God, we give thanks, we bless God's name, we ask
for forgiveness, we ask God to receive our prayer. The dominant
note of this symphony of acclamations and supplications remains the
glorification of God. The text begins with *Glory to God in the highest*

and finishes with *in the glory of God the Father.* All the other prayers of the hymn are thus placed in the ambiance of the glory that we acclaim; the Eastern liturgies call the *Gloria* the "Great Doxology."[8]

In as much as it is a doxology, the *Gloria* belongs to the highest form of Christian prayer. Before the transcendence of the Father who dwells in inaccessible light, before the marvels of salvation that God has accomplished among his people, before the mystery of the Eucharist through which the Lord Jesus dwells in the midst of human poverty, human beings can only repeat: "Glory to God!" There is nothing that we can add to or take away from the divine glory, but human greatness consists precisely in recognizing and proclaiming God's greatness and opening ourselves to the radiance of that enveloping glory by our human "Amen."

In singing: "We give you thanks" *(eucharistoumen),* the Christian community, for the first time since the beginning of the Mass, clearly proclaims that the heart of its celebration is to give thanks, to celebrate "Eucharist."

Music

We insisted above on the importance of the music for the hymn.

In theory, all forms of music are possible for the *Gloria,* from a simple melody to a very ornate harmony in several voices. Melody, harmony, and rhythm must work together to create a festive atmosphere. The *Gloria* must be festive.

The *Gloria* of the Gregorian repertoire reached a level of perfection in musical genius. Think of the tenderness and freshness of the *Gloria* of the Easter Mass *Lux et origo,* of the glory of the *Gloria* of Mass II, *Fons bonitatis,* of the supplication of the *Gloria* of Mass IX, *Cum jubilo:* we can never forget these even if we have heard them only once.

We may also mention the polyphonic Masses of the classical epoch. Josquin des Près, Palestrina, Lassus—all knew how to clothe the *Gloria* in a robe of glory and jubilation. Or the ecstatic *Gloria* of Bach's B-minor Mass! Not all pieces of the classical repertory are masterpieces, but what magnificence is found in those that are!

Yet today it is not a question of imitating the Gregorian or polyphonic styles, nor imposing on our communities the aesthetics of yes-

---

[8] As opposed to the same doxology (Glory to the Father . . .) that is said at the end of the psalms.

terday. But the lyricism and jubilant festivity of these ancient pieces must spring forth from the new melodies, harmonies, and rhythms that we create. In the *Gloria,* music in the service of the liturgy must attain its highest point.

Participants

The text of the *Gloria* is not reserved for a special person (as, for example, the preface is reserved for the priest, or the *Sanctus* for the whole celebrating assembly); it is not even essential to use it in the Eucharistic celebration: many Masses do not have the *Gloria.* This is another way of saying that the question of who sings the *Gloria* is not a problem. The Missal's GIRM 31 states that it can be sung either "by the congregation, or by the congregation alternately with the choir, or by the choir alone."

Further Reflections

We may resolve the rubrical question by saying that the community should recite or sing the *Gloria* each time the rubrics prescribe it.

Yet, having said this, we may also ask another question: Is it desirable to keep the *Gloria* in the Mass? Is it desirable to keep it in its present place in the Mass? Here are some reflections.

We have insisted on the beauty of the *Gloria.* Dom Cabrol called it "a liturgical pearl . . . one of the most venerable of the prayers of Christian antiquity."[9] However, the beauty of a piece and its value in the tradition are not sufficient reasons for keeping it in the contemporary liturgy. A prayer or rite is to be kept insofar as it fulfills a precise ministerial function in the celebration. The goal of the liturgical celebration is not to preserve yesterday's prayers today, however beautiful they may be. The community is not a group of music lovers meeting together to listen to ravishing musical pieces founded on moving texts, but a community of the baptized who have been called together to celebrate and praise God.

Besides, when Dom Cabrol spoke of a "liturgical pearl," he was referring, I suppose, to the primitive Greek or Latin text, texts that have their own rhythmic pulses and colors and are impossible to translate. The English translation remains the translation of a text in

---

[9] F. Cabrol, *Le Livre de la prière antique* (Paris: Oudin, 1900) 154, 156.

a dead language, fruit of a dead culture, into contemporary English. In seeking to reconstruct a masterpiece from the debris of the past, one may create an antique but not necessarily a living liturgical work.

Let us pose the question in another way: If the English text were simply a modern composition, would Christian communities eagerly accept it as a "pearl"? They would not much appreciate the lyricism of its poetry. They would cast suspicion on the orthodoxy of its theology of the Holy Spirit. No one would accept it without rubrical coercion.

The *Gloria* creates a doublet, for several of its themes already figure in other prayers of the Mass:

Gloria	Other Prayers
. . . we worship you, we give you thanks, we praise you for your glory.	See the preface.
Lord Jesus Christ . . . *have mercy on us. . .*	*Lord have mercy (Kyrie)*
Lord Jesus Christ, only Son of the Father,	
Lord God, *Lamb of God, you take away the sin of the world: have mercy on us. . . .*	*Lamb of God, you who take away the sins of the world: have mercy on us (Agnus Dei).*
For you alone are the *Holy* One, you alone are the *Lord* . . .	See the *Sanctus*.

It is perfectly possible to express the same prayer several times in the course of a celebration, but one cannot pretend that the *Gloria* gives the community themes for prayer that are not present elsewhere. The only original theme of the *Gloria,* and that which gives it its weight of tenderness and rich affectivity, is the song of the angels at Bethlehem. This link ties it to the context of the nativity of the Lord.

We have already spoken of the inordinate "weight" of the entrance songs. The entrance song itself, the penitential rite with the *Kyrie,* the *Gloria,* in which we first acclaim the glory of God (first part), then implore the mercy of the Son (second part), and finally, acclaim his holiness, "with the Holy Spirit in the glory of God the Father" (third part)—all this before the presidential prayer, risks weighing on the assembly, and what is more, demands of the assembly a tremendous effort of attention and agility. This coming-and-going among the jungle of feelings and prayers is more favorable to flitting about like a butterfly than to deep and reverential adoration in spirit and in truth. The entrance song and penitential rite have well-defined ministerial functions; the *Gloria* appears as a gem without precise ministerial function.

This is confirmed by the fact that it is tied rubrically to Masses on feastdays and Sundays outside of Lent and Advent. Yet this link is a loose one. A song that is fitting for every feast does not really express the particular mystery of any of them. There is no real reason to reserve it for Sundays and feasts.

This is particularly true when the *Gloria* is not sung but only recited. In these cases it loses its function as a hymn. It no longer has the festive character necessary for a feast.

Finally, the weight of the *Gloria* is sometimes slighted by the fact that even the words are shortened by musical tricks. This happens often in polyphonic Masses, when one phrase begins before the preceding phrase is finished: it makes the text incomprehensible. Sometimes this trick goes to the utmost limit. The polyphonic Mass *Missa Brevis Sti Johannis de Deo,* by J. Haydn (1732–1809), who was in fact a devoted member of the faithful, offers the following example: after the intonation *Gloria in excelsis Deo,* the bass part takes up *Et in terra pax hominibus,* etc.; at the same time, the tenor part sings *Domine Deus, Agnus Dei,* etc.; the alto part sings *Domine Fili Unigeniti,* etc.; and the soprano part, at the same time, sings *Gratias agimus tibi,* etc. Finally, the four parts sing together *Cum Sancto Spiritu.* All the words of the *Gloria* are sung, but only God the Father could understand them. It is sad to see the text of the *Gloria* humiliated in such a mess.

We do not know today how the *Gloria* will evolve in the parish liturgical celebrations of the future. But it is always possible to express some desires and hopes for that future.

It should be possible, *ad libitum,* to keep or omit the *Gloria.* This would allow communities to give greater weight to the entrance rites on certain feast days or to simplify them, at other times, in the context of achieving a more balanced celebration and better prayer.

It could be used as an entrance song for Christmastime. This would give back to it its significance as the "Song of the Angels."

It could also be used as the hymn after communion, which would emphasize its character of praise, of what the Eastern liturgies have called "the Great Doxology."

THE HYMN RELATED TO THE GOSPEL

The Tradition

It is possible to envision a hymn in which the community expresses again, in a lyrical manner, the message it has just heard, and responds to in prayer. The sequences that have come down to us from the Middle Ages give numerous examples.

They are not intended to anticipate the gospel or to repeat it mechanically. They highlight it by clothing it with beauty, and they comment on it by revealing its multiple riches for Christian life; these are the preludes that echo the melody of the good news in order to emphasize its beauty and enhance its affective power.

The pastoral importance of these hymns connected to the gospel may be great. These popular hymns mark the people and form their piety. Is it our homilies that remain in their minds and nourish their souls? Not necessarily, nor the "truths" of the catechism learned in the past, nor theological discussions. Often it is the texts of popular songs and hymns that come to mind in their hearts when they meet God in the things of everyday life.

Certain ancient sequences that were customarily connected to the reading of the gospel are pure masterpieces. Think of the *Victimae paschali laudes* (which has given birth to "Christ Lay in the Bonds of Death") that comments so perfectly on the mystery of Easter. Or the sequence of Pentecost, *Veni Sancte Spiritus,* one of the most beautiful prayers to the Holy Spirit in existence. Here, from the Eastern tradition of the fifth century, is a hymn for Easter night:

O night more radiant than the day,
O night more resplendent than the sun,
O night more dazzling than the snow,
O night more brilliant than our flames of fire!

O night more sweet than Paradise itself;
O night that delivers from darkness,
O night that chases sleep away,
O night that makes us watch with the angels!

O night terrible for every demon,
O night toward which the whole year turns,
O night that leads the Church to her Spouse,
O night, mother of the enlightened ones!

O night in which the devil,
while he slept, was despoiled,
O night in which the Inheritor
introduces the inheritees to the inheritance![10]

In our own time, some of the black spirituals testify to the immense possibility of the people to rethink and re-create the gospel in a way at one with their own sensibilities. Is not the following gospel song an authentic meditation on the passion?:

They have taken our blessed Lord,
the blessed Lord,
they have taken him, our blessed Lord,
who uttered not a single word.

Not a word, not a word.

And they have crowned him with thorns,
the blessed Lord,
and they have crowned him with thorns.
He uttered not a single word.

Not a word, not a word.

And they have nailed him to the Cross,
the blessed Lord,
and they have nailed him to the Cross.
He uttered not a single word.

Not a word, not a word.

The tears ran down his cheeks,
the blessed Lord,
The tears ran down his cheeks,
He uttered not a single word.

Not a word, not a word.[11]

Liturgical Problems

Is the introduction of a hymn "related" to the gospel desirable in the context of the Mass? In other celebrations?

[10] Asterios (d. 410), bishop of Amassis, *Homily 19 on Psalm 5,* PG 40.436c.
[11] See J.-P. Foucher, *Poésie Liturgique: Orient et Occident* (Paris: Mame, 1963) 296–97.

Before the Gospel: Responsorial Psalm, Alleluia, and Hymn

The songs that belong to the structure of the celebration of the Word are the responsorial psalm—which responds to the Word—and the Alleluia (or a similar acclamation) as the processional song of the gospel. Both songs fulfill, respectively, their own ministerial function. In these conditions, the hymn related to the gospel, because it does not have a ministerial function that is solidly rooted in the celebration, risks appearing superfluous. The liturgy should not be encumbered with useless additions, even beautiful ones, that slow down the action. Nor the faithful, whose devotion is strictly regulated by the clock. A song that precedes the gospel must be an exception. Just as the sequences *Victimae paschali laudes* and *Veni, Sancte Spiritus* were exceptions. They must also be as beautiful.

RESPONSORIAL PSALM OR HYMN

We have spoken above of the profound veneration with which the liturgy surrounds the responsorial psalm: it venerates the psalm as an authentic Word of God, discovering in it the face of Jesus Christ. In this regard no human text, however beautiful, can replace the responsorial psalm, the "song of the Covenant."

It can happen, however, that a community might replace the psalm with a hymn because the psalm is too difficult for the community to understand; this can happen in celebrations with children or in catechumenal assemblies.

If such a substitution is contemplated for pastoral reasons, the decision must be gravely weighed, for it is a serious decision to make.

ALLELUIA OR HYMN

The text of the Alleluia (or another gospel acclamation) does not have the same biblical density as the responsorial psalm. Neither does it have the same liturgical function. Therefore it does not seem so undesirable, at least at first glance, to replace the Alleluia and its verses with a hymn. The most we must ask is whether a hymn with a strophic structure can fulfill the role of a processional song for the gospel as well as an acclamation.

After the Gospel

In the "Liturgy of the Hours," the song finds a natural place after the readings in the form of a response. These *respond* like an echo of the Word and prolong it in the form of acclamations, praise, or petition.

In the Mass, the gospel is prolonged by the homily and by the prayer of the faithful (and sometimes by the *Credo*). If we decide to add a hymn as a "response" to the gospel, we must make sure that it can be harmoniously integrated into the structure. Too many songs or words, instead of highlighting the dignity of the gospel, easily overshadow it.

We may also envisage a song—an acclamation, for example, the gospel acclamation—which could be used during the proclamation of the gospel (or even during the homily[12]) and which would emphasize different parts of it.

In this area, it is always better to surprise the assembly by sobriety than to overwhelm it with overkill.

Outside the context of the liturgical celebration, it is possible to envision prayer meetings in which a song related to the Gospel might play an important part. Think of Bach's Passions, in which the gospel text is continually commented upon and made real by the choir or soloists. Thus, in the *Passion According to St. John,* when Jesus affirms that he is ready to do the Father's will and to drink the cup presented to him, the choir sings: "May your will be done on earth as in heaven!" When he is arrested and bound, the choir sings: "To liberate me from the chains of my sins, my Savior was chained." When it is said that Peter and another disciple followed Jesus, the soprano sings: "I, too, will follow you with joy." Throughout the account the community shares in the passion of Jesus Christ.

I remember certain prayer meetings in Africa in which I was able to participate. They did not have the musical splendor of Bach, but they manifested the same sense of celebrating the gospel. On Sunday evening, at the hour when the day was beginning to fade, and when the great song of the animals in the bush began to rise, the Christian community and the catechumens gathered around the catechist for prayer. People were chattering, laughing, praying. When the atmosphere had become favorable, and the moon and the stars began to shine, the "soloist"—a charism is necessary for this function—began an invocation to Christ, taken from the gospel of the day. The whole community took up the invocation in the almighty rhythm of a single beating heart. Immense improvisation began: the soloist seemed to

---

[12] See J. Lebon, *Dans vos assemblées,* 424–25.

invent the gospel heard that morning at Mass anew, proclaiming it in short phrases to accompany the notes of the instruments. The community acclaimed the gospel unendingly. It was of incomparable beauty because the community expressed itself with all its authentic humanity. Sometimes the soloist, as if overcome by his own inspiration, added and put the final touches to the Gospel according to Mark or Matthew in his own way. He sometimes echoed the Mass homily—amazing liturgy in which the Word sown in the heart flourished in praise, adoration, and ecstatic joy in innumerable variations!

THANKSGIVING HYMN AND FINAL SONG

The thanksgiving hymn after communion is a new thing in the Roman liturgy. The charter of its foundation can be said to be the instruction of May 4, 1967:

> At Masses with the people, according to what is judged opportune, before the prayer that follows the communion, there may be a pause with a time of sacred silence, or a psalm or song of praise may be recited or sung (art. 15).

In introducing this hymn, the thanksgiving is given full value:

The time of silence favors *individual* thanksgiving.

The communion song expresses a *collective* thanksgiving.

The postcommunion prayer represents the *presidential* thanksgiving.

The introduction of such a song depends on a pastoral judgment: "what is opportune." We cannot put into effect all the good suggestions at every Mass; we cannot sing all the songs that taken individually are excellent but an accumulation of which would weigh down a celebration.

The Final Song (Recessional)

Most parish communities are accustomed to singing a final hymn. In speaking of this song, the instruction *Musicam Sacram* states that it should not only be "Eucharistic" but also that it should reflect the mystery of the feast being celebrated (art. 36). In other words, one cannot tag on any song at the end of the Mass, especially as it will be the last song the faithful will carry with them in their hearts when they leave and return home. It is necessary that the song chosen can be organically integrated into the celebration, whether it expresses the thanksgiving of the community or sings about the feast or liturgical season being celebrated.

The final song may be brief, in the genre of an acclamation sung by all the community, or a strophic hymn. Too much singing, especially at the end of the celebration, may produce fatigue. It is better to experience a certain eager hunger to sing than to suffer indigestion at being overfed. It is better at the end of Mass that people say "We should have sung another verse," than "They wear us out with singing!"

13

The Credo

For the liturgical mentality before Vatican II, the *Credo* had a great symbolic value: a community proclaiming its faith in unison with a thousand voices in the great gatherings at Lourdes or Rome, or even in festive Sunday celebrations, which showed forth a living image of the unity of the Church. It was thrilling to experience everyone singing the same melodies in the same "sacred" language of the Roman Church. It was also a little romantic, for many confused the language of the Roman Church with the language of the entire Church, and would have been incapable—except for the theologians—of judging the theological weight of certain formulas. In the context of the reform after Vatican II, the problem of the *Credo* arose not only because the ancient formulas, dense with the weight of the faith, are recited in the vernacular and lose their theological aura but also because their recitation seems less useful in the Eucharistic celebration.

The majority of our Masses do not have the *Credo,* and this absence in no way threatens the equilibrium of the entire celebration: on the contrary, it is the equilibrium of the Sunday celebration with the *Credo* that is problematic. Is not each celebration in itself a proclamation of faith?

THE HISTORY OF THE CREED

The Roman liturgy before Vatican II used three credal statements:

The so-called Apostles' Creed, since the fifth century in the Church in Rome, was part of the preparatory rites for baptism. It is centered on the proclamation of the three divine Persons and on the history of Jesus Christ, born of the Virgin Mary, who suffered under Pontius Pilate, and rose on the third day.

The so-called Athanasian Creed that was used especially to combat the Nestorian heresy, condemned first at the Council of Ephesus in 431, and with Eutyches, condemned at the Council of Chalcedon in 451. This Creed was introduced about the eighth century into the Romano-Benedictine Office. It was recited on Sundays at Prime. It was taken out of the Office by the decree *De rubricis ad simpliciorem formam redigendis* of March 23, 1955.

The Nicaean-Constantinopolitan Creed added the affirmations of the Councils of Nicaea (325) and Constantinople (381).

These three different statements of the Creed signify at least that there are different ways to proclaim the same faith. The "obedience of faith," as Paul calls it (Rom 1:5), has greater importance than the mere recitation of the words.

The insertion of the *Credo* at Mass happened only slowly, and with resistance. In the sixth century, the patriarch Timothy of Constantinople (511–517) prescribed, not without polemical designs,[1] that the Creed was to be recited at all solemn Masses. In the West, an identical prescription was formulated by the Third Council of Toledo (589) in reaction to Arianism: the recitation of the *Credo* was placed just before the Lord's Prayer as a preparation for communion. In 794, Charlemagne, in a fervor of orthodoxy, introduced this usage at his court in Aachen. In 1014 the emperor Henry II, having come to Rome, pressured Pope Benedict VIII to adopt the same custom in Rome.

At the end of this development, whereby the Creed was definitively accepted into the Eucharistic liturgy, the profession of faith appeared as a "response to the Word of God in the West (and as) a purification of faith before the celebration of the Mysteries in the East."[2]

---

[1] Timothy had Monophysite tendencies himself. Jungmann writes of him: "He would have acted in this way to show up his Catholic predecessor as being wrong and to display his own zeal for orthodoxy," *Missarum Solemnia*, vol. II, p. 270.

[2] See Cabié, "L'Eucharistie," in A. G. Martimort, *L'Eglise en Prière*, vol. II, p. 163.

Biblical and Liturgical Significance

Each Sunday celebration, as memorial of the Pasch of the Lord, reenacts the death and resurrection of the Lord Jesus. As such it is the baptismal feast of feasts and is for every Christian the anniversary of his or her own death and resurrection in Christ Jesus.

It is fitting that on the feast of their baptism Christians should proclaim their faith in the dead and risen Christ. We know how important the "transmission of the Creed" *(traditio symboli)* was in the fifth century, when the catechumens who were preparing for baptism received the statement of the Christian faith on the fifth Sunday of Lent and gave it back to the community *(redditio symboli)* by proclaiming it before the community at the Easter Vigil. The Creed of the Sunday Mass is, as it were, the "giving back of the Creed" by the entire celebrating community on the day of its baptismal anniversary. This is why, even when it is sung or recited together, each person says in his or her own name, "Credo = I believe," and not "We believe."

Rather than becoming weighed down under the anti-heretical aspects of the Creed, we shall concentrate on the biblical elements that outline the history of salvation realized in Jesus Christ. The Creed gives a theological and polemical profession of the faith in which orthodoxy expresses itself in a way that attacks the errors of past ages, errors of which most Christians are not even aware. These anti-heretical formulas barred the way to heresy. For example, the accumulation of images and affirmations about Christ pronounced at the Council of Nicaea in 325 sought to refute those who refused to recognize the Son as *homo-ousios,* that is, "consubstantial" with the Father:

> God of God, Light of Light,
> true God of true God,
> begotten, not made,
> of one substance with the Father.[3]

They came out of the particular historical situation of the fourth-century Church. Today, they remind us of our continuity with the tradition of the early Christian period. Yet, are they really appropriate for the Sunday parish celebration? Actually, they present the faith in an anti-heretical mode, whereas the faith is first of all "pro-Christian." The realities of the faith are often richer than the definitions worked out to

---

[3] *The Sacramentary* (published in 1985) gives "one in Being with the Father."

combat specific heresies. If it is good to proclaim Christ as consubstantial with the Father, a more existentially rich and living theology would proclaim that God is a Father full of tenderness, that his mercy is eternally present for us in his Son, and that his Spirit lives in our hearts.

The truths proclaimed in the Creeds are certainly immutable and true, but their formulas are more related to the times in which they were composed. Words are fragile, passing, and change in use and meaning as time passes. The Church has no particular hold on them: it simply uses them as conceptual material with which to work. Nor can the Church resist the evolution of vocabulary and its meaning: the word "substance" does not have the same meaning for a contemporary person trained in chemistry as it had for a Greek of the fourth century. We can say the same for the terms "nature" and "person." We cannot say, therefore, that we are authentically conserving the faith simply by repeating the words of the ancient formulas. For example, when we say Christ "descended into hell," the majority of the faithful probably misunderstand what is meant: the statement was correct in its time, but the meaning of the terms used has evolved, so that it is no longer correct to express the ancient faith in such a way today. In order to be faithful to the tradition itself, we need to reexpress the statements of the faith in contemporary language and to take notice of the evolution of language.

A last remark. An *act* of faith cannot be reduced to the singing of a formula, but must be expressed as *act*. Christian faith is neither primarily recited nor sung; it is lived. The true *Credo* of the Sunday celebration takes place when the Christian, receiving the Body and Blood of Christ, responds "Amen!" We only receive the Body of Christ when we commit ourselves to putting into practice the Word of God that has been proclaimed to us.[4] The true profession of the Creed for Christians is their Christian life.

TEXTS

The liturgy gives two texts that may be used: the Nicaean-Constantinopolitan Creed or the so-called Apostles' Creed. The first is more marked by the early trinitarian and christological controversies.

---

[4] For the relationship between Word and Eucharist, see Deiss, *Celebration of the Word*.

The Apostles' Creed is shorter, and centered on the history of salvation realized in Jesus Christ. Let us be aware that tradition has conserved many other Creeds.[5] Some of them are remarkable. Others have withered with the passing of time.

We also need to remember that the New Testament contains professions of faith used in early baptismal celebrations. They have the enormous advantage of being simple and of bearing the incomparable dignity of the Word of God. They may also serve as the Creed in ecumenical celebrations or other celebrations of the Word.

One of the most ancient formulas is found in the Letter to the Romans (10:9):

> If you confess with your lips that Jesus is Lord, and believe in your heart that God raised him from the dead, you will be saved.

Prodigious affirmation! Salvation, the fullness of salvation, depends simply on faith in the lordship of Jesus, risen from the dead.

There is also the profession of faith in the Letter to the Ephesians (4:4-6). It is the hymn of Christian unity:

> There is one body and one Spirit, just as you were called to the one hope of your calling, one Lord, one faith, one baptism, one God and Father of all, who is above all and through all and in all.

Finally, in the First Letter to Timothy (3:16) we find the hymn on the "mystery of faith":

> The mystery of our religion is great:
>
> [Christ] was revealed in flesh,
>   vindicated in spirit, seen by angels,
>   proclaimed among Gentiles,
>   believed in throughout the world,
>   taken up in glory.

We must not forget these ancient professions of faith: they bear the savor of eternity: "The grass withers, the flower fades," as all hu-

---

[5] For example, that of: Eusebius of Caesarea (ca. 325), cf. Denzinger, 32nd ed., 40, cited in abbreviated form; Cyril of Jerusalem (ca. 348: *D.S.* 41); Epiphanus (*D.S.* 42–43); Pseudo-Athanasius (*D.S.* 46–47); the Armenian Church (*D.S.* 48–49); the Antiochean baptismal creed (*D.S.* 50); Theodore of Mopsuestia (*D.S.* 51); Macarius the Great (*D.S.* 55), without counting the creeds contained in the liturgical books, such as the Gelasian Sacramentary (*D.S.* 36), *The Apostolic Constitutions* (*D.S.* 60), *The Testament of Our Lord Jesus Christ* (*D.S.* 61), the *Constitutions of the Egyptian Church* (*D.S.* 62–63), and the *Canons of Hippolytus* (*D.S.* 64). There is an abundance of professions of faith!

manly composed creeds wither, "but the word of our God will stand forever" (Isa 40:8).

MUSIC

The Instruction *Musicam Sacram* classifies the *Credo* on the same secondary level of participation as the *Kyrie,* the *Gloria,* and the *Agnus Dei* (art. 30). In so doing, the Instruction gives the *Credo* great honor—perhaps too much. No doubt the importance of the *Credo* in the past played a large part in this evaluation rather than its usefulness in the present. Since the council, communities have been asking various questions regarding it: Should we make an effort to continue to sing the *Credo* in Latin, at any cost? Should we teach it to the young? Or should we sing it in the vernacular and use a modern tune? Is such an investment liturgically worthwhile, or would it be better to simply recite the Creed and reserve our energies for more important songs?

Some Problems

In favor of a simple recitation—which is usually the case in Eastern liturgies—there are a number of arguments:

It is a proclamation of faith, a text that is not rhythmic, so that it demands to be sung. A simple recitation is more in keeping with its literary genre. In addition, singing gives the Creed an exaggerated importance: it thus becomes the longest common song! Furthermore, it is then inserted between the homily and the prayer of the faithful as an enormous division, separating even more drastically two elements that are organically linked, breaking up the path that should lead the people from the first reading to the prayer of the faithful, thus threatening to disfigure the harmonious structure of the celebration of the Word.

In favor of singing the *Credo,* an argument of great weight can be advanced:

Once a community reaches a certain number, the only way of pronouncing a text together in unity, as befits the dignity of the liturgical celebration, is to sing it. A monotone recitation, in which everyone recites as they think best, tends to resemble the murmurings of leaves in a forest blown by the evening wind, even if we think it has a rhythm.

Let us return to the ministerial function of singing: Singing is a means of creating unity.

This ministerial function is not a question in certain tonal languages of equatorial Africa or the Far East. These languages are so musical in themselves that common recitation is not a problem: every word is sung and all singing is rhythmic. One can remember the experience of assemblies "singing" the common prayers and the Apostles' Creed with tuneful and moving inflections, and with a great and wonderful rhythm that made the words swirl.

Some Solutions

For the pastor who does not live in the shade of palm trees but in the din of the city, the problem remains. There seems to be no ideal solution. Here are some reflections:

Song

The Creed can be sung in exceptional circumstances where we want to highlight the profession of faith. Such could be the case at great gatherings, or at celebrations centering on the profession of faith.

It is preferable to choose simple melodies, like a recitative. The Gregorian *Credo I* and its variant, *Credo II*, give excellent examples.[6] Vernacular language compositions might well take them as models. The very popular *Credo III* and *Credo IV* present beautiful melodies of the fifteenth century. But they are probably closer to being a good Gregorian chant than a good profession of faith!

We must not snatch the bread from children's mouths: if a community has the custom of singing the Creed and does it together in the joy of an adult faith, without asking questions, let them sing it without asking them questions! Let us use our energy for essential questions. The time when the questions begin to arise is the time to communally discuss finding new solutions—if the community is try-

[6] H. Hucke, in *Eglise qui chante* (Paris, 63–64, p. 51) states that "the melody of the *Credo* of the Vatican edition undoubtedly has narrow links with the music of an ancient popular ballad of Bluebeard, known across Europe." This shows that the Church has had the custom of using melodies that are part of the idiomatic usage of different peoples for their participation in the liturgy.

ing to move toward an authentic practice of liturgical rites, these questions will eventually arise.

Recitation

Recitation is always possible in the context of a small community. It is even preferable. In the context of a larger community, the mumble created by common recitation may be lessened by having a soloist—or a small group—alternate with the rest of the assembly. The soloist can set a certain rhythm, quickening a pace that is dragging or slowing down a recitation that is rushing. Without such alternation, it is not possible to control the recitation: once it has begun, the recitation has a life of its own and is impossible to direct if it takes a wrong turn. We can only resign ourselves and wait for the final Amen.

It is sometimes possible to control the movement by using a microphone. This requires discretion and ability. The microphone is an instrument to be used with care and know-how. The overuse of decibels is a worse remedy than the original evil.

PARTICIPANTS

The Creed is the profession of faith of the entire congregation of the baptized. It is therefore normal that it should be recited by the entire assembly.

Nothing prevents its recitation by two alternating choirs. It still remains the expression of the faith of all present, just as a psalm that is sung by alternating choirs still remains the prayer of the entire assembly.[7]

FURTHER REFLECTIONS

The Text

The first question is that of the text. The question is simple: Does the Church judge that Christians today must express their faith—until

---

[7] In the tenth century the *Credo* was sometimes sung only by the clergy, which seemed that much more natural in that it took the place—they thought—of the sermon; see Jungmann, *Missarum Solemnia*, vol. II, p. 246.

the Parousia of the Lord!—in affirmations elaborated in the fourth century at Nicaea (325) and at Constantinople (381)? Or can it be hoped that, without denying the treasury of the faith, it is possible to express the faith in a language and manner better suited to our own age, by referring directly to the Word of God? Nicaea and Constantinople are like precious vases in which the living water of tradition is kept, water that flows directly from its source in the Scriptures. The Scriptures are the source. The question is whether third-millennium Christians must necessarily draw the living water via tradition if they can go directly to the source.

Another consideration: the history of the Church shows us that creeds are always formulated in reference to errors that threaten the faith at any determined point in history. What are the errors threatening the Church today? How can we formulate our faith so as to respond to these errors? For example, the world threatens to destroy itself by war, it divides itself by social and racial segregation, and poor countries are stricken with famine. Is there not a magnificent *Credo* that needs to be formulated in reference to Christ, who by his incarnation brought peace (Luke 2:14), who came to gather the children of God, dispersed by sin, into unity (John 11:52), who was sent to preach the good news to the poor (Luke 4:18)? Would not such affirmations engage the faith of contemporary people better than singing that Christ "descended into hell," a statement that no one contests and that is not directly threatened by any heresy?

At All Sunday and Feastday Masses?

The second question concerns the Creed at Sunday and feastday Masses.

The Creed is only one possible expression of the faith, one among a multitude of others. The whole Eucharistic celebration is also *mysterium fidei,* the mystery of faith. Eucharistic Prayer IV presents an excellent history of salvation: its presentation seems vastly superior to that of the Apostles' Creed.

The Extent of the Problem

These are important problems, but they must not be exaggerated. Scholastic theology affirmed that the act of a believer surpasses what is stated and attains to the Person affirmed:[8] it is a luminous principle. Beyond all that can be said, beyond the propositions of any Creed, and of any material conception, it is the Subsisting Truth, God, the most personal Being of beings that could possibly be, who is both affirmed and attained. The dynamism of faith is not restricted by the difficult propositions of the *Credo,* nor by the partial degree to which the mysteries of faith are enunciated, but tends, with all the force of love, toward the God of tenderness and compassion whom we affirm.

This means that the affirmations of the Creed, even of the most perfect Creed possible, are only crutches to aid us paralytics to walk. We certainly need to perfect these crutches, but most of all, to place our hands in the hands of God, who will lead us along the path to the trinitarian God.

---

[8] Thomas Aquinas, *Summa Theologica* IIa–IIae, 1,2, 2m: *Actus credentis non terminatur ad enuntiabile, sed ad rem.*

14

The Cantillation of the Readings

By "cantillation" we mean a recitative "in which the rhythmic elements and melodies exist only in the service of the words pronounced, which respect the semantic structures, syntax, and poetry of the words."[1]

There is a problem in the cantillation of the biblical readings in vernacular languages, but this discussion specifically concerns the problem in European languages. In other languages the problem is not present in the same way. In certain African or Far Eastern languages, the meaning of words depends on the relative pitch at which sounds are sung and linked. Each word is thus naturally cantillated. In a common recitation this cantillation can attain the fullness of a fifth on the melodic scale. Singing in its proper sense must simply accentuate the natural melody of the words if it is not to destroy the meaning of the phrase. It is a fuller cantillation.

The principles enunciated here can, however, illuminate the proclamation of the Word in any language.

THE PROBLEM OF CANTILLATION

The proclamation of the Word of God before the Christian community is a *liturgical act*. As such, it is distinguished from the private reading of Scripture and requires a minimum of solemnization. "The

---

[1] M. Veuthey, *Dans vos assemblées,* vol. 1 (Paris: Desclée, 1989) 156. This introduces a subject developed in Deiss, *Recitatifs pour la Proclamation de la Parole de Dieu et Psalmodies* (Paris: Ed. du Levain, 1964); Spanish translation, *Recitativos Salmodias* (Madrid: Ed. Berit, 1965).

liturgical reading (of Scripture)," wrote Jungmann, can never remain for long a prosaic declaration, seeking only to be understood practically. The recitation is stylized. . . . The reader must not introduce his own sentiments into the sacred text; it is with a strict objectivity, and with a sacred respect that he must present the Word, as on a golden platter: it is the Word of God that he proclaims."[2]

As long as the Word of God was proclaimed in Latin, there was little difficulty. The proclamation was rendered using the *toni communes missae.* The language and the official character of the Gregorian cantillation prevented the priest from ridicule for maltreatment of the text. The most awful errors could be committed—misplacements of Latin accents, defective cadences, breaking of the text in ways that made no sense, omissions that made it incomprehensible—without upsetting either the devotion of the faithful or the continuation of the celebration. It was a symbolic presentation of the Word of God. The community venerated this symbolic presentation even if it did not understand it.

But since the reading has been in the vernacular, the proclamation has had to be done in a way that, while preserving the solemnity of the liturgical action, is immediately intelligible. The one who sings can no longer simply execute a rubric but must accomplish a prophetic ministry: they are the mouthpieces of God.[3]

It is an awesome undertaking, for it is a question of incarnating, in human notes arranged according to human laws, the transcendent Word of God. If the recitative is too ordinary, it can perhaps cast a cloud over the transcendence of the message. Yet if the melody is too forceful, the music can distract one from the text, the frail but seductive human beauty can veil the splendor of the message, and the musical ornamentation can hide the person of Jesus Christ, whom it seeks to honor.

This cantillation of the Word of God is a continual search for a balance between text and music, the balance being the full and joyful subordination of music to text. Here more than anywhere the music serves the text or, more exactly, the interior message it announces. "The sung word . . . is not an art in itself; it is not an ornamentation of worship but a kind of bridge between human beings and God."[4]

---

[2] Jungmann, *Missarum Solemnia,* vol. II, p. 174.
[3] See the article "Musique" by E. Gerson-Kiwi, in *Dictionnaire de la Bible* (Paris: Letouzey et Ané) *Supplement,* vol. 5 (1957) col. 1436.
[4] S. Corbin, *L'Eglise à la conquete de sa musique* (Gallimard, 1960) 61.

In the Old Testament, the reading of the sacred text is rarely conceived without cantillation. The Mishna teaches that the one who recites Scripture without "cantillating" it is guilty of idolatry. This tradition of singing the reading is so deeply rooted that popular language spoke indiscriminately of the *singing* or *recitation* of a canticle.[5] The proclamation of the Word of God is conceived of as a divine music bursting upon the earth, just as the angels at Bethlehem proclaimed the glory of God through *song*. Clement of Alexandria cried out with enthusiasm: "The prophets *speak:* the sound of music resounds everywhere!"[6]

Text

Our starting principle is this: *The cantillation of the Word of God is the solemnization of the proclamation of that Word.*

If we accept this principle, the first requirement is that the biblical text itself should possess a minimum of solemnity, that it should itself belong to the literary genre that is called "cantillation."

Let us explain this: It is clear that the whole Bible is inspired by the Holy Spirit and therefore possesses the incomparable dignity of the Word of God. Yet this dignity does not automatically give any text a solemn and formal character—or lyrical qualities—of a pericope. For example, the list of David's officers and associates (2 Sam 23), while inspired by the Holy Spirit, is not a rhythmic passage that needs cantillation.

It is also clear that although the Bible is inspired in its entirety and in each of its parts, certain texts have greater value in terms of the faith. We do not have to say that everything that is an article of faith is necessarily solemn and formal, and therefore needs to be cantillated. On the contrary, it is likely that the more catechetical parts need only a mere reading.

Lastly, it is clear that some texts possess an interior rhythm and a lyrical quality that call for cantillation. For example, the Prologue to the Gospel of John (1:1-18, Gospel of Christmas), the hymn in the Letter to the Philippians (2:6-11, Palm Sunday), the poem in Isaiah

---

[5] Strack-Billerbeck, *Kommentar zum Neuen Testament aus Talmud und Mishna,* vol. 4, part I (München: Beck, 1961) 394, 398. Rabbi Aquiva taught: "Sing, sing without ceasing," in the sense of *"study"* without ceasing by singing the text of the Bible and the Mishna."

[6] *The Protrepticus* XIII, 119; SC 2 (1949) 189.

60:1-4 (Epiphany), and the Gospel of the Beatitudes (All Saints), are all examples of texts that call for cantillation.

In regard to the Gospels, here again, when a simple reading is required, there is no reason to use cantillation. We need to remember, however, that all the historical accounts in the Gospels do not belong to the same redactional level, and that some have been transmitted in a formal style that calls for cantillation, that some had this formal style even in the pre-Synoptic tradition, memory techniques having been used to remember and transmit them.

Thus, while Mark gives the account of Jesus' baptism in a simple narrative style, Matthew transmits his text in three-line stanzas:

> And when Jesus had been baptized,
> just as he came up from the water,
> suddenly the heavens were opened to him
>
> and he saw the Spirit of God
> descending like a dove
> and alighting on him.
>
> And a voice from heaven said,
> This is my Son, the Beloved,
> with whom I am well pleased (3:16-17).

Here is Matthew's introduction to the Sermon on the Mount (three stanzas of two lines):

> When Jesus saw the crowds,
> he went up the mountain:
>
> And after he sat down,
> his disciples came to him.
>
> Then he began to speak,
> and taught them, saying . . . (5:1-2).

It is necessary that translations keep this rhythm of the original. But it also requires that the recitative not only does not break the rhythm but highlights and underlines it. Then, thanks to the cantillation, we shall be able to understand and value more than by a simple reading the three stanzas of Jesus' temptation (Matt 4:1-11), the five stanzas built on the verb "to worry" of the Sermon on the Mount (Matt 6:25-34), and the peaceful joy of the hymn of jubilation (Matt 11:25-27; Luke 10:21-22).

MUSICAL ELEMENTS OF THE RECITATIVE

The musical elements of the recitative consist of rhythm and melody.

The Rhythm

Like ancient cantillation, the rhythm of the recitative must follow the rhythm of the text it proclaims.

An infinitely flexible rhythm, with the spontaneity of a bird in flight or a child at play.

Ever renewed rhythm that does not allow itself to be chained down in predetermined measures. The recitative invents its rhythm as it goes along, founding itself on the support the text gives, concerned only with a satisfactory proclamation.

A rhythm that nevertheless is not chaotic. For if the recitative is the solemnization of the Word, the rhythm of the recitative will be the solemnization of the rhythm of the Word.

The Melody

A recitative is not a song that seeks to develop a musical argument. It is not interested in proclaiming a tune but in proclaiming the Word of God.

The musical elements must therefore serve to punctuate the phrases of the text, not as ornamental elements with a value in themselves.

The cantillation of the Word of God must constantly seek a balance between text and music, a balance in which the music submits fully and joyfully to the needs of the text and its interior message, and is its servant, as we have said above.

Elements of the Recitative's Melody

The recitative includes a *reciting tone* and a *final cadence*. There may also be an *introductory formula,* one or several *modulations,* and *passing tones* or *ornamentation.* Here, as an example, is a recitative in which the reciting tone is A:

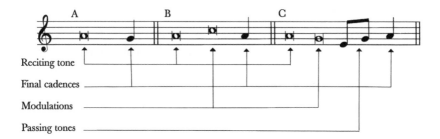

Classification

We can distinguish the punctuated recitative, a strophic recitative, and a decorated recitative.

In the *punctuated recitative,* the phrase is sung on a single note (the reciting tone) with a final cadence at the end that "punctuates" the proclamation. The most typical example is the Latin recitative used for proclaiming the gospel.[7]

In the *strophic recitative,* the biblical pericope to be proclaimed is divided into a certain number of "strophes" or "stanzas," that are each given the same melodic treatment. The best examples of this kind of recitative are the psalms when they are divided into three- or four-line stanzas.

The *decorated recitative* is when a text, to use the expression of H. Hucke,[8] is *durch-komponiert,* composed syllable by syllable on a melody. The recitatives of the *Pater Noster* of the Great Lamentation for Holy Saturday *(Incipit oratio Jeremiae prophetae)* or of the *Exsultet* are good examples of this type of recitative. At the same time, they are masterpieces that surpass any category of recitative. They cannot be executed by memory, but must be read note by note.

---

[7] See, for instance, *Liber Usualis Missae et Officii* (Paris, Tournai, Rome: Desclée et Socii, 1936) 102–3, for the *Tonus Prophetiae.*

[8] See "Le Récitatif liturgique en langue moderne," in *Musique sacrée et langue moderne,* Coll. Kinnor (Paris: Fleurus, 1964) 61.

Range[9]

The melody of a recitative must move according to the limited range of each voice, so that the text can be proclaimed in a pleasing and full sound.

In Latin recitatives, these limits do not exceed a fifth (in the tones for chapters or prayers) or a sixth (preface and the *Pater*).

It seems that the ancient five-note scale (C, D, E, G, A), which does not exceed the limits of a sixth, whatever the position of its notes, is a better range, and fully adapted for cantillation—because the five-note scale is the easiest musical scale to sing and to listen to, and a normal voice easily sings well within its limits.

Each reader must choose the most suitable pitch, and should not hesitate to raise or lower the key according to the requirements of the cantillation. It needs to be remembered that there is a fundamental difference between the interpretation of a work of art, in which it is necessary to be faithful to the intentions of the composer, and the execution of a liturgical recitative, which requires that the "ministry" be authentically performed.

Reciting Chord or Tone

Normally, cantillation is done on a *single* chord or reciting tone. It is certainly possible to begin the phrase with good intoning, add passing notes, and end with a final cadence, yet these variations, far from undermining the reciting tone must highlight and support it by always gravitating towards it.

There are *exceptions*. They attempt precisely to break out of a too rigid structure by seizing the attention.

Structured raising of pitch is one such technique, sometimes used in Eastern liturgies. Usually, the melody does not vary much but is just sung contrastingly higher. Sometimes this is accomplished by scarcely perceptible changes in the middle of the phrase, of a third or a quarter of a tone, an act that places the recitatives in the strange and mysterious world of Eastern music, which is unhindered by our "tempered" Western scale. In other cases, there is a systematic rise at the beginning of phrases. This procedure gives the reading a life and

---

[9] Range refers to 1) the span of notes that constitute the texture of a melody; 2) the span of notes best suited to a given voice.

a brilliance that places it above the reaches of ordinary cantillation: it is the expression of an ever-increasing solemnity.

Moderated by Western discipline, this procedure appears in the Roman liturgy:

> in the triple *Ave, sanctum chrisma* of the Chrism Mass of Holy Thursday;

> in the triple *Ecce lignum crucis* of Good Friday;

> in the triple *Lumen Christi* of the Easter vigil.

Let us also note that in popular song, whether ancient or modern, this technique is often used—proof that it really works! It is hardly used in contemporary liturgy.

Passing Tones and Ornamentation

S. Corbin notes that the "ornamentation of the cantillation, and even the extent of the decoration, varies infinitely from place to place, and especially from rite to rite. There is a whole world between the 'bare-boned' cantillation of the Latin tradition and the Eastern world where ornamentation has its own particular feel."[10]

It is presumed that Western communities will want to use ornamentation moderately rather than in excess, and that English liturgical song goes well with a certain reserve and moderation.

A Question as Conclusion

Before Vatican II the biblical texts were cantillated—whether well or poorly—because this was what the rubrics demanded. With the introduction of the vernacular, the cantillation of the biblical readings has almost disappeared. The only problem today seems to be the quality of the translation.

Meanwhile, the use of microphones has become normal. Used with intelligence, this permits a personalized proclamation of the Word of God that can encompass an almost private communication to an overly solemn proclamation. The amplification of the voice means that good diction and singing are amplified as well as the weaknesses of both.

---

[10] *Révue de musicologie*, 47 (1961) 11.

The question remains whether in certain special celebrations a moderate use of the microphone and of cantillation might emphasize the beauty of the Word of God.

This question is not considered a great problem. It is only a problem of beauty in the proclamation of the Word of God. But is it not true that a problem of beauty is always important in our celebrations?

Postlude

O sing to the LORD a new song;
sing to the LORD, all the earth (Ps 96:1).

Vatican II spoke of the *perennis reformatio,* the "permanent reform" of the Church.[1] This permanent reform of the Church requires the permanent reform of the Church's liturgy and, therefore, of its song. It will always be urgent and necessary to invent "a new song" with which to celebrate God's gift of salvation in the continual adaptation of the Church to each era, an adaptation that is the constant joy of the Church's ever-renewed youthfulness.

The fundamental criterion of this renewal is that of ministerial function. It can be summarized in the simple and banal questions: What use is this? What is the purpose of this song, and for which assembly can it be of service? And if a certain song does not fulfill its ministerial function, what can replace it?

For the reform to be successful, there are two essential conditions. The first is a knowledge of the tradition, a tradition that is the wisdom of the past. The second is the peaceful observance of the liturgical laws presented by the Church. We have insisted on both. Tradition and obedience trace the only sure path to an authentic renewal.

Just as the knowledge of the vocabulary and grammar of a language does not automatically create literary masterpieces, the knowledge of the tradition does not spontaneously produce new masterpieces of song and rite. Yet such knowledge allows us to avoid faults of grammar and spelling, which is already extremely precious in the

---

[1] Decree on Ecumenism, *Unitatis redintegratio,* 6.

237

liturgy. It may also help us to invent authentic new forms. Authentic tradition is never just a material repetition of the past but an inspiration for future solutions.

Obedience to liturgical laws is the price to pay for the unity of the Church. Of course, it is the Spirit who is at the root of our unity. Yet this interior unity also expresses itself outwardly. It is important that this "new song" should reveal the unity of the Church.

What is the future of liturgical song? After the explosion of vernacular songs in the liturgy in all the communities of the world, what hope should the prophet have? Liturgical song depends on the future development of the liturgy itself. The great question for the Church today, beyond those of inculturation, acculturation, and adaptation, is that of the Church's own conformity to the will of Christ, or in another way of speaking, the problem of the Church's permanent attempt to reform its life so that it is ever in greater conformity with the teachings of the gospel. Liturgists and musicians must also remain humble.

There remains, however, the joyful challenge of seeking to clothe the Church and its liturgy with God's own beauty.

Index